Cromosys Publication

Teach Yourself Tally

NIRANJAN JHA SHOWMAN

Founder - Niranjan Jha Showman

+91-9561450045
Learn Advanced Skills
And Get Job Instantly
GERMAN
Python
FRENCH
C++
SPANISH
Java
ENGLISH
HTML5
RUSSIAN
CSS
JavaScript
Cromosys
Education and Technology Research Center
Nallasopara (W), Mumbai

Learn Web Programming
Demo-Class Free
HTML
CSS
React
JavaScript
Typescript
Bootstrap
Cromosys
20 Years of Experience
Nallasopara (W), Mumbai
+91-9561450045

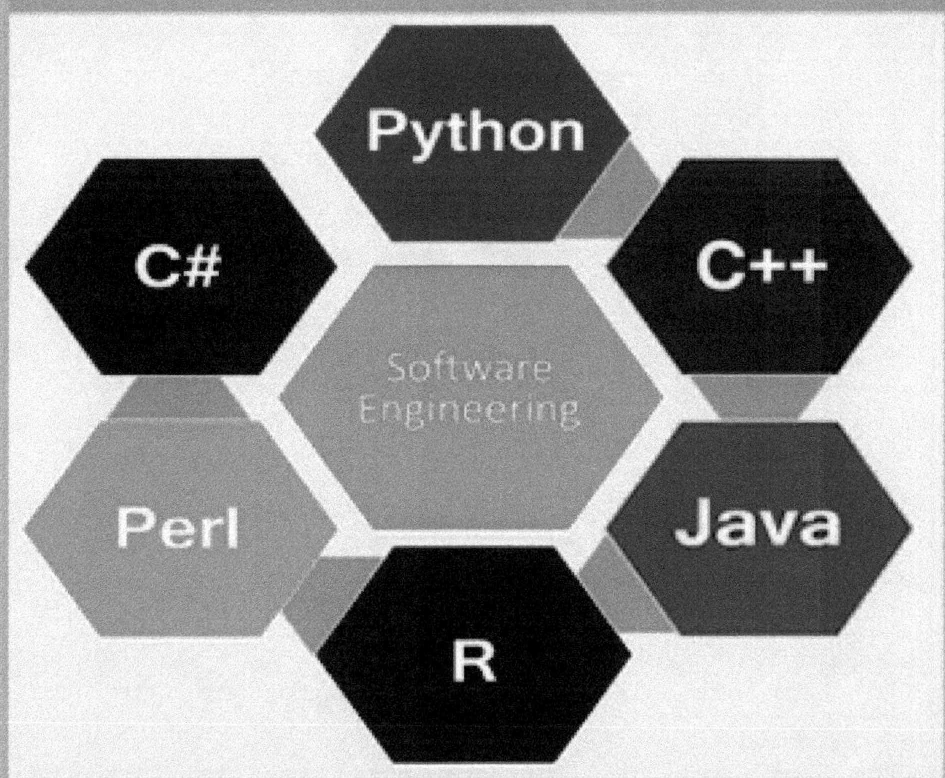

+91-9561450045
Learn Software Engineering
Demo-Class Free
Python
C#
C++
Software
Engineering
Perl
Java
R
Cromosys
20 Years of Experience
Nallasopara (W), Mumbai
+91-9561450045

25 Years of Experience
Learn Visual Multimedia
Animation VFX
Movie Editing
Game Development
Cromosys
+91-9561450045
Education and Technology Research Center
Nallasopara (W), Mumbai
www.facebook.com/cromosys

Jobs Available
For Candidates Who Know

German

French

Spanish

Vacancy in Germany, France, Spain

For Hospitality, Engineering, IT Sector

With Free Visa, Airfare and Accommodation

Cromosys

Education and Technology Research Centre

Nallasopara (W), Mumbai

+91-9561450045

20 Years of Experience

Book: Teach Yourself Tally
Author: Niranjan Jha Showman
Publisher: Cromosys Publication
ISBN: Acquired
Date: 2020
Category: Computer Education

Preface

Cromosys Publication's **Teach Yourself Tally** book is an optimal quality guide to the beginners and advanced learners of Tally. We are the leading eBook publisher of languages and technology. Our research and education center working for last fifteen years has made tremendous effort to simplify the learning of Tally, and so, we assure you that this book will walk you through in the simplest way in your entire course of learning. Whether you are using Tally ERP 9 or the latest version, this book will make you a master of it in just one month of time. The tutorials in the chapters will lead you step-by-step giving pictures of every move and will help you create all financial entries starting from the real basic of creating a company to the opening the balance sheet. Tally is an accounting software that is designed to integrate and automate all the business transactions of a company as it helps the management in taking quick and correct decisions and allows to have a better control of the business. It is an accepted financial system for a decade that this accounting software simplifies, integrates, and streamlines all business transactions in an easy and cost-effective manner. That is why it is compulsory for every company to have Tally Operating Accountants as it created job opportunities for millions of people of the world. And what is noticeably true is that Tally doesn't require from you be educated in commerce stream, which means you can learn and work on Tally having any educational background. It's cool, simple, and sublime!

Niranjan Showman, the author of this and twenty other eBooks published online, is the founder of Cromosys Corporation. His dedication in technological and linguistic research is significantly known to the millions of people around the world. This book is the creation of his avowed determination to make the learning of Tally easy to the people. After you install this program on your system, you just have to follow the instructions doing the same on your computer, and you will see that you are quickly learning everything. Just an hour of practice per day, and in a month of time you'll get a lot of knowledge, tips and tricks to work with this software. This is an unmatchable unique book of its kind that guarantees your success. The lessons are magnificently powerful to bring you into the arena of accounting. It is the need of time, and that's why many people have been sharpening their knowledge to be good in it. Since a recent past, Tally has become an academic element of commerce education and we have seen a great increase in the number of students interested in learning this software. As we have been teaching Tally for past ten years, so we are quite sure about the usefulness of this book. The method, lessons, examples, and explanations of this book are hundred percent easy, correct, and comprehensive.

One thing is necessary to say that Tally is software that one cannot learn playing around it but they have to learn from the beginning. And it is also true that there is nothing to play in Tally. The simplicity of this software definitely makes the things easy to learn provided one has the interest, patience, and curiosity for it. Seeing the improvement in multimedia and conventional reading going old, the students also like to read and share the things through electronic system; therefore we decided to bring out a book of this kind which serves their all purposes. Tally ERP 9 is the latest version of Tally, which comes with various enhancements to make handling and processing of business transactions even easier and quicker. It can handle the accounts of more than one company simultaneously. It is very simple to use and allows you to enter data in various formats. In addition, you can view information of any period, compare data across companies and financial periods, maintain account details, and generate reports. In other words, with Tally ERP 9, accurate and up-to-date business information is literally at your fingertips. Installing Tally is quite easy and when you do that, a folder named Tally is created by default in which program files required to run this program are saved. The user can specify the location of the data directory to save these files and install program files on any drive. It does not take more than a minute to install Tally ERP 9 on the local hard disk and uses up only about 40 MB of space. For installation, you must have sufficient user-rights so that you can make necessary changes during the installation process.

Cromosys, our education and technology research center, saving human efforts from being wasted, is committed to help you gain profound and contemporary knowledge. We strongly believe that this book is useful for the people working in a company's accounting department. After you start the lesson, you don't need to worry about anything but just follow each and every step carefully. This eBook is designed to fulfill the instant need of learners in a very economical way, as it is easy to find on internet and affordable to buy and share. Cromosys, our path-breaking pioneer training institute for Computer Courses, English Speaking, Mass Communication, Foreign Languages, and Competition Coaching, is dedicated to enlightening human mind with educational endeavors, and we are doing the same for last successful fifteen years. And recently we have come up with 'Worldwide Online Teaching System' for languages and technology. We not only hope but believe that your success is in your hand now, as this book will take you miles ahead in your expectation. We always respect the views and comments of readers, so for any communication with regards to assistance, enquiry or collaboration, we are always there at your reach as it helps us improve our quality.

Niranjan Jha Showman
Founder: Cromosys Corporation
Web: facebook.com/cromosys
Contact no.   +91-9561450045
Email address: cromosys@yahoo.com
Nallasopara (W), Mumbai, India

Books by the same author
Teach Yourself Maya, Teach Yourself Adobe Flash, Teach Yourself 3ds Max, English Voice Accent and Pronunciation, Teach Yourself Spanish, Teach Yourself French, Teach Yourself German, English Word Power, Dynamic Grammar of English, English Dictionary of Modern Slang, English Accent and Diction

Cromosys
Education and Technology Research Center
Education, Technology, Publication, Healthcare, Realtor, Filmmaking
Nallasopara (W), Mumbai, India

Caution: All the writing works that include all the educational, non-educational books, novels, and articles of the author Niranjan Jha, are the registered contents of Online Digital Services and also published contents of his registered magazine FACE OFF - Inventing Truth, which carries registration no. MAHENG12112/13/1/2009-TC and the endorsement no. 3244 28/5/2009 with the Ministry of Information and Broadcasting, Govt. of India. Any plagiarism in this regard will attract strict legal action. Any further publication of any of these books requires his written permission. Copyright certificate of this book is attached at the end of this book.

Lesson 1
Creating a Company

The first thing that you do in Tally is creating a company, which means providing the basic information about the company whose accounts are to be maintained. Let's look at the steps to reach Company Creating screen.

1. To open Tally on your computer you can go to Start> All Programs and select Tally. It opens first screen of Tally, as shown in picture 1.1.

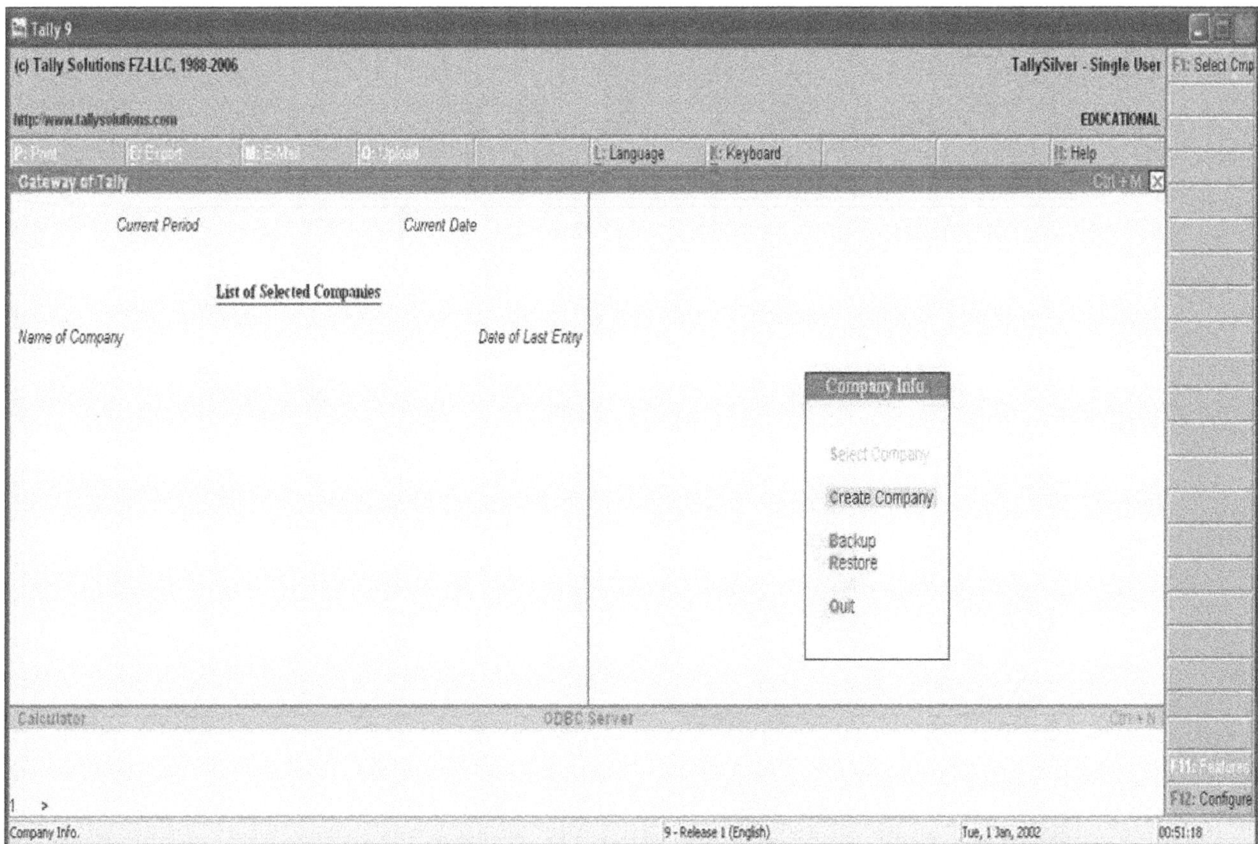

Picture 1.1

2. On the first screen, you can select and press enter on the option **Create Company** in the Company Info menu. You can use the arrow key of the keyboard or mouse click for that.

3. Pressing enter on Create Company opens Company Creation screen, as shown in picture 1.2. In this screen you are required to fill the company information.

4. Enter the name of the company in the Name option. In our case, we enter **Cromosys Corporation** as the company's name.

5 Enter the **Mailing Name** of the company if it is a different name. You can use the same name if you press enter of Tab key. Pressing Tab lets you go one option ahead and Shift+Tab take you one option back. Using keyboard is highly recommended than mouse in Tally because you have to enter a lot of details and toggle between so several options.

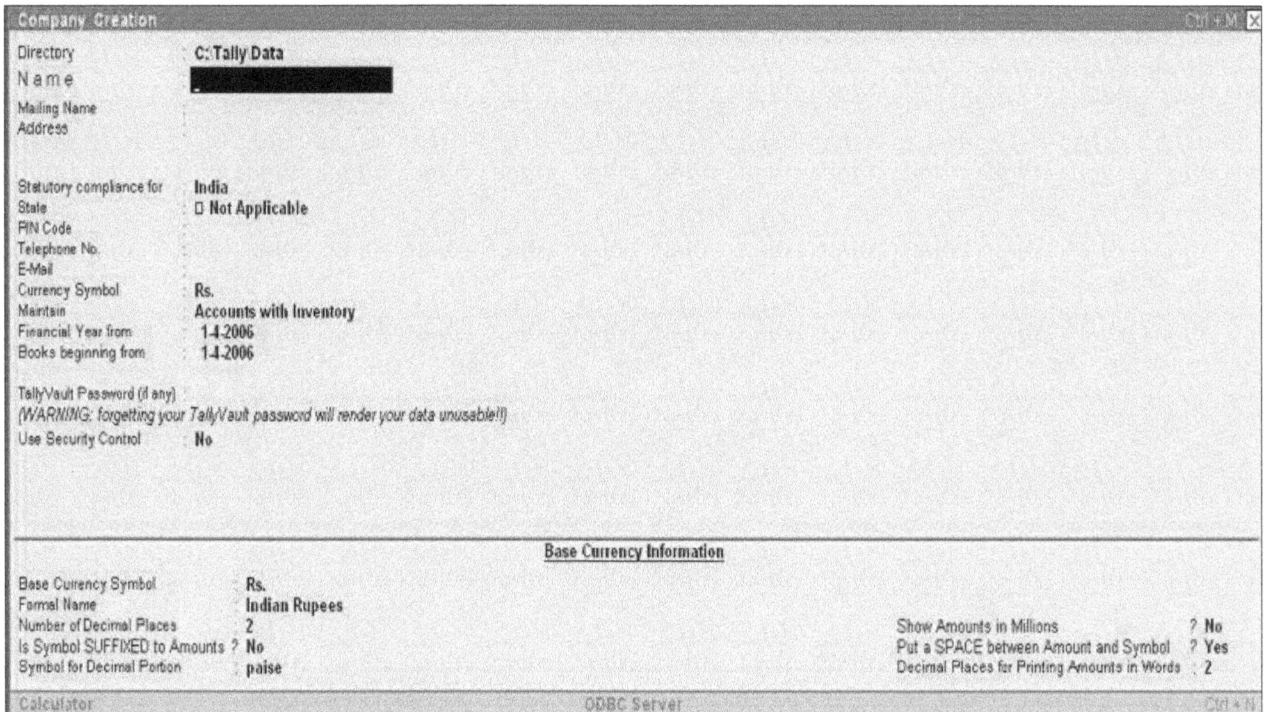

Picture 1.2

6. Enter the address of the company. Select the name of the country for the option: **Statutory compliance for**, and select the state.

7. Enter PIN Code, Telephone Number, and E-Mail Address.

8. Depending upon the country you select, the option beside the **Currency Symbol** changes automatically. And it makes changes in **Base Currency Information** section at the bottom of the screen.

9. Beside the **Maintain** option select **Accounts with Inventory**. Enter the date beside **Financial Year from** and **Book beginning from**.

10. Leave the option blank of **Tally Vault Password**. Vault is used when Tally works on Network System.

11. Enter **Yes** beside **Use Security Control**. Enter Administrator Name, Password, and set **Yes** next to **Use Tally Audit Features**.

12. Press Tab key to move to the **Base Currency Information** section and verify the information displayed under this section. Press Enter key till the end and select **Yes** on **Accept**.

It saves the data and opens the company on the **Gateway of Tally**. If you want to close this company, you can press Alt+F1 or click **Shut Cmp** at the top right corner of the screen. In order to close Tally, you can press **Esc** and select **Yes**, or select **Quit** at the bottom of Gateway of Tally. To understand next chapter better you can go ahead and close Tally for now.

Opening a Company

Let's open Tally again by selecting Start> All Programs> Tally. If there is only one company created in Tally of your computer, then this time it'll directly open the **Company Login** screen when the Tally starts, and it will ask you to enter User Name and Password. If there is more than one company created, then you will see Company Info screen open when Tally starts, as shown in picture 1.1. Even if you close all companies and have Tally open, you'll still see this Company Info screen.

1. Under Company Info the first option is **Select Company**. When you can press enter on that you see the List of Companies with all the companies created in your computer, as shown in picture 1.3. You can select Cromosys Corporation and press enter.

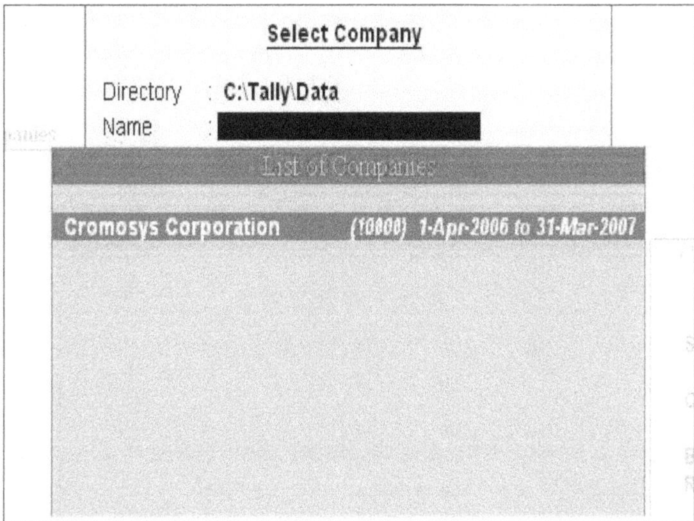

Picture 1.3

2. It opens Company Login screen where you can enter the User Name and Password. Make sure you enter correct User Name and Password.

3. Now you see Gateway of Tally with your company opened and listed at the left-hand side.

Altering Basic Info of a company

Suppose that you want to make some changes in the Basic Information that you entered while creating a company then there are the steps to follow.

1. When you are on Gateway of Tally with your company opened at the left-hand side, you have to press Alt+F3 or select **Cmp Info** at the top right corner. Some shortcut options listed in red color at the top right corner are underlined, which means they need **Alt** key to be pressed with them.

2. In Gateway of Tally you come across another Company Info screen. You can arrow down to the option **Alter**, or press the shortcut **A** because A is highlighted in red, or double click with the mouse.

3. Select your company from the List of Companies and you will have **Company Alteration** screen open with the cursor blinking in it. You can make changes you want and select Yes on Accept at the end.

Lesson 2
Creating a Stock Group

Stock refers to the supply of items in a company. The Stock Group that you create can assemble the stock item as per their functionality. It is used to locate stock items easily. You can create, display and alter single as well as multiple stock groups.

1. Go to **Gateway of Tally**, select **Inventory Info**> **Stock Groups** and press enter on **Create** under Single Stock Group. It opens Stock Group Creation screen, as shown in picture 1.4.

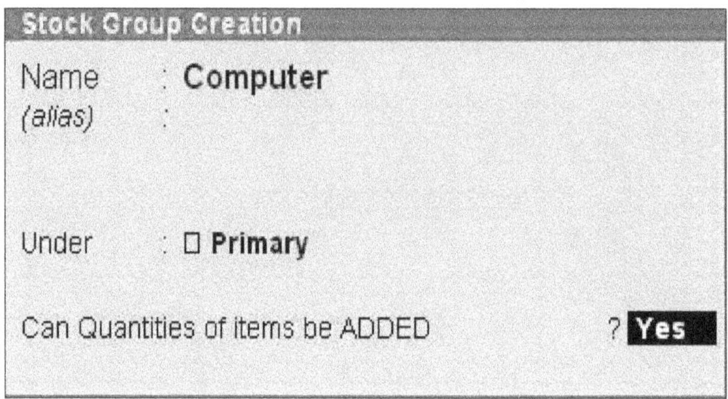

Picture 1.4

2. Type the name of stock group beside Name: **Computer**. You can leave the alias blank and for Under: select **Primary**, as it is going to be the primary stock of the company.

3. Select **Yes** beside Can Quantities of items be ADDED. When you save it by selecting Yes on Accept, another blank screen of the same Stock Group Creation appears. You can create another stock group if you want or simply press Esc to come out of it.

Displaying and Altering a Stock Group

1. Go to **Display** under Stock Groups (Single Stock Group), and then select the stock group **Computer** under List of Groups. It will open the stock group that you created. Pressing **Esc** will let you close the Stock Group Display screen.

2. You can select **Alter** under Stock Groups (Single Stock Group), and then select the stock group **Computer** under List of Groups. The blinking cursor allows you to make changes that can be saved by selecting Yes on Accept. You can press Esc if you do not want to change anything, as it is not required. In case if the change is made, then you can go to Display mode again to see if the change is saved.

Creating Multiple Stock Groups

In the multiple stock groups, the new tock groups are crated under a single parent group. We will create multiple stock groups in **Computer** stock group.

1. Go to **Gateway of Tally**, select **Inventory Info**> **Stock Groups** and press enter on **CReate** under Multiple Stock Groups. It opens Multi Stock Group Creation screen as shown in picture 1.5.

2. Select the parent stock group name beside **Under Group**, under which you want to create multiple stock groups. You can make a choice from the **List of Groups** of the right-hand side.

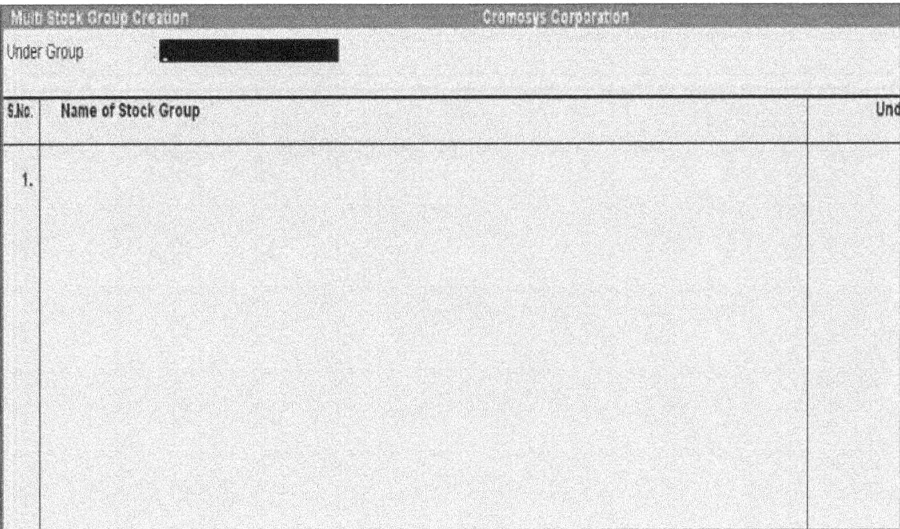

Picture 1.5

3. You can select **Computer** for Under Group, and then type the name of two sub stock groups as **Monitor** and **Hard Drive**. Select **Yes** when it asks you if **Items are Addable**. And select Yes on Accept.

4. Go to **DIsplay** option under <u>Multiple Stock Groups</u> and select **Computer**. It will show all the sub stock groups you created under Computer.

Creating a Single Stock Category
Stock categories are used to store similar type of stock items. At the time to creating a stock category, you need to specify information such as name of the stock category, and the primary category of sub-category under which under which you want create a stock category. To create a stock category, first you need to enable the Maintain Stock Categories option that you can do following the steps below.

1. When your company is open and you're on Gateway of Tally, you need to press **F11** which opens Company Features menu looking similar to the picture 1.6.

Picture 1.6

2. In Company Features menu you need to arrow down and press enter on **Inventory Features** which opens Company Operations Alteration screen, as shown in picture 1.7.

Company : **Cromosys Corporation**

Inventory Features

General		Invoicing	
Integrate Accounts and Inventory	? Yes	Allow Invoicing	? Yes
Allow Zero valued entries	? No	Enter Purchases in Invoice Format	? Yes
		Use Debit/Credit Notes	? No
Storage & Classification		Use Invoice mode for Credit Notes	? No
Maintain Multiple Godowns	? No	Use Invoice mode for Debit Notes	? No
Maintain Stock Categories	? Yes	Separate Discount column on Invoices	? No
Maintain Batch-wise Details	? No		
(set Expiry Dates for Batches)	? No	**Purchase Management**	
Use different Actual & Billed Qty	? No	Track additional costs of Purchase	? No
Order Processing		**Sales Management**	
Allow Purchase Order Processing	? No	Use Multiple Price Levels	? No
Allow Sales Order Processing	? No	**Additional Inventory Vouchers**	
		Use Tracking Numbers (Delivery/Receipt Notes)	? No
		Use Rejection Inward/Outward Notes	? No

F1: Accounts	**F2:** Inventory	**F3:** Statutory

Picture 1.7

3. For the **Maintain Stock Categories** option under **Storage & Classification** type **Yes** and press enter till Accept.

4. Go to Gateway of Tally (press Esc once if needed), select Inventory Info and then select **Stock Categories**. Press enter on **Create** under Single Stock Category.

5. It opens Stock Category Creation screen. Type the Name of Stock Category: **Intel**. You can leave the alias blank and for Under: select **Primary**, as it is going to be the primary stock category.

6. To see the stock category, you need to select **Display** under Single Stock Category in Stock Categories. Similarly, you can arrow down to **Alter** under Single Stock Category to make changes if required. You can also create Multiple Stock Categories following the same steps.

Lesson 3
Creating a Single Stock Item
Stock items are either the products of your company or the company deals in. The stock items can be bought, sold, or issued for a production purpose.

1. In Gateway of Tally, go to Inventory Info> **Stock Items** and select **Create** under Single Stock Item. It opens Stock Item Creation screen, as shown in picture 1.8. Here you need to enter the name of the stock item, the parent stock group as well as parent stock category under which you want to crate a stock item, and unit in which the stock item is measured.

Picture 1.8

2. In Stock Item Creation screen type the Name of stock item: **Motherboard**, leave alias blank, Under: **Computer** (select from the List of Groups).

3. Beside Category: **Intel** (select from the List of Categories). You can also create a new category by pressing Alt+C which you don't need at this moment. Alt+C lets you create a new entity of anything.

4. Press Alt+C on Units to create one as it can be left out. It opens Unit Creation screen. Type beside Symbol: **S**, Formal Name: **My System**, Number of Decimal Places: **2**, and save it on Accept. Now it'll show Units: **S** in Stock Item Creation screen.

5. Now the cursor moves to Tax Information area. Enter Rate of Duty: **5**, Tariff Classification: **No**, Quantity: **10**, Rate per: **10,000**. It will show the Value automatically. Select Yes on Accept.
If it opens *Stock Item Allocation* screen, for Godown select Main Location (or create one pressing Alt+C), and all the other entries will remain same as previous screen. Press enter till Yes on Accept.

You can try **Display** and **Alter** options of Single Stock Item. You can also create Multiple Stock Items following the same steps.

Creating a Single Godown

The Godown is like a warehouse where stock items are stored. It has different kinds of stock summary, and all material expenditure from godowns is displayed in the godown summary. The godowns can give you current stock position at any time because it is updated with every transaction.

1. You need to activate Godowns first, and for that press **F11** on Gateway of Tally and select **Inventory Features.** In Company Operations Alteration screen, type **Yes** for Maintain Multiple Godowns and press enter till Accept.

2. Now you have to set Cost Centres, and for that press **F11** on Gateway of Tally and select **Accounting Features**. Under Cost/Profit Centres Management, type **Yes** for <u>Maintain Cost Centres</u>, as shown in picture 1.9.

Company : Cromosys Corporation

Accounting Features

General		Invoicing	
Integrate Accounts and Inventory	? Yes	Allow Invoicing	? Yes
Income/Expense Statement instead of P & L	? No	Enter Purchases in Invoice Format	? Yes
Allow Multi-Currency	? No	Use Debit/Credit Notes	? No
		Use Invoice mode for Credit Notes	? No
Outstandings Management		Use Invoice mode for Debit Notes	? No
Maintain Bill-wise Details	? Yes		
(for Non-Trading A/cs also)	? No	**Budgets & Scenario Management**	
Activate Interest Calculation	? No	Maintain Budgets and Controls	? No
(use advanced parameters)	? No	Use Reversing Journals & Optional Vouchers	? No
Cost/Profit Centres Management		**Other Features**	
Maintain Payroll	? No	Enable Cheque Printing	? No
Maintain Cost Centres	? **Yes**	Set/Alter Cheque Printing Configuration	? No
Use Cost Centre for Job Costing	? No	Allow Zero valued entries	? No
More than ONE Payroll / Cost Category	? No		
Use Pre-defined Cost Centre Allocations during Entry	? No		

Picture 1.9

3. Now to create a single godown, Go to Gateway of Tally> Inventory Info> **GoDowns** and select **Create** under Single Godown.

4. Type the Name: **New Delhi**, and select for Under: **Main Location** (from the List of Godowns). Press enter till Accept. You can check Display and Alter options for this godown you created.

Creating Multiple Godowns

The multiple godowns can be created by specifying the name of the parent godown. You can create many godowns under one parent godown.

1. Go to Gateway of Tally> Inventory Info> **GoDowns**, and select **CReate** under <u>Multiple Godowns</u>. It opens Multi Godown Creation screen.

2. Select **New Delhi** (from the List of Godowns) for Under Godown, and type the name of sub-godowns under the **Name** column.

3. You can type three names under name column – **First Branch**, **Second Branch**, **Third Branch**. And select Yes to save multiple godowns.

To display multiple godowns, you can select **DIsplay** under <u>Multiple Godowns</u> and select **New Delhi** in the List of Godowns. You can alter multiple godowns by selecting AlTer in Multiple Godowns.

Lesson 4
Creating a Single Group

Groups are basically known as account groups which are the collection of ledgers of the same nature. An account group is a method of coordinating ledger accounts into a tree-structured hierarchy. Each account group is a component of assets, liabilities, income, or expenditure.

1. Go to Gateway of Tally> **Account Info**> **Groups** and select **Create** under Single Group. It opens Group Creation screen, as shown in picture 2.0.

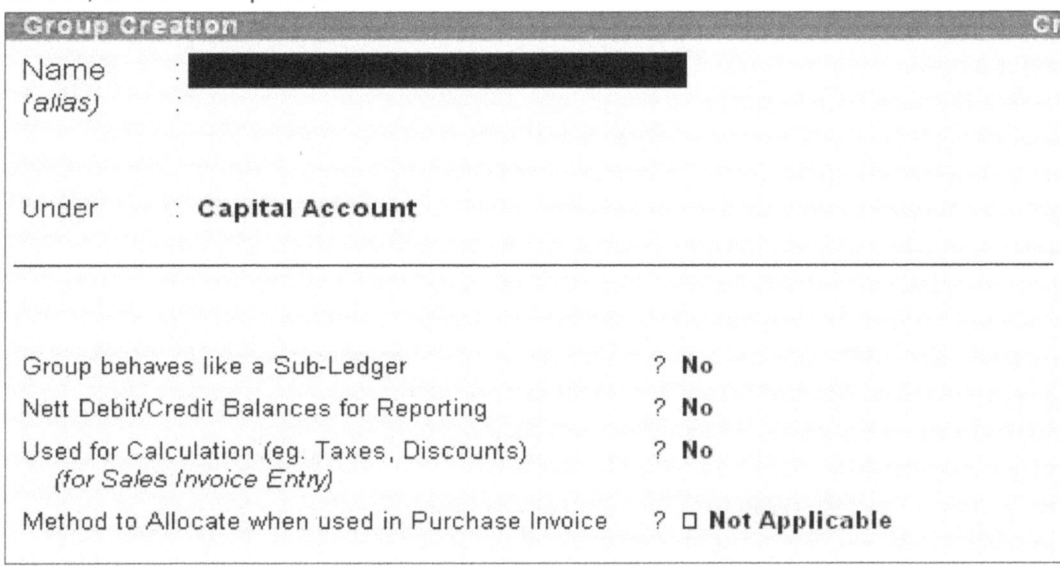

Picture 2.0

2. Type the name of the group: **Banking Detail** and leave alias blank. For Under, you need to select **Current Assets** from the List of Groups at the right-hand side. You can use Tab or Shift+Tab key to undo and redo things quickly.

3. Leave all the other options set to **No**, and go ahead to select Yes on Accept at the end. You can try Display option under Single Group to open Banking Detail group on the screen again.

Creating a Sub-Group

A sub-group is a group inside another group. You need to select the name of the parent group under which you want to create a sub-group.

1. Go to Gateway of Tally> Account Info> Groups> and select Create under Single Group. Enter the name of the sub-group: **Finance Paper**, leave alias blank, and for Under: **Banking Detail**. This means you're creating a sub-group named Finance Paper under the group named Banking Detail.

2. Leave all the other options set to **No**, and save it on Accept. Now select **Display** under Single Group and open **Finance Paper** sub-group which will be shown under Banking Detail-Current Assets. You can always press Esc key or click the Close button to return to the previous screen.

Creating multiple groups

In multiple groups, the sub-groups automatically inherit the features of their parent groups. While creating multiple groups, you have to specify the name of parent group and they all will be saved under parent group.

1. Go to Gateway of Tally> Account Info> Groups> and select **CReate** under <u>Multiple Groups</u>.

2. Select **Banking Detail** for Under Group from the List of Groups. After you press enter, you can type at least three sub-groups name under the **Name of Group** column. In our case we type, **Associate One**, **Associate Two, Associate Three**, and press enter till Accept.

You can go to **DIsplay** under <u>Multiple Groups</u> and select **Banking Detail** to see the name of all the sub-groups you created. You can always make necessary changes by selecting Alter option under <u>Multiple Groups</u>.

Lesson 5
Understanding Ledgers

A ledger is the most important part of your company's financial records. It is organized into hierarchical levels in account groups to represent assorted, summarized, and balanced transactions of a company. When you make a transaction of a company in Tally, you need to specify its ledger name. This helps in maintaining consistency in accounts related information. A ledger constitutes the records of each transaction through vouchers. Before moving ahead, you need to know about the accounting, inventory, and statutory and taxation features to use a ledger in Tally. You can open **Accounting Features** by pressing F11 on Gateway of Tally and read all the options. Similarly, you can open **Inventory Features** and **Statutory & Taxation Features**.

Setting Accounting Features

Accounting Features allows you to set the features related to accounting. It contains a number of headings and each heading contains some options. Some of the important options are explained below.

A. The options under the **General** heading are:
Integrated Accounts and Inventory: Enables you to integrate or separate account and inventory.
Income/Expense Statement instead of P & L: Enables you to prepare the income and expenditure statements rather than profit and loss statements.
Allow Multi-Currency: Allows you to include multiple currencies in the records.

B. The options under the **Outstanding Management** heading are:
Maintain Bill-wise Details: It activates Sundry Debtors and Sundry Creditors in Ledger Master.
Activate Interest Calculation: Allows you to calculate interest automatically when it is set you Yes.

C. Other important options:
Cost/Profit Centres Management: Allows you to create a payroll for an employee.
Invoicing: Allows you to make voucher transactions inside the invoice mode.
Budgets and Scenario Management: Allows you to maintain budgets.
Other Features: Allows you to print some documents.

Setting Inventory Features

A. The options under the **General** heading are:

Integrate Accounts and Inventory: Allows you to integrate accounts and inventory features.

Allow Zero valued entries: Allows you to use zero value entries in your vouchers.

B. The options under the **Storage & Classification** heading are:

Maintain Multiple Godowns: Allows you to create multiple godowns and track movements of the stock in these locations.

Maintain Stock Categories: Allows you to maintain Stock Categories when it is set to Yes.

Maintain Batch-wise Details: Allows you maintain batch details of your stock.

Set Expiry Dates for Batches: Enables you to set expiring date for batches.

Use different Actual & Billed Qty: Specifies received or delivered quantities during invoicing.

C. The options under the **Order Processing** heading are:

Allow Purchase Oder Processing: Enables you to create a Purchase Order.

Allow Sales Order Processing: Enables you to create a Sales order.

Setting Statutory & Taxation Features

The options of Statutory & Taxation features are:

Enable Excise: Allows you to enable the Excise feature. And another option under this **Set/Alter Excise Detail:** Enables you to add or modify information related to excise.

Follow Excise rules for Invoicing: Allows you to set excise rules for invoicing. If this option is set to Yes, Tally will create the invoice with excise rules.

Enable Value Added Tax (VAT): Allows you to enable VAT features. And another option under this **Set/Alter VAT Details:** Allows you to add or modify information related to VAT.

Enable Service Tax: Allows you to set the service tax features for the company. The other option under this **Set/Alter Service Tax Details:** Enables you to add information related to service tax.

Enable Tax Deduction at Source (TDS): Allows you to collect income tax if the employees of your company come under the norms and regulations of the Income Tax Department. The other option under this **Set/Alter TDS Details:** Enables you to add or modify information related to TDS.

Enable Tax Collected at Source (TCS): Allows the company to make any sort of deductions from the employee's wage. The deductions could be in the form of tax and contribution towards savings. The other option under this **Set/Alter TCS Details:** Enables you to add or modify information related to TCS.

Enable Fringe Benefit Tax (FBT): Allows you to enable taxable benefits, other than wage, which are given to the employees. Any benefits or perks that employees (current or past) get as a result of their employment are to be taxed which depends upon the employer. Such taxable benefits include entertainment, club membership, telephone, and hotel boarding and lodging.

The other option under this **Set/Alter FBT Details:** Enables you to add or modify information related to FBT.

Setting Ledger Configuration

There is a Configuration setting in Tally to add fields in ledgers.

1. You need to press **F12** or click on **Configuration** button on Gateway of Tally which opens **Configuration Menu**, as shown in picture 2.1.

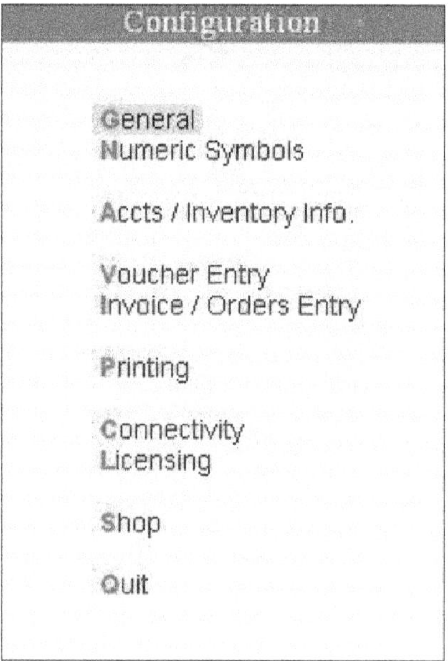

Picture 2.1

2. In Configuration menu, you can select the option that you want to make the change in. In our case, we select **Accts/Inventory Info** option and press enter on that.

3. It opens **Master Configuration** screen in which you can set the options as per your requirement or leave it as it is. We quit this screen by pressing Esc.

Creating a Single Ledger

A ledger is a book in which business transactions are posted in the form of double entry book-keeping system. Without a ledger, we can not record any transaction. There are three ways to create ledgers, such as single ledger, multiple ledgers, and ledgers in advance mode.

1. Go to Gateway of Tally> Accounts Info> **Ledgers** and press enter on **Create**. It opens Ledger Creation screen, as shown in picture 2.2.

2. Type beside Name: **Business Element**, and beside alias: **BS**. Alias helps you access the ledger by its alias name also.

3. For Under: select **Capital Account** as parent account group from the List of Groups. You can type **Yes** for Inventory Values are affected, and set **No** for Cost centres are applicable.

4. When the cursor moves to Mailing Details section, type the mailing address, state, PIN Code, PAN/IT No. and Sales Tax No.

5. Enter Opening Balance: **9, 00,000 Cr**. (Cr abbreviation is used for Credited). Then select Yes on Accept to create the ledger. Press Esc when another empty ledger creation screen appears.

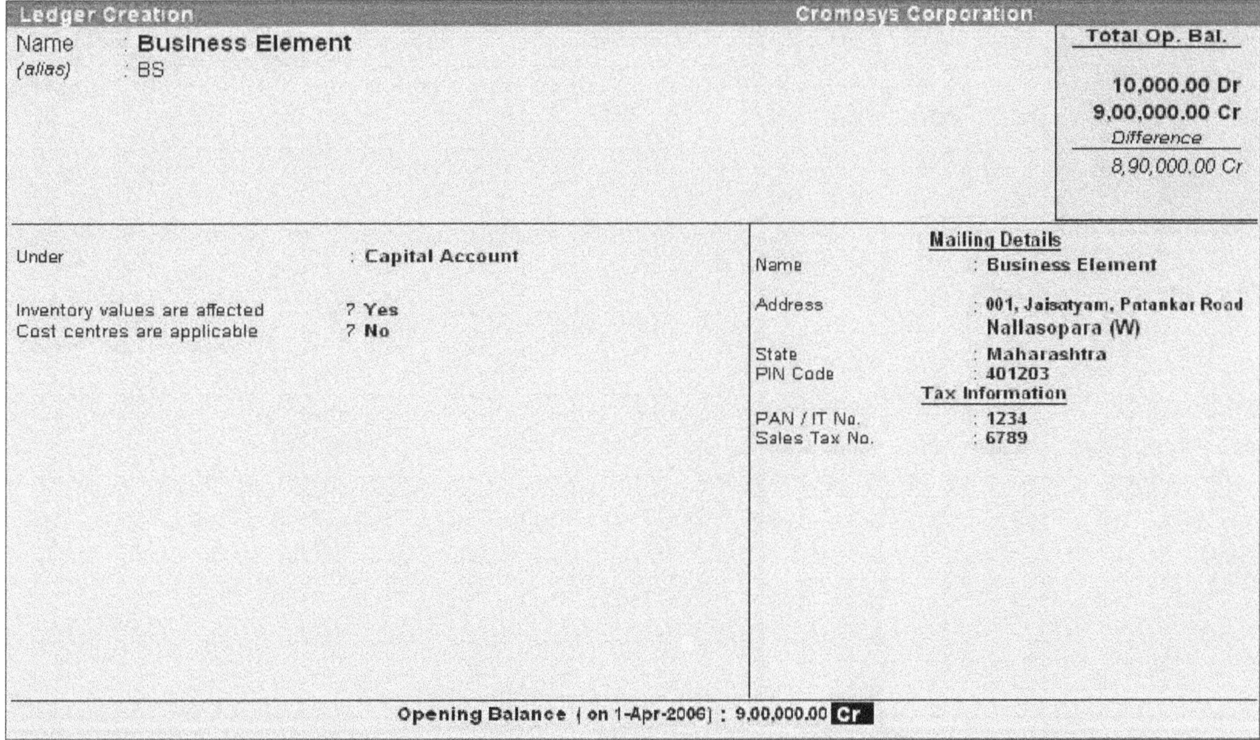

Picture 2.2

6. To display the single ledger you created, you can select **Display** under **Single Ledger** in the **Ledger** menu, and select the name **Business Element**. You can go to Alter mode to make changes if you want.

Creating Multiple Ledgers

When you are creating a multiple ledger, you need to specify the parent account group in which the ledger is being created.

1. Click **CReate** option under **Multiple Ledgers** in the **Ledgers** menu. It opens the Multi Ledgers Creation screen as shown in picture 2.3.

Picture 2.3

2. For Under Group, select the name of account group **Banking Detail** from List of Groups. In the column of Name of Ledgers, you can type the name of two ledgers: **Prism Cellular** and **Streamline InfoTech**.

3. Enter the Opening Balance: **1, 00,000** (Dr) or (Cr). And select Yes on Accept at the end. You can use Display and Alter options under Multiple Ledgers to see the multiple ledgers you created.

Deleting a Ledger Account
You can delete a ledger only in the **Alter** mode by pressing Alt+D on the selected ledger. If a ledger is used in any account, it cannot be deleted.

Deleting a Company
You do not need to delete things so often in Tally, and you should not even do also, therefore you were not told about deleting a company till now. In case you really want to delete a company, you have to go to **C:\Tally\Data** and in Data folder select the Company's folder you want to delete.

Lesson 6
Creating Sales Ledgers for Services
Sales ledgers are created for keeping the records of sales. If you are selling a service, then create a ledger for the service provided. These ledgers can be created under Sales Accounts or Direct Incomes group.

1. Go to Gateway of Tally> Accounts Info> Ledgers and select Create. It opens the same Ledger Creation screen, as shown in picture 2.2.

2. Type the ledger name beside Name option: **Legal Consultancy**. For Under, you can select **Sales Accounts** or you can even select **Direct Incomes** from the List of Groups.

3. Set the **Inventory values are affected** option to **Yes**. Set the **Is Service Tax Applicable** option to **Yes**. It opens <u>Category Name</u> screen. Using a different version of Tally may hide some options of this chapter.

4. Select the **Charted Accountants** option for Category Name from the List of Service Categories. Set the **Is Abatement Applicable** option to **Yes**. Type the Notification No.: **01**, Percentage: **2%**.

5. Enter Mailing Details and Tax Information, and Opening Balance: **50,000**. Select Yes on Accept. This is how you create a Sales Ledger. You can use Display option to check.

Creating Purchase Ledgers for Service
Purchase ledgers for service tax are created under the Purchase Accounts or Direct Expenses group. Any payment made for the purchasing and hiring the services, such as professional and consultancy are recorded in the purchase ledger.

1. Go to Gateway of Tally> Accounts Info> Ledgers and select Create.

2. Type beside Name: **Appliance Purchase**, select for Under: **Purchase Accounts** and set the **Inventory values are affected** option to **Yes**. Then set the **Is Service Tax Applicable** option to **Yes**.

3. Select the **Charted Accountants** option for Category Name. Set the **Is Abatement Applicable** option to **Yes**. Enter the Notification No. and Percentage.

4. Enter Opening Balance: **20,000** and select Yes on Accept. This is how you create a Purchase Ledger. You can use Display option to check.

Creating a Voucher

A voucher is a primary document that contains the details of account transactions. The transactions are recorded in vouchers and affect the profit and loss account and balance sheet. Now you are going to create a voucher by performing these steps:

1. Go to Gateway of Tally> Accounts Info> **Voucher Types** and select **Create**. It opens Voucher Type Creation screen which is divided into three sections – General, Printing, and Name of Class (shown in picture 2.4).

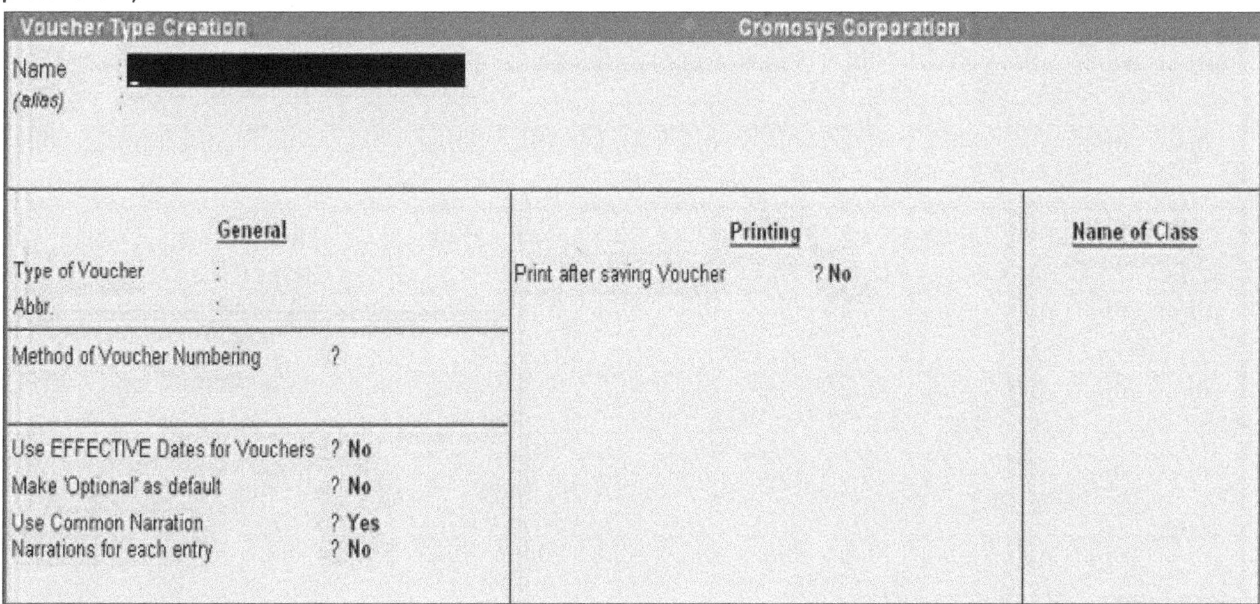

Picture 2.4

Now let's look at the sections present in the Voucher Type Creation screen. The options under the General section are as follows:

Type of Voucher: Gives you the list of voucher types to define the type of your voucher.

Abbr.: Sets a default name to a voucher which is specially used for unformatted reports.

Method of Voucher Numbering: Provides three methods of voucher numbering – Automatic, Manual, and None. If you select **Automatic** option and set the advance configuration to **Yes**, vouchers would be numbered automatically. If you select Manual option, then the numbering has to be done manually. You can use the None option to disable the voucher numbering option.

Use EFFECTIVE Dates for Vouchers: Allows you to enter the effective dates for the vouchers.

Make 'Optional' as default: Allows you to set your voucher to optional voucher by default.

Use Common Narration: Gives a common narration for all entries or a separate narration for each entry.

Narrations for each entry: Allows you to provide a separate narration for each entry when you se this option to Yes. This option is used for vouchers with multiple entries with separate details for each entry.

The options under the <u>Printing</u> and <u>Name of Class</u> section are as follows:

Print after saving Voucher: Allows you to print a voucher when you set this option to Yes. Selecting this option would first save the voucher and then generate its printout automatically. Select **No** if you do not want to print the voucher.

Name of Class: Allows you to classes for voucher type. You can use a voucher class in sales invoicing where the nominal ledger account to be credited for each item of sale is defined once. You can also use the voucher class to automatically round off values and enter values to predefined ledger accounts.

2. Coming back to the Voucher Type Creation screen, you can enter beside the Name option: **Electronic**, and type the alias name if you want: **Et**.

3. Select the parent voucher beside the Type of Voucher: **Purchase**, type the Abbr.: **Purc**, select the Method of Voucher Numbering: **Automatic**. Set the other options under the General section as per your requirement.

4. Set Print after saving Voucher: **No**, and enter the Name of Class if you have created a Voucher Class, or else you can skip it. Select Yes on Accept.

You can use Display and Alter options to view and edit the details you entered while creating a voucher in Tally.

Some commonly used vouchers
There are some (parent) vouchers that are commonly used in Tally. You see the list of these parent vouchers at the time of selecting a **Type of Voucher** in Voucher Creation screen, as shown in picture 2.5. Let's see the options in the List of Voucher Types.

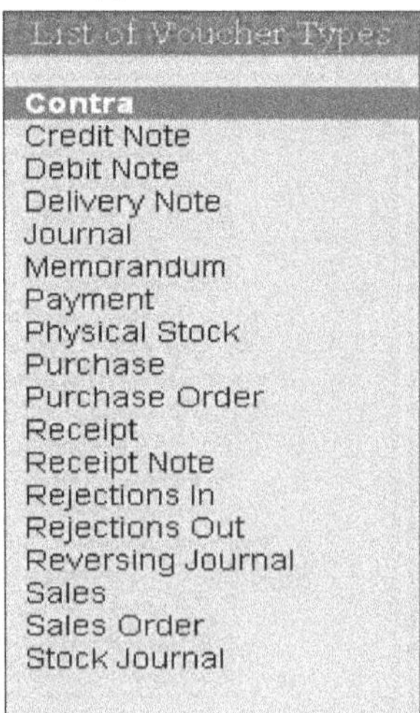

Picture 2.5

Contra Voucher: Indicates transactions related to the transfer of funds from Cash Account to Bank Account, Bank Account to Cash Account, and Bank Account to Bank Account.

Journal Voucher: Indicates where the company requires to adjust the debit and credit amount without involving the cash or bank accounts. Therefore, they are referred as adjustment entries.

Payment Voucher: It records the transactions related to payment. When a company settles the expenses of conveyance and stationary through cash in one voucher, you can enter these details in the payment voucher.

Purchase Voucher: Allows you to record purchase-related entries.

Sales Voucher: Allows you to record sales-related entries. When a sales transaction takes place, a document detailing the transaction (item name, tax, etc.) has to be given to the buyer (debtor) as a proof of purchase. This document is called an **Invoice** or **Bill** or **Cash Memo**.

Lesson 7
Creating a Voucher Entry
A voucher is a document that contains the detail of financial transactions. When you enter data in Tally though the voucher entry mode, it is known as voucher entry. You can use the suitable voucher to enter the details into the ledgers for each transaction. There are two kinds of vouchers in Tally – Accounting Voucher and Inventory Voucher.

Create an Accounting Voucher
Accounting vouchers contain entries related to accounting transactions. Perform the following steps to create an accounting voucher in Tally:

1. Go to Gateway of Tally and select **Accounting Vouchers**. It opens Accounting Voucher Creation screen which is divided in three parts: Main Voucher Entry Area, button bar, and Calculator Area, as shown in picture 2.6. Now we can see how these parts function.

Main Voucher Entry Area: Allows you to enter all your transactions. It includes date, name of the ledger, amount, and the screens depending on your voucher configuration.

Button Bar Area: Displays various buttons for quick interactions.

Calculator Area: Allows you to enter any number of mathematical formulae for complex calculations.

2. In Accounting Voucher Creation screen, you need to select the name of the account. As you have not created a ledger for an account in Tally yet, so go ahead and press Alt+C on Account option. It opens Ledger Creation (Secondary) screen.

3. Type beside Name: **HDFC Bank**, leave alias blank, and select for Under: **Bank Accounts** from the List of Groups. When you select Bank Accounts, it says Current Assets below the Under option. Set Cost Centres are applicable to: **No**, and enter Account Number, Address, State, and Pin Code. Select Yes on Accept. It selects HDFC Bank beside Account option in Accounting Voucher Creation screen.

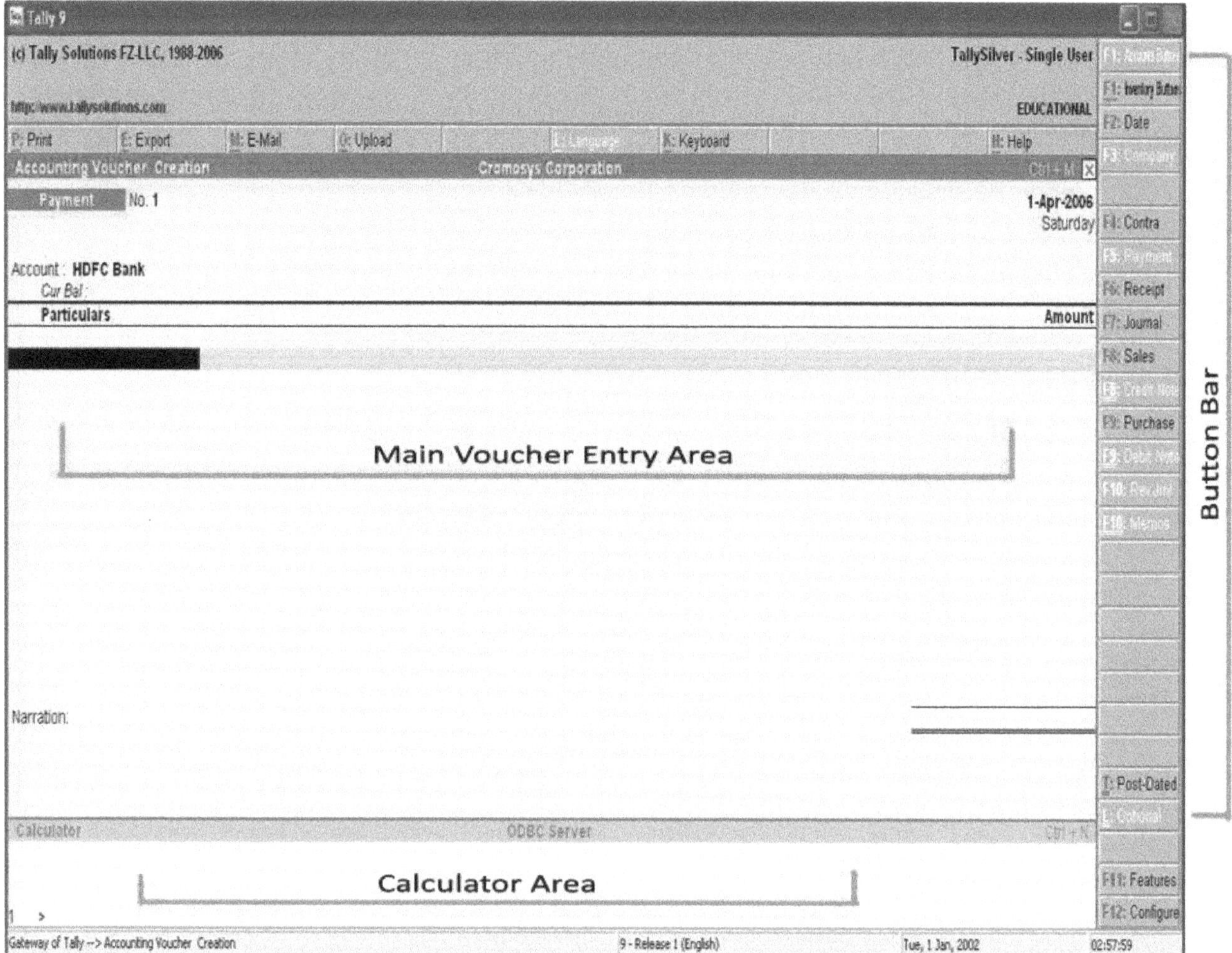

Picture 2.6

4. Now in <u>Particular</u> section you need to select the thing which is being sold, but Tally will list only those things which have their ledgers already created. In accounting voucher creation, every entry needs a ledger associated with it. So you can press Alt+C when the cursor is blinking under Particulars, and type beside Name: **Soundcard**. Select for Under: **Banking Detail**, Inventory values are affected: Yes, Cost centres are applicable: No, and select Yes on Accept. It opens <u>Inventory Allocation screen</u> for Soundcard.

5. In Inventory Allocation screen, select **Motherboard** for <u>Name of Item</u>. It opens Items Allocation Screen. Select under Godown: **New Delhi**, Quantity: **10**, and Rate and Amount will be filled automatically. Press enter till it brings you back on Accounting Voucher Creation screen.

6. On Accounting Voucher Creation screen, press enter to go to Narration section where you can enter cheque number or additional detail if necessary. And then, select Yes on Accept. If you are using a different version of Tally, the options may be a little dissimilar.

This is how you create an Accounting Voucher in Tally. The next chapter will help you create an Inventory Voucher. Doing practice over these lessons is necessary as that is the only way of getting familiar to the functions in Tally.

Create an Inventory Voucher

This is the second type of voucher in Tally. Let us go ahead and create an Inventory Voucher following these steps:

1. First you have to configure Inventory Voucher, and for that press F11 on Gateway of Tally, select Inventory Features. Go to **Storage and Classification** and set **Yes** to: <u>Maintain Multiple Godowns</u>, and set **Yes** to <u>Maintain Stock Categories</u>. Select Yes on Accept at the end.

2. Go to Gateway of Tally and select **Inventory Vouchers**. It opens Inventory Vouchers Creation screen, as shown in picture 2.7. This screen is divided into two parts.

Source (Consumption): Records the data of items that are consumed under the Source part.
Destination (Production): Records the data of items that are produced under Destination part.

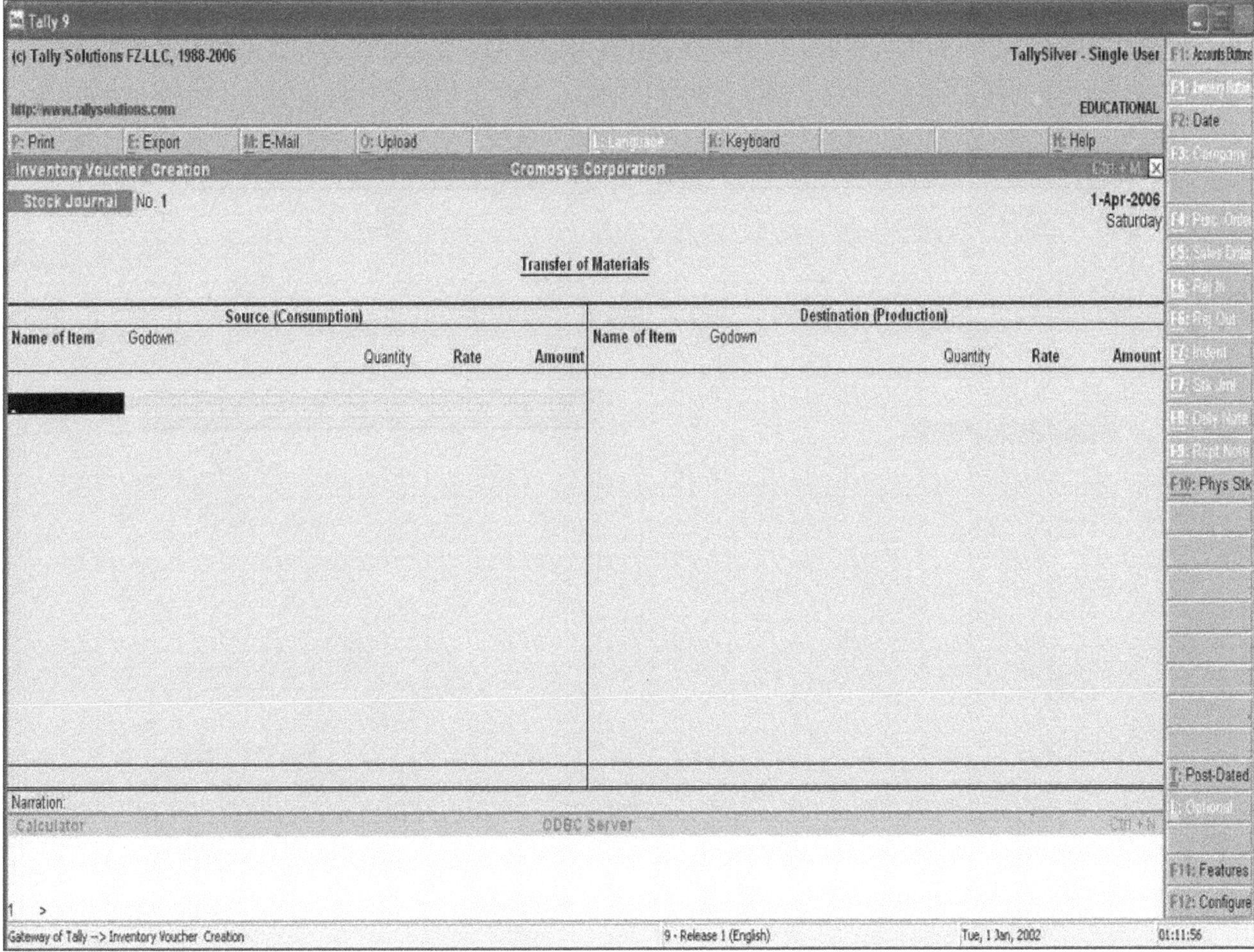

Picture 2.7

3. Type under Name of Item: **Motherboard**, Godown: **Main Location**, and Quantity: **10**. The Rate and Amount will get automatically filled. Press enter till the cursor moves to Destination section.

4. Enter the same information in Destination section as you did in Source section. If you want, you can enter additional detail in Narration at the bottom. Select Yes on Accept at the end.

Lesson 8
Working with Purchase Orders

A Purchase Order is an order that is created in Tally and directly sent to the supplier. The order that you place can be seen in the Stock Summary screen. The purchase order book lists all the purchase orders placed and sales order book lists all the sales orders received.

Creating a Purchase Order

In order to create a purchase order, you have to activate this option in Inventory Features following these steps:

1. Press F11 on Gateway of Tally and select **Inventory Features**. Go to the section that says **Order Processing** and set **Yes** to Allow Purchase Order Processing and Allow Sales Order Processing. Select Yes on Accept at the end.

2. Go to Gateway of Tally, press enter on **InvenTory Vouchers** and click the button **F4: Purc. Order** located on the vertical button bar. It opens the Purchase Order in Inventory Voucher Creation screen, as shown in picture 2.8.

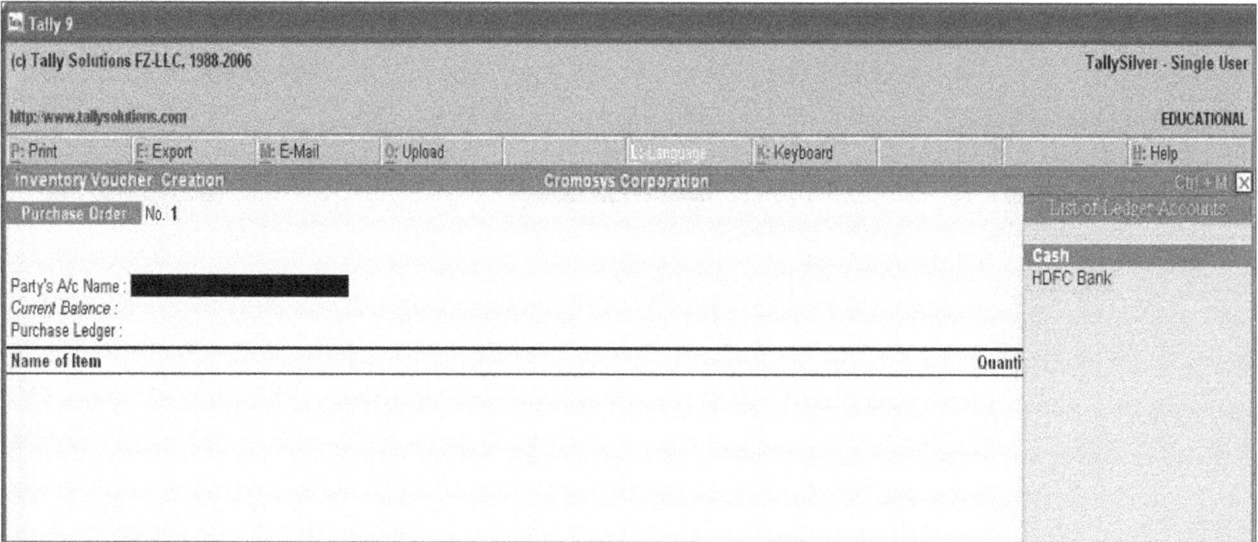

Picture 2.8

3. To make a selection beside Party's A/c Name, you have to create a party's (supplier) account. For that, press **Alt+C** on Party's A/c Name which will open a Ledger Creation screen. Enter Name: **Odyssey Company**, Under: **Bank Accounts**, and Opening Balance: **2, 00,000**. Select Yes on Accept at the end which will reopen Inventory Voucher Creation screen and add Odyssey Company as Party's A/c Name.

4. Pressing enter once will open **Supplier's Details** screen. It automatically fills the supplier's name and address. Press enter to go to Order Details section. Enter beside Mode/Terms of Payment: **Cash**, Other Reference: Leave it blank, Terms of Delivery: **30 Days**, Dispatch through: **Roadways**, and Destination: **Chennai**. When you press enter, the Inventory Voucher Creation screen reappears.

5. Enter Order No.: **233**. It will automatically show the amount beside the Current Balance option. Now you are supposed to select a Purchase Ledger which you need to create. Press **Alt+C**, Name: **Direct**

Purchase, Under: **Purchase Accounts**. Select Yes on Accept which will bring Inventory Voucher Creation screen back.

6. Sect the name of item from the list. In our case we select **Motherboard**. When you press enter, Item Allocation screen appears. Select Godown: **Main Location**, Quantity: **10**. Rate and Amount will be automatically filled. Press enter till the end which will open Inventory Voucher Creation again. Press enter till Accept.

To display or alter the purchase order you created, you need to go to **Gateway of Tally> Display> Day Book** and press enter on Odyssey Company entry under Particulars.

Deleting purchase order
If you do no need the purchase order any more, then you can delete it in Tally. But for now, you should not delete it because the next lesson will require a purchase order created in Tally.

To delete a Purchase Order, you can go to Gateway of Tally> Display> Day Book. Select the purchase order that you want to delete and press **Alt+D** on that. If the purchase order is in use by any other company, then it can not be deleted.

Working with Sales Orders
You create a Sales Oder the same way as you created the Purchase Order. Before moving ahead, you need to select **Inventory Features** by pressing F11 on Gateway of Tally, and make sure that under **Order Processing** section the option Allow Sales Order Processing is set to **Yes**.

1. Select **InvenTory Vouchers** from Gateway of Tally and click the button **F5: Sales Order** located on the vertical button bar. It opens the Sales Order in Inventory Voucher Creation screen.

2. Press Alt+C on Party's A/c Name which will open a Ledger Creation screen. Enter Name: **LG Worldwide**, Under: **Bank Accounts**, and Opening Balance: **1, 00,000**. Select Yes on Accept at the end which will reopen Inventory Voucher Creation screen and add LG Worldwide as Party's A/c Name.

3. Pressing enter once will open **Buyer's Details** screen. Press enter to go to Order Details section. Enter beside Mode/Terms of Payment: **Cash**, Terms of Delivery: **15 Days**, Dispatch through: **Airways**, and Destination: **Kanpur**. When you press enter, the Inventory Voucher Creation screen reappears.

4. Press enter on Order No.: **1** which will automatically show the amount beside the Current Balance option. Now select for Sales Ledger: **Legal Consultancy**. This ledger you had created in lesson 6 and saved under Sales Accounts.

5. Sect the name of item from the list, if not available, you can create one by pressing Alt+C which will open Stock Item Creation screen. Name: **Graphic Card**, Under: **Primary**, Unit: **S**, and Rate of Duty: **5**. Select Yes on Accept at the end. It opens Item Allocation screen.

6. Select Godown: **Main Location** from the list. In case the list doesn't come up, you can press any key which will bring the list up. Select Quantity: **10**. Rate and Amount will be automatically filled. Press enter till the end which will open Inventory Voucher Creation again. Press enter till Accept.

To display or alter the sales order you created, you need to go to **Gateway of Tally> Display> Day Book** and press enter on LG Worldwide entry under Particulars. You can also delete a Sales Order by going to Gateway of Tally> Display> Day Book. Select the sales order that you want to delete and press **Alt+D** on that.

Lesson 9
Introducing Invoices

An invoice or bill is a commercial document issued by a seller to a buyer, indicating the products or services and their agreed quantities and prices. It also specifies the date and time on the payment that is due. The difference between an invoice and voucher is that in an invoice the stock information is primary and the accounting information is secondary. But a voucher accepts the information in the reverse order.

Creating an Invoice Entry

To create a purchase or sales invoice entry, you need to enable it in Inventory Features by following these steps:

1. Press F11 on Gateway of Tally and select **Inventory Features**. Go to the **Invoicing** section and set **Yes** to Allow Invoicing and Enter Purchases in Invoice Format, as shown in picture 2.9 A. Select Yes on Accept at the end.

Company : **Cromosys Corporation**				
Inventory Features				
General			**Invoicing**	
Integrate Accounts and Inventory	? Yes		Allow Invoicing	? Yes
Allow Zero valued entries	? No		Enter Purchases in Invoice Format	? Yes
			Use Debit/Credit Notes	? No
Storage & Classification			Use Invoice mode for Credit Notes	? No
Maintain Multiple Godowns	? Yes		Use Invoice mode for Debit Notes	? No
Maintain Stock Categories	? Yes		Separate Discount column on Invoices	? No
Maintain Batch-wise Details	? No			
(set Expiry Dates for Batches)	? No		**Purchase Management**	
Use different Actual & Billed Qty	? No		Track additional costs of Purchase	? No
Order Processing			**Sales Management**	
Allow Purchase Order Processing	? Yes		Use Multiple Price Levels	? No
Allow Sales Order Processing	? Yes		**Additional Inventory Vouchers**	
			Use Tracking Numbers (Delivery/Receipt Notes)	? No
			Use Rejection Inward/Outward Notes	? No
F1: Accounts		F2: Inventory		F3: Statutory

Picture 2.9 A

2. Go to Gateway of Tally> Accounting Vouchers and click the button **F8: Sales** located on the vertical button bar. It opens the Accounting Voucher Creation screen for Sales.

3. Now you need to click the buttons **As Voucher** and then **As Invoice** located at the bottom of the vertical bar. Your screen will look like the page shown in picture 2.9 B.

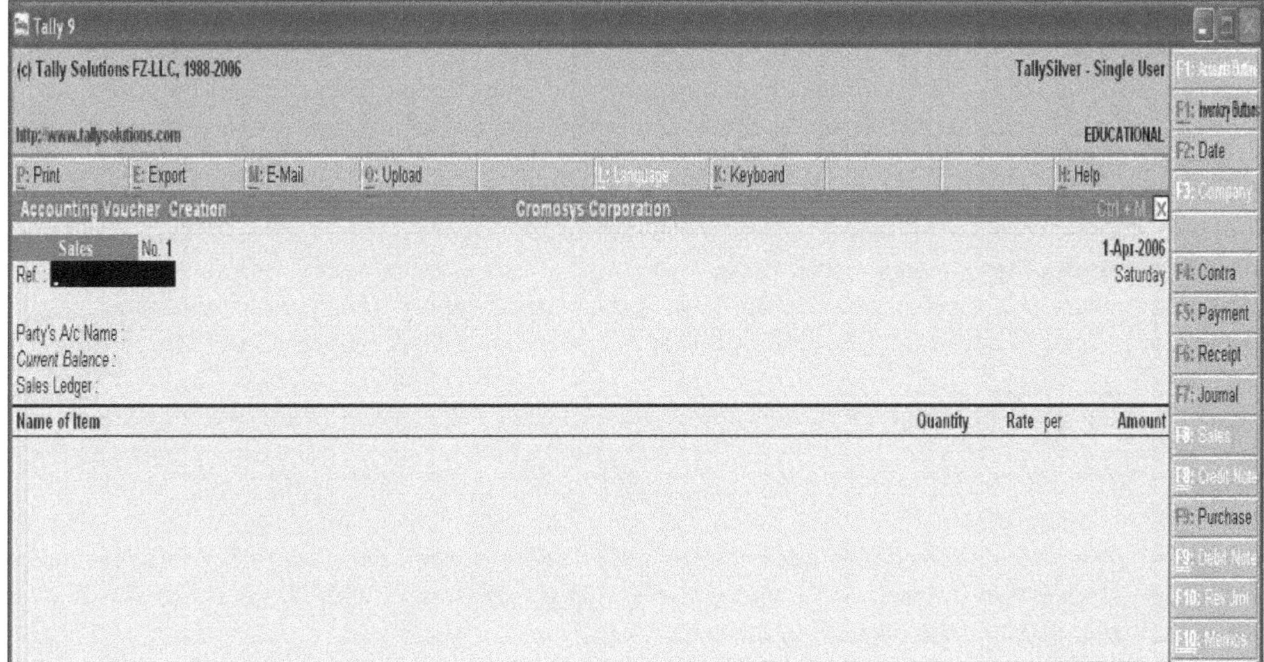

Picture 2.9 B

4. Enter the Reference Number: **123**, select the Party's Account Name from List of Ledger Accounts or you can create one by pressing Alt+C and save it Under <u>Bank Accounts</u>. In our case, we select **LG Worldwide**.

5. It opens <u>Dispatch Details</u> screen. Enter Delivery Note: **123**, dt.: **1-April-2013**, Dispatch Doc No.: **456** (Any Number), Dispatched through: **Roadways**, Destination: **Mumbai**, Order No: **End of list**, Mode/Terms of Payment: **Cash**, Terms of Delivery: **30 Days**.

6. Enter Sales Tax Number at the bottom, and when you press enter it will reopen Accounting Voucher Creation screen.

7. Select the Sales Ledger: **Legal Consultancy**, select Name of Item: **Graphic Card**. It opens Stock Item Allocation screen.

8. Select Order No.: **New Number**, enter New Number: **987** (Any number), Due on: **1-May-2013**, and press enter. Select Godown: **New Delhi**, Quantity: **10**, Rate: **1000**, the Amount will get automatically filled. Select Order No.: **End of List**. The Accounting Voucher Creation screen will reappear. Select Yes on Accept at the end.

This is how you create an invoice entry in Tally. To display or alter the Invoice Entry you created, you can select <u>Display</u> in Gateway of Tally, and then select <u>Day Book</u> and press enter on LG Worldwide. The best way to keep the steps in mind is to do the practice as much as possible.

Lesson 10
Introducing Balance Sheet
Balance Sheet is the financial reporting tool that allows you to perform a quantitative analysis of the company's assets, liabilities, and net worth at a particular date, such as the end of a financial year. We can say that a Balance sheet reflects the quantitative and summarized form of financial position of a company in a particular period. It also displays the owner's fund of a company, what a company owns, and its net worth in business.

The Balance Sheet is a kind of report in Tally, and a report is an organized and formatted presentation of data in the form of text, graphics, and calculations. Tally allows users to collate different types of data such as vouchers and invoices, and display them in the form of report. There are various categories of reports in Tally such as Balance Sheet, Profit & Loss A/c, Stock Summary, and Ratio Analysis.

Configuring a Balance Sheet
Now you knew what a balance sheet is, but before opening, you will have to configure it following these steps:

1. Go to Gateway of Tally, select **Balance Sheet** under Report section, and click **F12: Configure** button located at the vertical button bar. It opens the <u>Configuration</u> screen with some options in it. It is important to understand the purpose of these options.

Show Vertical Balance Sheet: Generates your balance sheet in the vertical format. If you set this to No, the balance sheet will appear in the horizontal format.

Profit or Loss, both as Liability: Displays Profit or Loss, both as liabilities. If you set this to No, Profit and Loss will be displayed as assets in the balance sheet.

Show Percentages: Displays balance sheet with percentage column.

Show Working Capital figures: Allows you to show the value of working capital. Working capital is the value obtained by subtracting Current Assets and Current Liability.
Method of showing Balance Sheet: Displays balance sheet in two formats – Assets/Liabilities and Liabilities/Assets.

Appearance of Names: Displays the item name in balance sheet, such as Alias (Name), Alias Only, Name (Alias), and Name Only.

Scale Factor for Values: Allows you to select the scale in order to display values. For example, if we select <u>Hundreds</u> for the <u>Scale Factor for Values</u>, all subtotals and grand totals in the balance sheet will appear in the multiples of hundreds.

2. You can go ahead and set **No** to <u>Show Vertical Balance Sheet</u> and leave other options unchanged or you can change as per your requirement. When you press enter to go to the end, it opens the Balance Sheet, as shown in picture 3.0.

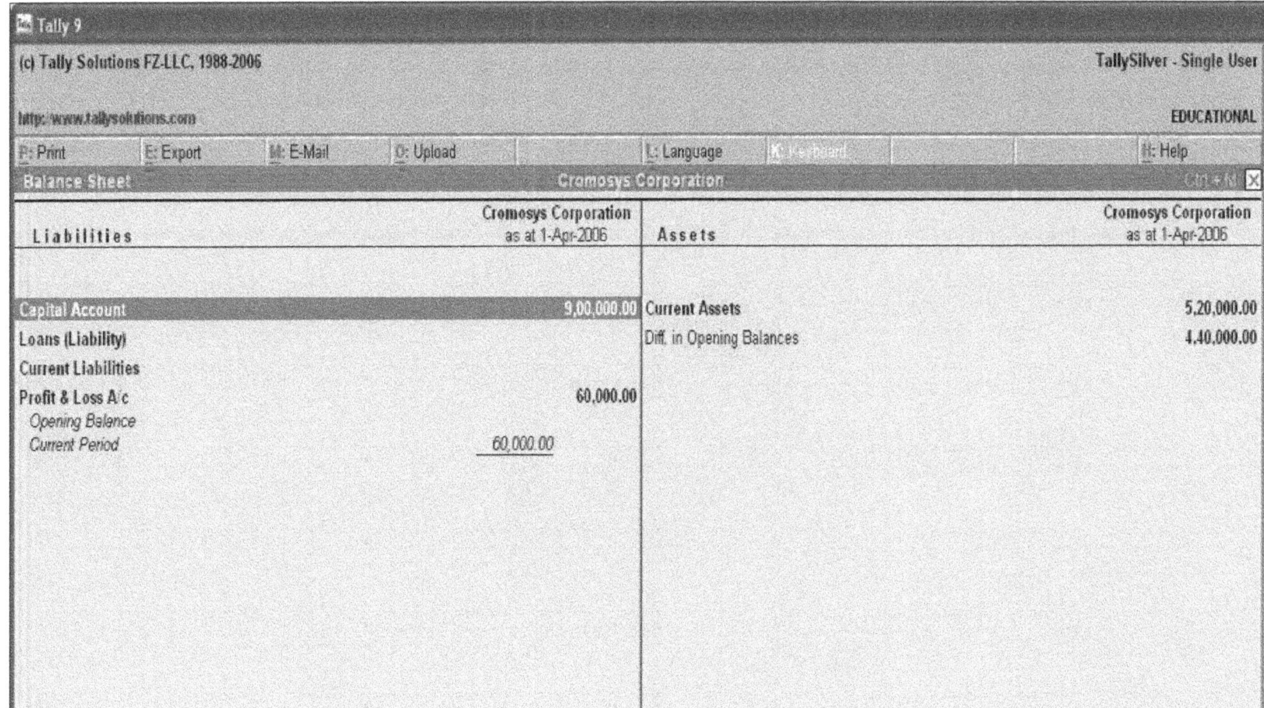

Picture 3.0

Displaying a Detailed Balanced Sheet

Tally ERP 9 also allows you to have a detailed view of balance sheet. To do so, first you have to open a balance sheet, and then press the button **F1: Detailed** in the button bar. Or you can press the shortcut key Alt+F1 also. Now you can see the detailed information of any entry you double-click on.

The **Liabilities** section contains the **Capital Account**, **Loans (Liability)**, and **Current Liabilities** subsection. Under the **Capital Account** subsection, you find three options – the **Customer**, **General Maintenance**, and **Tally Solution** option. Similarly, the **Assets** section contains the **Current Assets** and **Profit & Loss A/c** subsection. Under the Profit & Loss A/c, you find the **Opening Balance** and **Current Period** option.

Cross-checking a Balance Sheet

If you want to know whether your balance sheet is working properly, you can follow these steps mentioned below:

1. First you can go ahead and check the amount that shows beside **Total** option at the bottom of the balance sheet.

2. Now create a new ledger and save it Under: <u>Bank Accounts</u> with Balance: 1, 00000 (Credited).

3. Open the balance sheet again and you will see the amount of new ledger added to the Total amount in the balance sheet.

Working with Profit & Loss A/c

The Profit & Loss A/c report displays the net profit and loss of a company along with the opening and closing stock. To view the Profit & Loss A/c report, you can go to Gateway of Tally and select **Profit & Loss A/c** under <u>Reports</u> section. The picture 3.1 shows the Profit & Loss A/c.

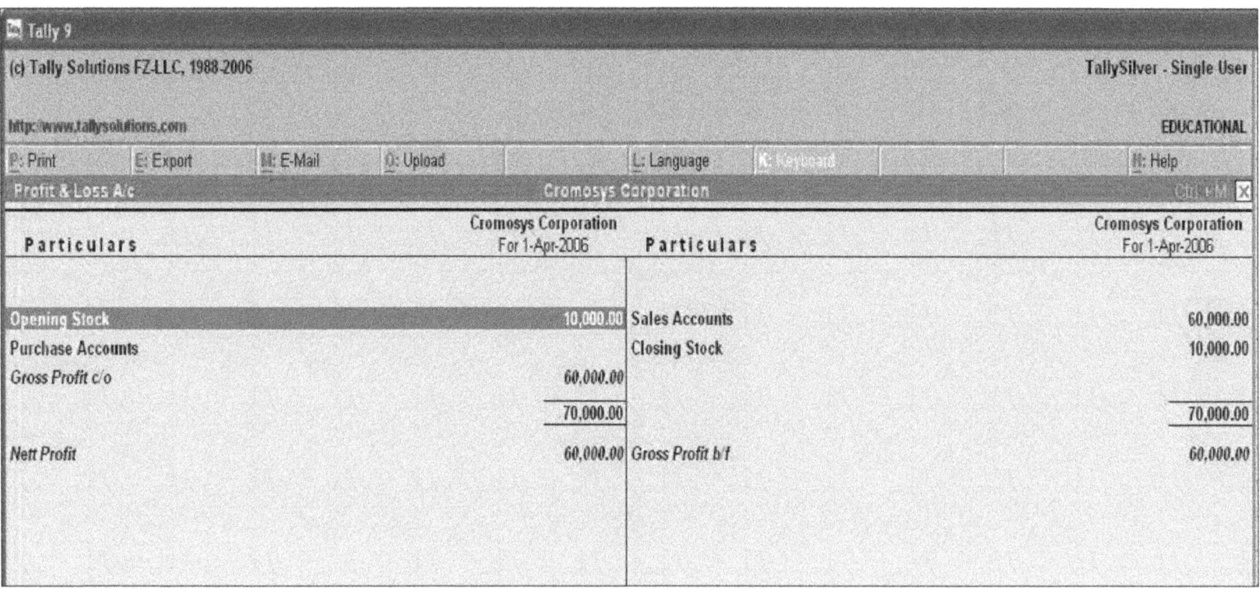

Picture 3.1

You can configure the Profit & Loss A/c by clicking the **F12 Configure** button in the button bar. And you can also display the detailed Profit & Loss A/c by pressing **Alt+F1** or clicking **F1: Detailed** button in the button bar.

Exporting Data to MS Excel

If you want someone to see the Balance Sheet or Profit & Loss A/c information of your company who doesn't have Tally installed in his computer, then exporting the Tally Data to MS Excel format can be the best option.

To do so, click **Export** button at the top of the Balance Sheet that you open. Select **Yes** on the confirmation page. Now go to **My Computer**, open **C: Drive**, and double-click on **Tally folder**. Then you need to right-click the document named **Bsheet** and left-click on **Open With** and select **Microsoft Office Excel**.

Lesson 11

Tax Structure

The act of practice of imposing taxes against any person, property, or activity for the support of government is called taxation. A tax is a financial charge imposed by a state or functional bodies governing a state. Funds are generated through taxation, and then states or other governing bodies perform various functions using these funds. These functions include enforcement of law and order, economic infrastructure, war expenditures, protection of historical properties, and many more.

Tax Deducted at Source (TDS)

TDS is a way of collecting income tax and you can generate different types of TDS reports in Tally. It helps you handle complex cases and calculate the tax payable to the Income Tax Department. Tally calculates the tax of all parties or suppliers where TDS deduction is required.

Enabling TDS in Tally

1. Press F11 on Gateway of Tally and select **Statutory & Taxation**. It opens Company Operations Alteration screen for Statutory & Taxation, as shown in picture 3.2. In this screen, you need to set **Yes** to the options Enable Tax Deducted Source (TDS) and Set/Alter TDS Details, and then press enter.

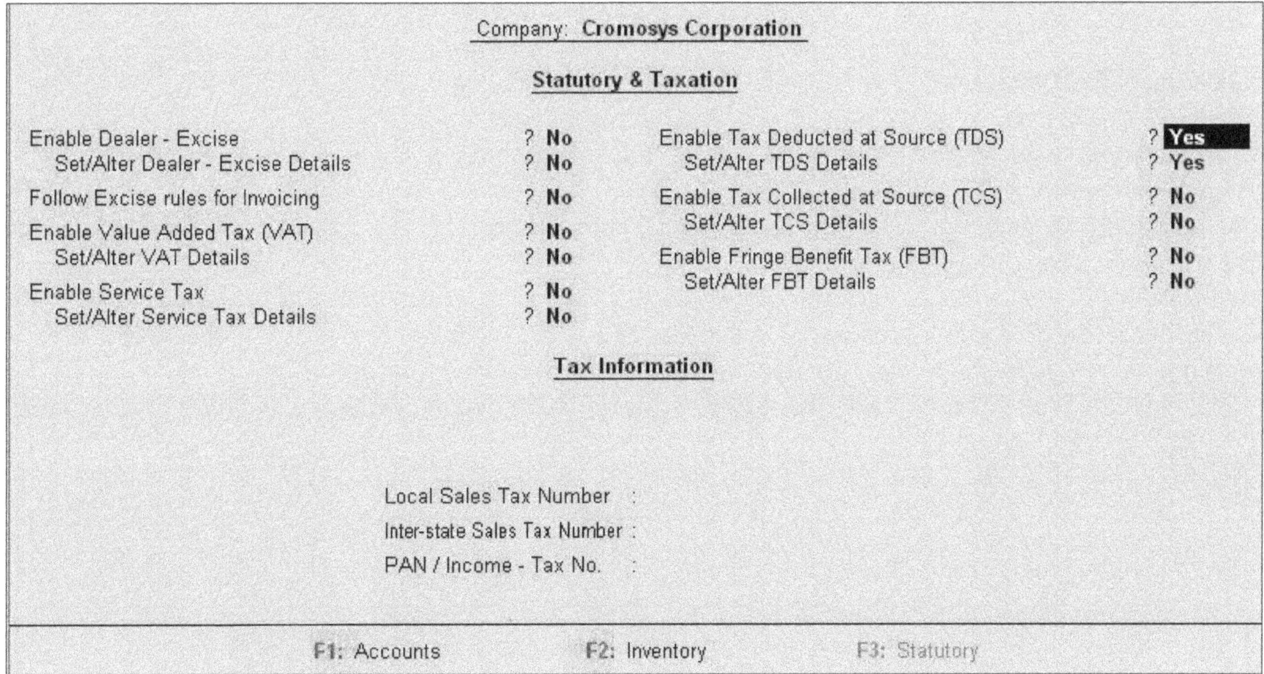

Picture 3.2

2. It opens Company TDS Deductor Detail screen. You can enter the Tax Assessment Number: **BRJL458544** (Any number), type for Income Tax Circle/Ward (TDS): **DTSI-TDS**, Deductor Type: **Other**, Name of person responsible: **Mr. Steve**, Designation: **Account Manager**.

Let us understand what these options are under Company TDS Deductor Details screen:

Tax Assessment Number (TAN): Allows you to enter the 10-digit alphanumeric number that is issued by the Income Tax department to the deductors.

Income Tax Circle/Ward (TDS): Allows you to enter the Income Tax Circle/Ward details.

Deductor Type: Allows you to select the deductor type depending on the organization from the list whether it is Government or Other.

Name of person responsible: Displays the name of the person responsible to file the TDS Returns of your company.

Designation: Displays the designation of the person responsible for the filing of the TDS Returns.

3. When you press enter at the end of Company TDS Deductor Details screen, the Statutory & Taxation screen comes back again where you need to enter tax information such as – Local Sales Tax Number, Inter-state Sales Tax Number, and PAN/Income – Tax Number. Select Yes on Accept at the end.

Creating a Tax Ledger

The Tax Ledgers have to be created using the **Duties and Taxes** group. This group is automatically used for the calculation of tax. The tax ledger holds the entire automatic calculation for TDS tax deductions at the vouchers entry level. It is internally enabled to calculate tax. But the option to specify the tax type is available only for ledgers under the **Duties and Taxes** group. The tax ledger master screen can be created by following these steps:

1. Go the Gateway of Tally> Account Info> **Ledgers** and select **Create** option under Single Ledger section of the screen. It opens the Ledger Creation screen as shown in picture 3.3.

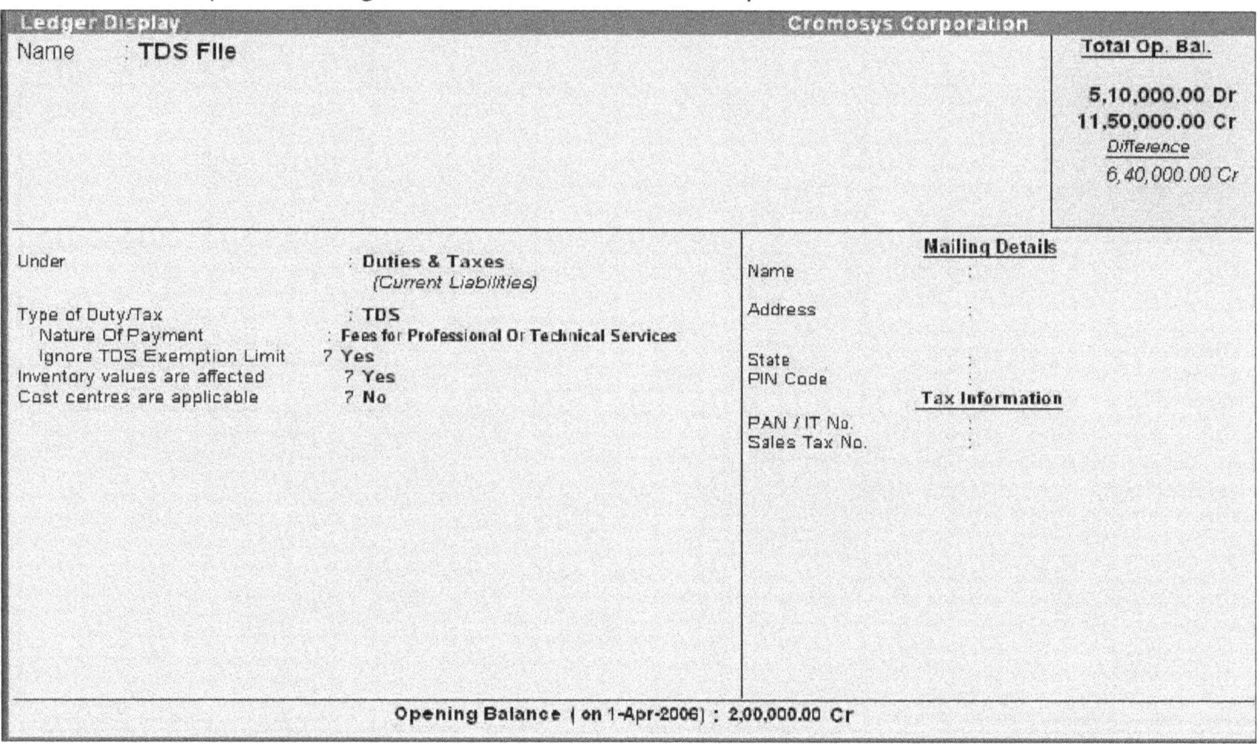

Picture 3.3

2. Enter beside Name: **TDS File**, Under: **Duties and Taxes**, and Type of duty: **TDS**. Nature of Payment: **Fees for Professional or Technical Services**, Ignore TDS Exemption Limit: **Yes**, Inventory values affected: **Yes**, Cost centres are applicable: **No**. Enter Opening Balance: **2, 00000**, and select Yes on Accept.

Lesson 12
Creating a TDS Party Ledger
The TDS Party Ledger is used for recording transactions related to parties. The party ledger can be created following these steps:

1. Go to Gateway to Tally> Account Info> **Ledges** and select **Create** option from the list. Now you need to enter the name of the party whose TDS ledger you want to create.

2. Enter beside Name: **Sigma Creditors**, Under: **Sundry Creditors**, Maintain balance bill-by-bill: **Yes**, Default Credit Period: leave blank, Cost centres are applicable: **No**.

3. Select for Is TDS Applicable: **Yes**. After you press enter, it opens TDS Details screen when you need to fill the other options.

4. Select for Deductee Type: **Body of Individuals**, Is Lower/No Deduction Applicable: **No**, Ignore Surcharge Exemption Limit: **Yes.** If other options appear, set them to No and press enter. It opens the Ledger Creation screen again.

5. Enter mailing details and Tax Information. Enter Opening Balance: **20,000** and press enter at the end. It opens Bill-wise Breakup Form.

6. You can leave the date as it is and press enter on that. Enter beside Name: **Tax Deduction**. It will automatically fill the Due Date and Amount. You can select Yes on Accept at the end.

You can check the display option to make sure the TDS Party Ledger with the name Sigma Creditors is created. Now we will move to the next chapter of this lesson.

TDS Vouchers
TDS Vouchers help you to compute TDS amount. By using TDS Voucher, you can book the expenses incurred or made on a particular type of service or product and directly deducts the amount. This way, the net payable amount is conveyed to the party who is making the final payment as well as end-user who receive the payment.

Creating a TDS Voucher
At the time of creating a TDS voucher, you should be aware of the nature of payment for which you are making TDS deduction. You can perform these steps to create a TDS Voucher:

1. Select **Accounting Voucher** in Gateway of Tally, and click **F7: Journal** button in the middle of the button bar. It opens the Journal in Accounting Voucher Creation screen as shown in picture 3.4.

2. In Particular section of the Journal screen, you can select the ledger **Sigma Creditors** from the List of Ledger Accounts. If you want to create a new ledger for Journal by pressing Alt+C, make sure that you save it Under: Sundry Creditors.

3. When you press enter, the cursor moves to the Debit section where you can enter the amount: **50,000** and press enter after that.

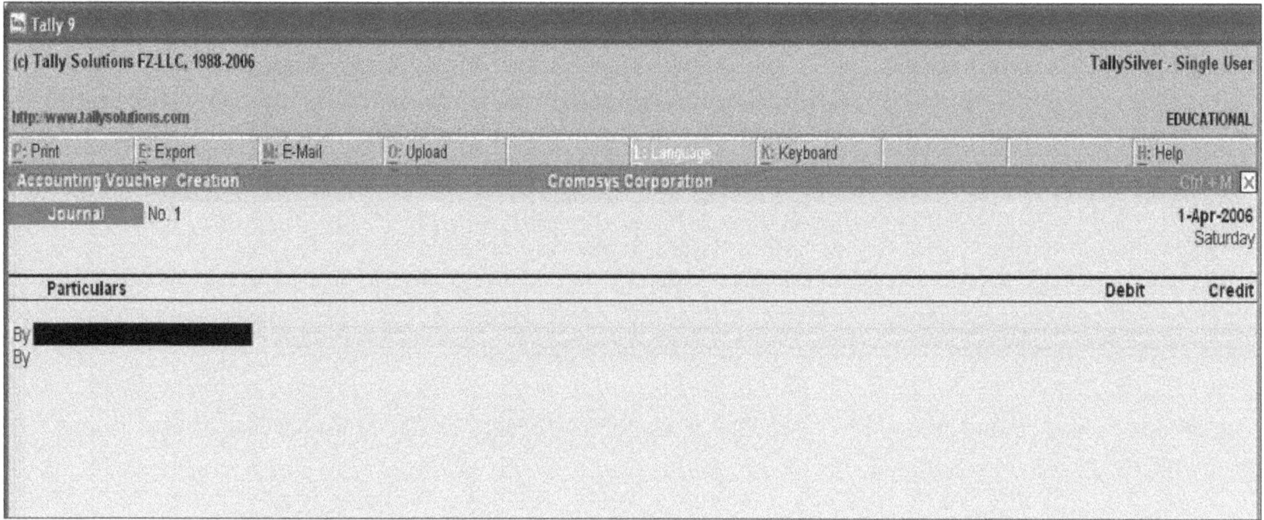

Picture 3.4

4. It opens Bill-wise Detail screen for Sigma Creditors. Select under <u>Type of Ref:</u> **On Account**, and Amount will get filled automatically. You can press enter twice to come back to Journal screen. The Journal screen will want you to select a second ledger in the Particulars section. You can select **Business Element** which opens Inventory Allocation screen.

5. Select under Name of Item: **End of List** and keep pressing enter till the end. In Narration, you can type any detail you want, or you can leave it blank. Press enter again and select Yes on Accept.

You can go to **Display> Day Book** from Gateway of Tally to view and print the entry you crated in Tally. The print option is below the title bar.

Lesson 13
Creating a Payment Voucher in TDS
Payment vouchers are multifunction vouchers, which are used to enter/record all TDS-related transactions. All transactions related to payer through bank, are recorded in the payment voucher. There are mainly two kinds of payment vouchers:

TDS challan payment: Specifies the payment of TDS tax that is done through a government format paper known as challan. These challans are filled by businessman to the bank to pay their TDS tax.

Payment to the party while paying the advance: Specifies that the payment to the third party is recorded in the payment vouchers. These payments can be in the form of advance.

1. Before proceeding ahead, make sure that in Statutory and Taxation – both of the **TDS options** are set **Yes**. You have already done that in <u>Lesson 11</u> following the picture 3.2.

2. Now you can select Accounting Vouchers in the Gateway of Tally, and click **TDS Helper** button in the button bar. If it doesn't appear, you can close Tally program and open again. It opens TDS Filters screen.

3. In <u>TDS Filters </u>screen you can select the ledger from the list named **TDS File**. It will shows only those ledgers in the list which are saved under <u>Duties and Taxes</u>. The picture 3.5 shows the TDS Filter screen.

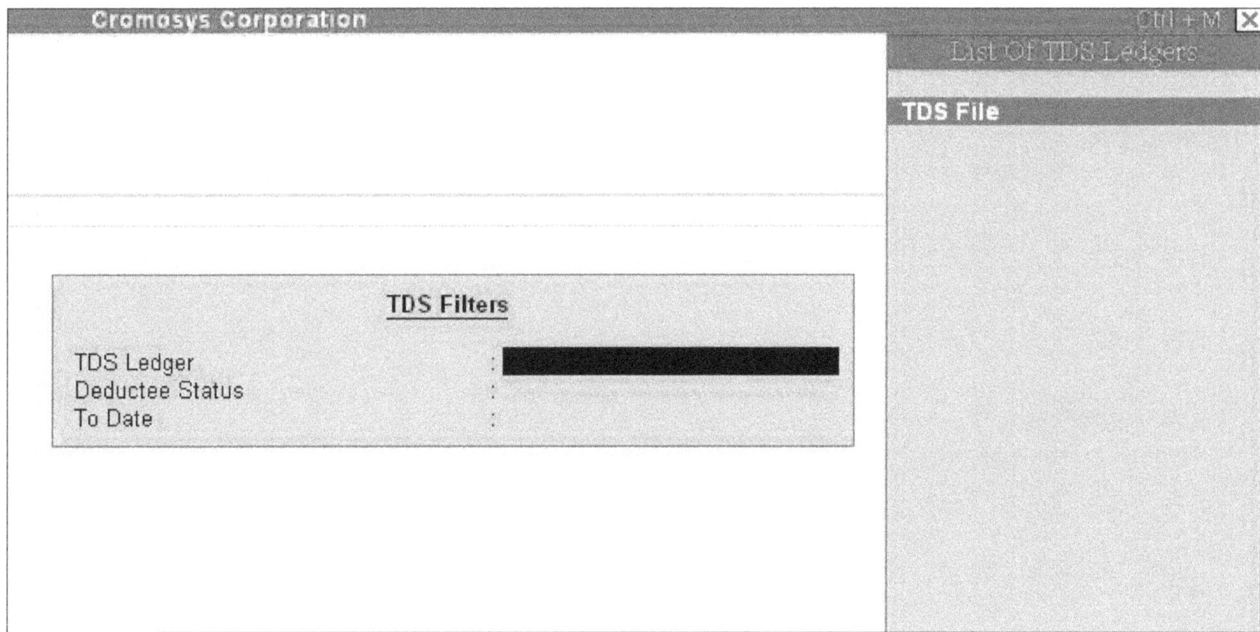

Picture 3.5

4. Select for next option, Deductee Status: **Company**, and enter the date (Any date) in **02.04.2013** format. When you press enter, it opens Accounting Voucher screen with Payment section.

5. Select beside Account: **Odyssey Company** from the List of Account. In case the list doesn't come up, you can press any key which will bring the list up. When you press enter, it does not allow you to edit the particular section but the cursor moves to narration section. For that, you can click **F7: Journal** button in the button bar.

6. Now under <u>Particulars</u>, the first ledger from the <u>List of Ledgers Accounts</u> you need to select is **TDS File**. You can press just enter on Inventory Allocation screen to skip the options. It will bring you back to the main screen of Account Voucher Creation. Type the amount for <u>TDS File</u> under <u>Debit</u>: **75,000** and press enter.

7. Select the next Ledger: **Business Element**. You can press enter on Inventory Allocation screen to skip, and then press enter three times to go to the end. Select Yes on Accept at the end.

To view the entry of this payment voucher, you can go to **Day Book** under **Display** option of Gateway of Tally.

While creating a payment voucher, any mistake on Accounting Voucher Creation screen will not let the detail get saved, and the error will come saying <u>No entries in voucher</u>. In case you see this error, check all the options using Shift+Tab key.

Lesson 14
Introducing TCS (Tax Collected at Source)

TCS is the tax collected by the seller from the buyer/lessee of the goods at the source. The goods are specified under the Section 206C of the Income Tax.

Enabling TCS

1. Press F11 on Gateway of Tally and select **Statutory and Taxation**. You need to set **Yes** to the options Enable Tax Collected at Source (TCS) and Set/Alter TCS Details, and press enter after that. The picture 3.6 shows both of the TCS options enabled.

<table>
<tr><td colspan="4" align="center">Company: Cromosys Corporation</td></tr>
<tr><td colspan="4" align="center">Statutory & Taxation</td></tr>
<tr><td>Enable Dealer - Excise</td><td>? No</td><td>Enable Tax Deducted at Source (TDS)</td><td>? Yes</td></tr>
<tr><td>Set/Alter Dealer - Excise Details</td><td>? No</td><td>Set/Alter TDS Details</td><td>? No</td></tr>
<tr><td>Follow Excise rules for Invoicing</td><td>? No</td><td>Enable Tax Collected at Source (TCS)</td><td>? Yes</td></tr>
<tr><td>Enable Value Added Tax (VAT)</td><td>? No</td><td>Set/Alter TCS Details</td><td>? Yes</td></tr>
<tr><td>Set/Alter VAT Details</td><td>? No</td><td>Enable Fringe Benefit Tax (FBT)</td><td>? No</td></tr>
<tr><td>Enable Service Tax</td><td>? No</td><td>Set/Alter FBT Details</td><td>? No</td></tr>
<tr><td>Set/Alter Service Tax Details</td><td>? No</td><td></td><td></td></tr>
<tr><td colspan="4" align="center">Tax Information</td></tr>
<tr><td colspan="4">Local Sales Tax Number : 4745125</td></tr>
<tr><td colspan="4">Inter-state Sales Tax Number : 745848</td></tr>
<tr><td colspan="4">PAN / Income - Tax No. : BNGH4521Y</td></tr>
<tr><td>F1: Accounts</td><td>F2: Inventory</td><td>F3: Statutory</td><td></td></tr>
</table>

Picture 3.6

2. When you press enter, it opens Company Deductor/Collector Details screen with the options automatically filled in. You can go ahead and press enter till the end which will reopen the Statutory and Taxation screen. Leave other options set to No.

3. You can press enter to the end as you already have Tax Information filled in. You had entered the details for these options while enabling TDS in previous lesson. Select Yes on Accept at the end.

Creating TCS Party Ledgers for Debtors/Creditors

1. Go to Gateway of Tally> Account Info> **Ledgers** and select **Create**. Enter the Name: **ABC TCS Ledger**, Under: **Sundry Debtors**.

2. Select for Maintain balances bill-by-bill: **Yes**, and Default Credit Period: **30**. Set Is TDS Applicable: **No**, and Is TCS Applicable: **Yes**. When you press enter, it opens TCS Details screen.

3. In TCS Details screen, select for the options – Buyers/lessee: **Association of Persons**, Is Lower/No Collection Applicable: **Yes**, Section: **206C**, TCS Lower Rate: **5%**, Ignore Surcharge Exemption Limit: **Yes**.

4. When you press enter, it opens Ledger Creation screen back. Enter Mailing Details and Tax Information. At the end, you can enter <u>Opening Balance</u>: **2, 00,000** and press enter.

5. The <u>Bill-wise Breakup</u> screen appears. Press enter on Date which is auto-filled. Enter the Name: **ABC TCS Ledger**, press enter till the end and select Yes on Accept.

Creating TCS Ledger under Duties and Taxes

You can create a TCS Ledger under <u>Duties and Taxes</u> as well. In order to create it, you need to follow these steps:

1. Go to Gateway of Tally>, Account Info> Ledger and select **Create**. Enter the Name: **BCD TCS Ledger**, Under: **Duties & Taxes**, Type of Duty/Tax: **TCS**.

2. Select for Nature of Goods: Select as per your requirement. In our case we select: **Scrap**. Inventory values are affected: **No**, and enter the Opening Balance: **1, 50,000**. You can go ahead and select Yes on Accept at the end.

Lesson 15
Calculating VAT

VAT is calculated by deducing tax credit from tax collected during the payment period. VAT is imposed on the difference between the sale price of the goods produced or the services rendered and the cost thereof – that is, the difference between the output tax and the input tax. When a company buys goods or services from another supplier, VAT is charged on the purchase price.

Enabling VAT

1. Select **Statutory & Taxation** by pressing F11 on Gateway of Tally, and set **Yes** for <u>Enable Value Added Tax (VAT)</u> and <u>Set/Alter VAT Details</u>, as shown in picture 3.7.

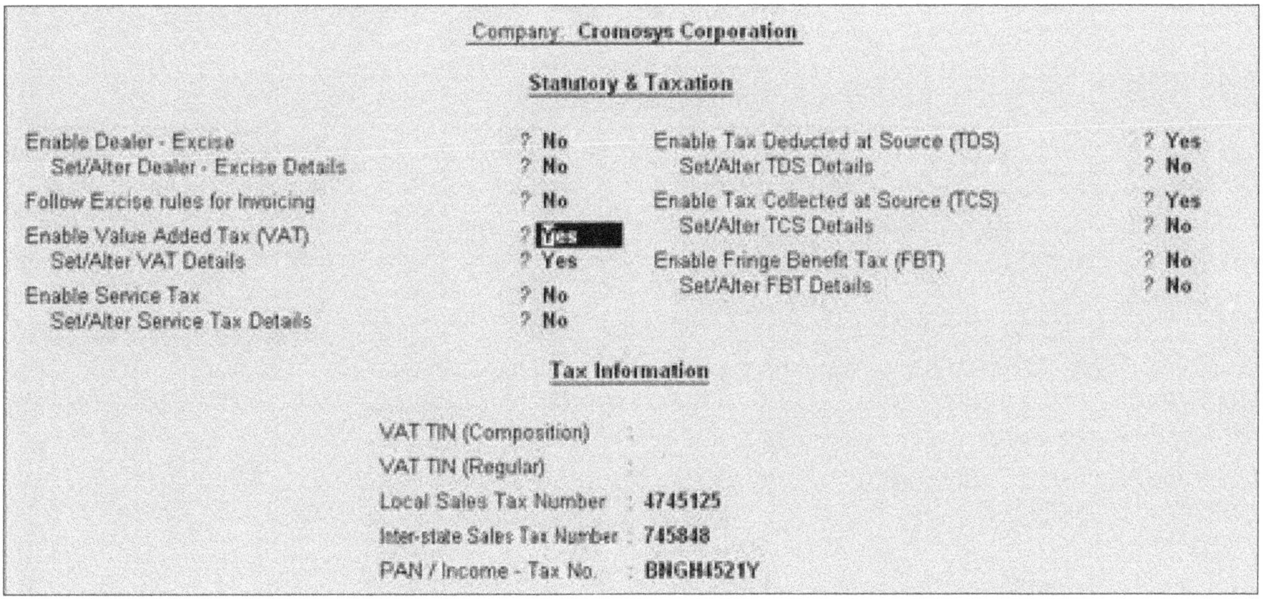

Picture 3.7

2. As you press enter, it opens <u>VAT Details</u> screen. You can select the state, Type of Dealer: **Regular**, Regular VAT Applicable From: press enter on auto-filled date.

3. It opens back the <u>Statutory & Taxation</u> screen. Leave other options set to No, and press enter to come down to Tax Information section. Enter VAT TIN (Regular) number and press enter to select Yes on Accept at the end.

Creating a Purchase Ledger for VAT

After VAT is enabled in Statutory & Taxation, you can now create a Purchase Ledger for VAT following these steps:

1. Go to Gateway of Tally> Account Info> **Ledger** and select **Create**. Type beside Name: **Purchase Ledger**, Under: **Purchase Accounts**, Inventory value affected: **Yes**, Cost centres are applicable: **No**, Used in VAT Returns: **Yes**.

2. It opens VAT/Tax Class screen. Select VAT/Tax Class: **Purchase @ 4%** from the list. Use for Assessable: · **Yes**, Duty/Tax type: **VAT**, Methods of Apportion: **Based on Value**.

3. Enter Opening Balance or leave it blank. Select Yes on Accept at the end.

Tally Installation

Your business and its needs are unique, so Tally is designed to be free of any rigid processes. Your business might need only one installation of Tally for one computer, or it might need multiple installations for many computers in your office network. Accordingly, you can purchase a suitable license of Tally and easily install it in your office. Setup Manager will take care of the installation and basic configuration.

Now in the next chapter, you will learn to install Tally application on your computer. For this, you require administrator rights (Create, Write, Update, Modify, and Delete permissions). If you are using multilingual features, ensure that the operating system supports multiple languages. The hardware and software requirements for a Client-Server system and a standalone computer are provided below. This is valid for all latest versions of Tally.

Lesson 1: System Requirements

1.1 Hardware Requirements

Processor	Intel Pentium IV and above or equivalent
Memory	256 MB RAM Recommended is 512 RAM MB or higher
Free Hard Disk Space	70MB Minimum (Excluding data)
Monitor Resolution	800 x 600 Recommended 1024 x 768 or higher

1.2 Operating System Requirements

Microsoft Windows 98/ME/NT/2000/2003/XP/Vista.

To get the maximum benefit of the Concurrent multilingual capability of **Tally.ERP 9**, we recommend Windows XP and above.

□ *Increasing RAM could improve the performance of **Tally.ERP 9**.*

□ *The **Tally.ERP 9 License Server** can be installed on Windows NT/2000/2003/ XP/Vista operating systems only*

Lesson 2:   Installing Tally.ERP 9 Silver

The installer will assist you with the installation of **Tally.ERP 9** on your computer. During the installation you can accept the default path to install the program, configuration and language files or specify a path of your choice.

2.1 Installing Tally.ERP 9 Silver

You can install **Tally.ERP 9** using any one of the following methods:

Method 1

❑   Double click the **INSTALL.EXE** icon available on the CD.

   Or

Method 2

❑   Click **START** from Windows

❑   Select **RUN**

❑   TYPE **<CD drive>:\INSTALL**

❑   Press **ENTER**

❑   *With **Tally.ERP 9 Silver** do not install **License Server**.*

❑   *To install **Tally.ERP 9**, you need to have administrator rights (to create, write, update, modify and delete) the Application, Data, Configuration and Language directory for Windows NT/ 2000/ XP/ 2003/ Vista operating systems.*

Follow the instructions displayed on your screen to proceed with the Installation of **Tally.ERP 9**.

1. The **Tally.ERP 9** Setup Wizard is displayed as shown.

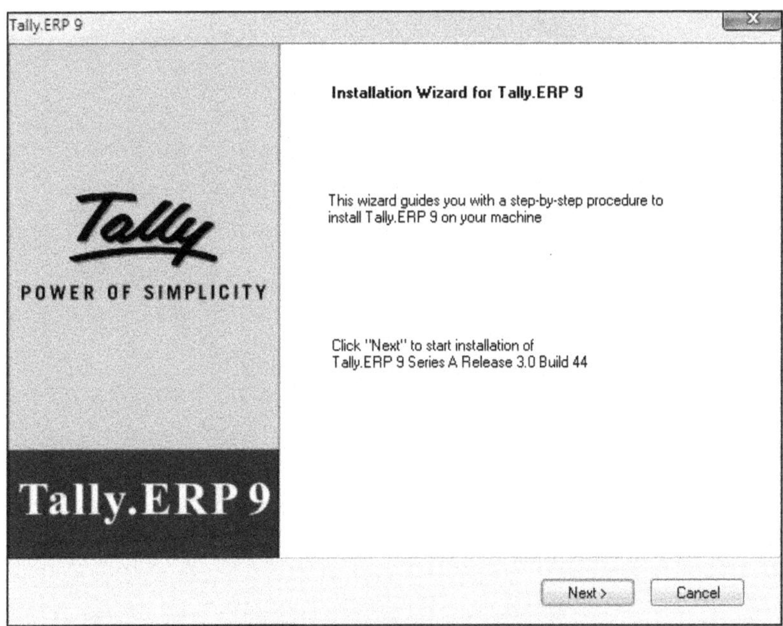

Figure 2.1 Tally.ERP 9 Setup Wizard

2. Click **Next** to continue with the installation.
The **Tally.ERP 9 Setup** screen is displayed as shown

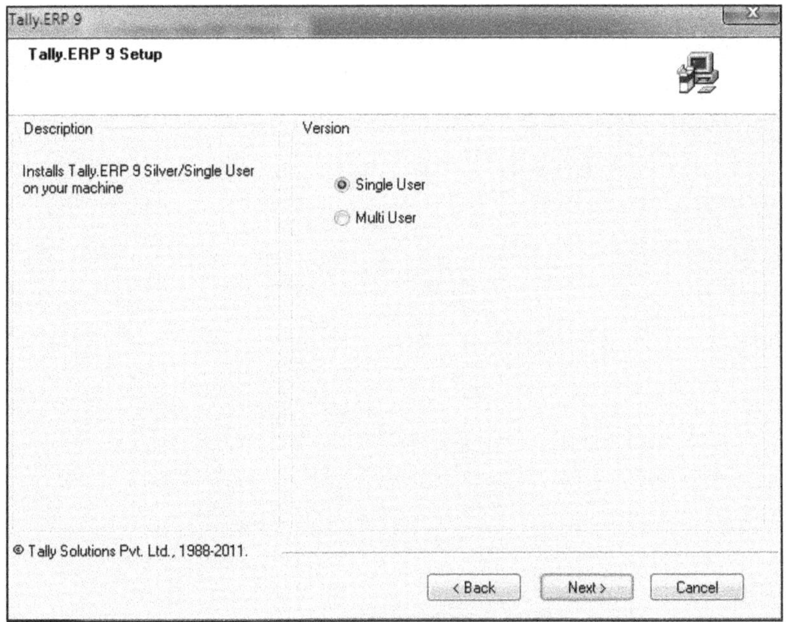

Figure 2.2 Tally.ERP 9 Setup Wizard

3. Check **Single User** to install Tally.ERP 9 **Single User/Silver** Edition on your computer.
4. Click **Next**

The **Tally.ERP 9 Setup** screen is displayed as shown.

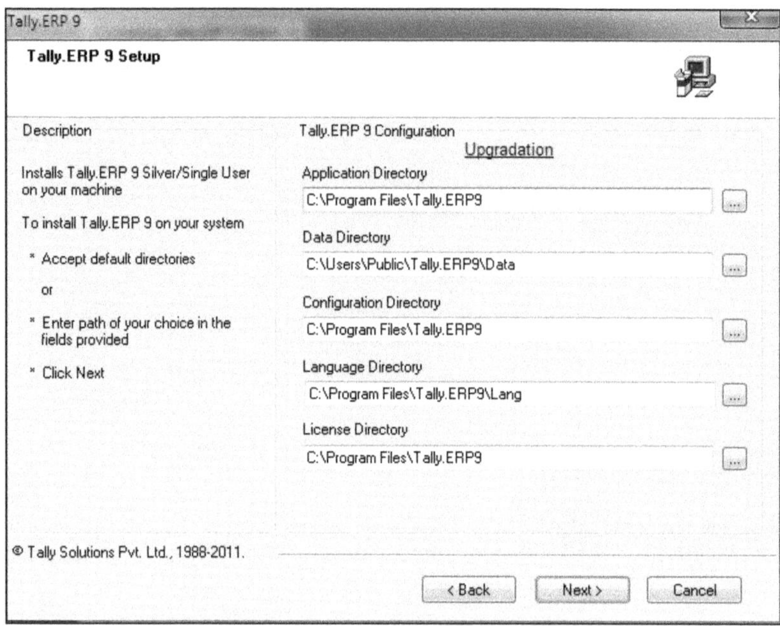

Figure 2.3 Tally.ERP 9 Setup

5. In **Tally.ERP 9 Setup** screen, you may accept the default directories or click on the buttons provided to change the path of **Application Directory,   Data Directory, Configuration Directory, Language Directory** or **License Directory** respectively.

   ▫ **Application Directory**: **Tally.ERP 9** program files reside in this directory.

   ▫ **Data Directory**: **Tally.ERP 9** data resides in this directory.

   ▫ **Configuration Directory**: **Tally.ERP 9** configuration file reside in this directory.

   ▫ **Language Directory**: **Tally.ERP 9** language files (.dct) reside in this directory.

   ▫ **LIcense Directory**: **Tally.ERP 9** license file (.lic) resides in this directory. By default the path of license directory is same as application directory.

*To run multiple instances of **Tally.ERP 9 Silver** on the same computer using single license file, ensure that an earlier version of Tally.ERP 9 is activated and enter path of the license file in **License Directory** while installing..*

6. Click **Next.**

The **Country/Language Selection** screen is displayed as shown.

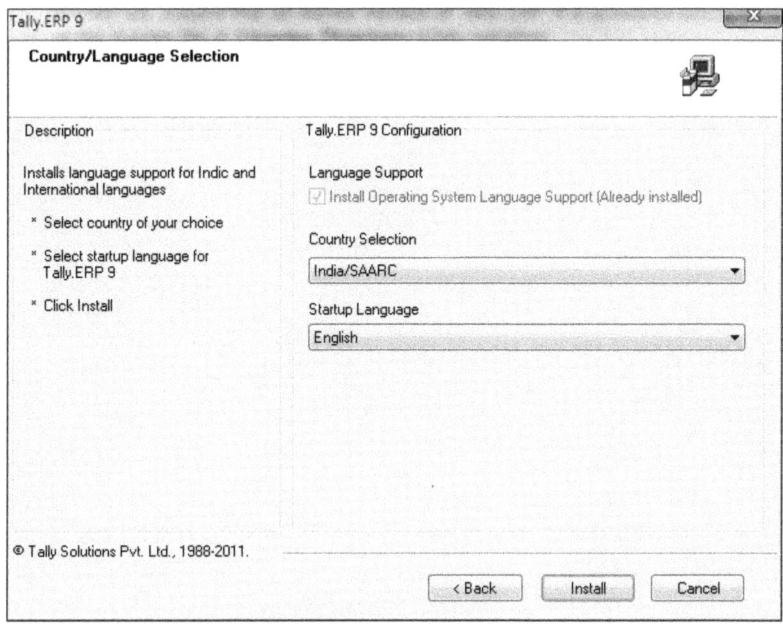

Figure 2.4 Country / Language Selection

7. In the **Country/Language Selection** screen, check **Install Operating System Language Support** to install **Tally.ERP 9** with multi-lingual support.

> □ *To use **Tally.ERP 9** in **English** only, uncheck **Install Operating Systems Language Support**.*
>
> □ *In **Country Selection** choose **India/SAARC,** if you are residing in India or SAARC countries, else choose **Others***

8. Click **Install**.

9. The **Setup Status** screen is displayed as shown.

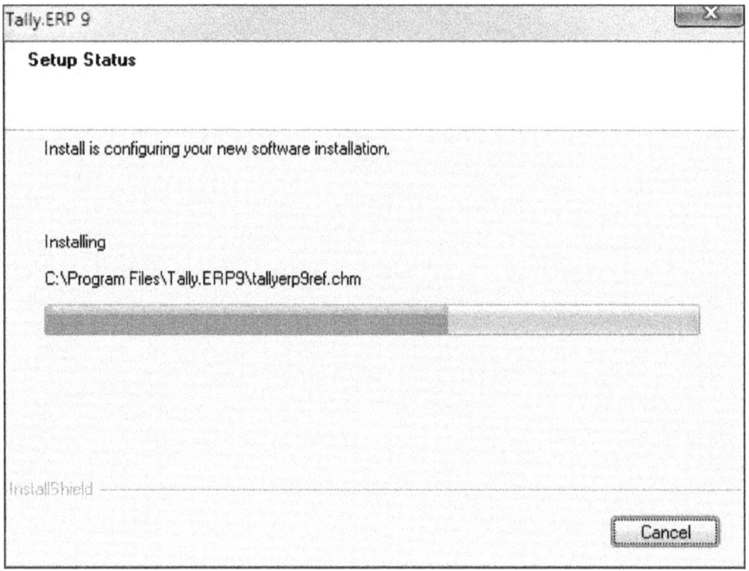

Figure 2.5 Setup Status

10. In case you are prompted for the language support files in the **Files Needed** screen, insert operating systems CD in the drive or click **Browse** and select the i386 folder where the required language support files reside on your computer.
11. Click **OK** to install **Language Support**.

- *The installer prompts for language support files in the **Files Needed** screen, insert operating systems CD in the drive or click **Browse** and select **i386** folder where the required language support files reside.*

- *Click **OK***

- *Click **Cancel**, if you do not have the operating system CD or if you do not want to install language support.*

The **Tally.ERP 9 Installed Sucessfully** screen is displayed as shown.

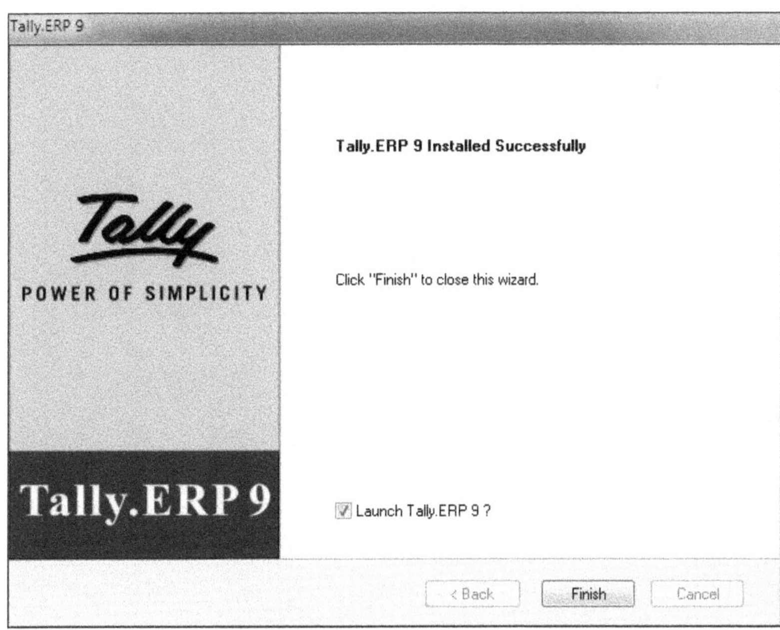

Figure 2.6 Tally.ERP 9 Installed Successfully

In **Tally.ERP 9 Installed Successfully** screen, **Launch Tally.ERP 9?** is checked by default.

12. Click **Finish** to complete installation and start setup **Tally.ERP 9**.

□ *Uncheck **Launch Tally.ERP 9**, to start Tally.ERP 9 later .*

□ *Double click **Tally.ERP 9** shortcut icon on the desktop to start Tally.ERP 9 later.*

Lesson 3:   Installing Tally.ERP 9 Gold

The installer will assist you in the installation of **Tally.ERP 9** and **License Server** on one system or on different systems.

3.1 Installing Tally.ERP 9 - Gold

Installing Tally.ERP 9 Multi-User/Gold is broadly classified into the following:

- **Installing Tally.ERP 9 on Server:** Installs the **License Service** and **Tally.ERP 9** on the computer designated as **License Server**.
- **Installing Tally.ERP 9 on Client:** Installs **Tally.ERP 9** only on a computer in the **LAN**. The user needs to provide the license server's **Name** or **IP Address** and **Port Number**.

We will first look at installing both components License Server and Tally.ERP 9 on the server followed by installing Tally.ERP 9 on the client.

*To install **Tally.ERP 9** on a computer with Windows XXXX operating system, it is essential that the user has administrator rights (create, write, update, modify & delete) for Application, Data, Configuration, License and Language Directories.*

3.1.1 Installing Tally.ERP 9 on Server

You can install both **Tally.ERP 9** and **License Server** by using any one of the following methods:

Method 1

- Double click the INSTALL.EXE icon available on the CD

Or

Method 2

- Click **START** from Windows
- Select **RUN**
- TYPE **<CD drive>:\INSTALL**
- Press **ENTER**

Follow the instructions displayed on your screen to proceed with the Installation of **Tally.ERP 9**.
The **Tally.ERP 9 Setup Wizard** is displayed as shown.

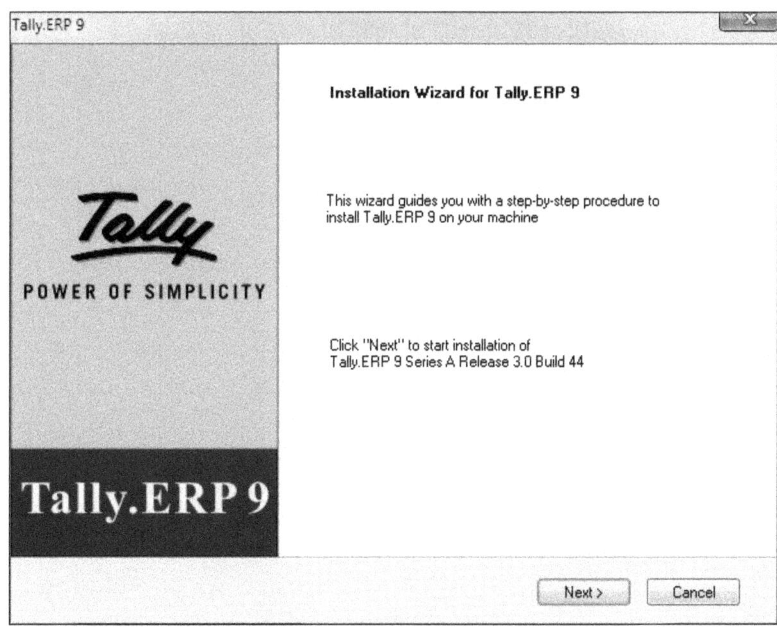

Figure 3.1 Tally.ERP 9 Setup Wizard

1. Click **Next** to continue with Installation.

The **Tally.ERP 9 Setup** screen is displayed as shown

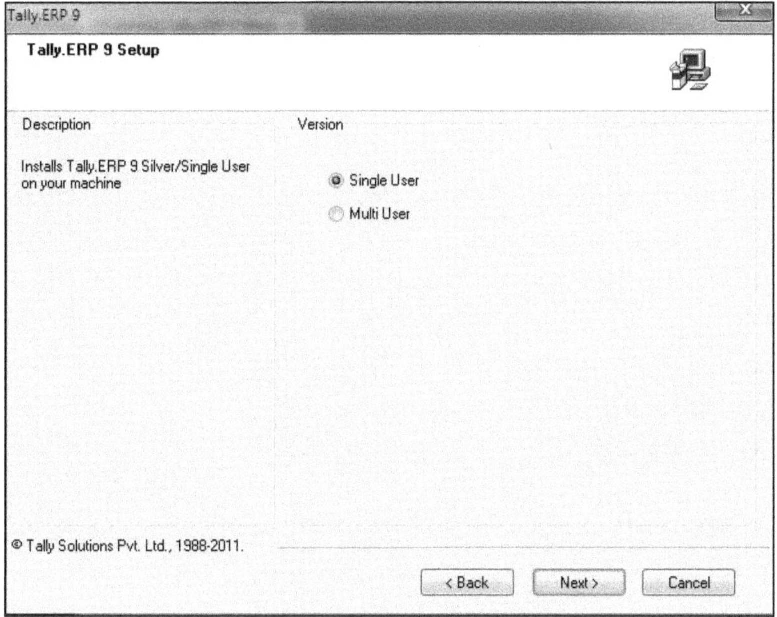

Figure 3.2 Tally.ERP 9 Setup

2. Select **Multi User**

3. Select **Server Machine**

The **Tally.ERP 9 Setup** screen is displayed as shown

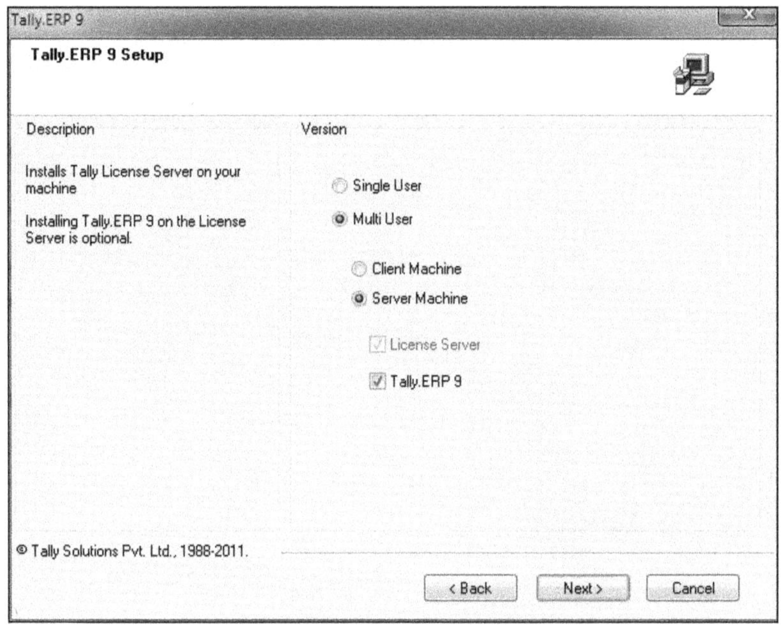

Figure 3.3 License Server Installation

*To install **License Service** only uncheck the option **Tally.ERP 9**.*

4. Click **Next**

The **Tally.ERP 9 Setup** screen is displayed as shown

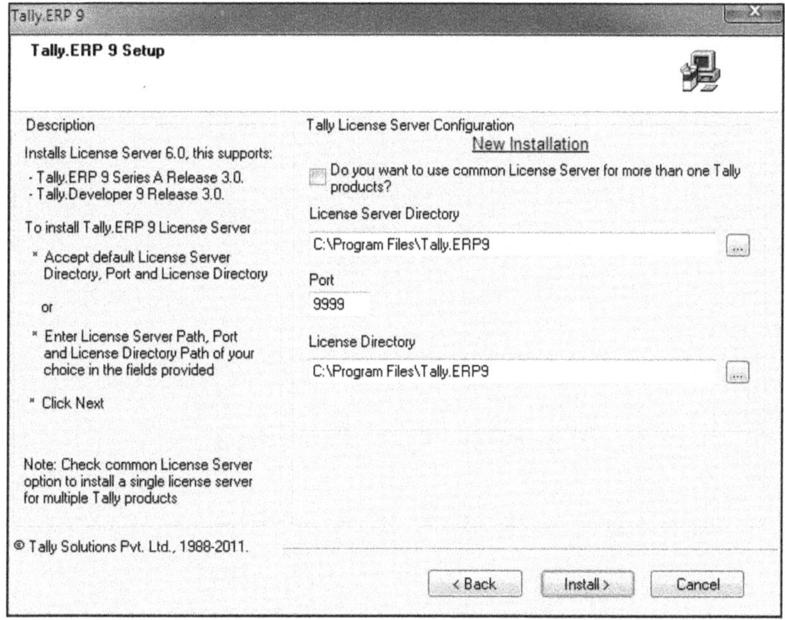

Figure 3.4 License Server Installation

5. In the **Tally License Server Configuration** section accept the default **License Server Directory**, **Port** number and **License Directory** or specify the **License Server Directory**, **Port** and **License Directory** of your choice.

To install the License Server 6.0 for more than one Tally product check Do you want to use Common License Server for more than one Tally product?

6. Click **Next**

7. On detecting earlier version(s) of License Server installed on your computer. The installer displays LicenseServers Installed.

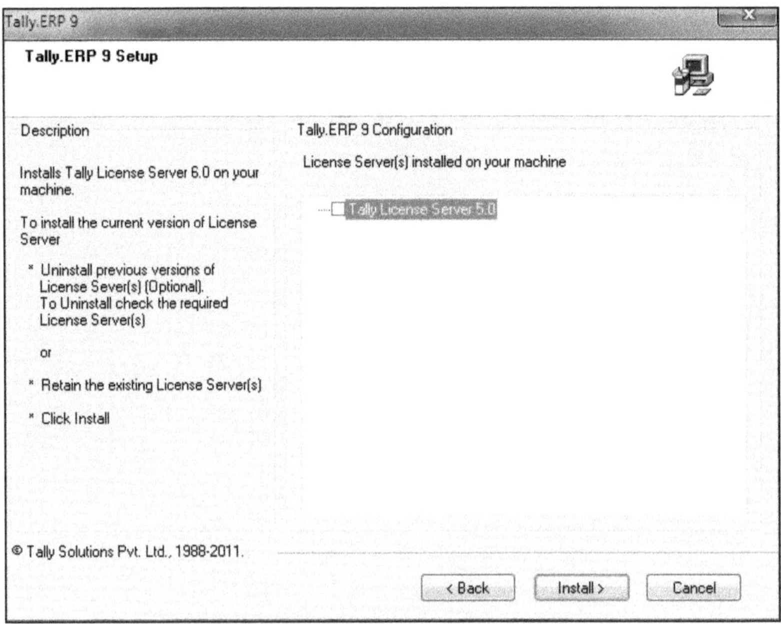

Figure 3.5 Earlier License Servers

8. Check the required version(s) of license server that needs to be uninstalled.
9. Click **Install**

The **Tally.ERP 9 Setup** screen is displayed as shown.

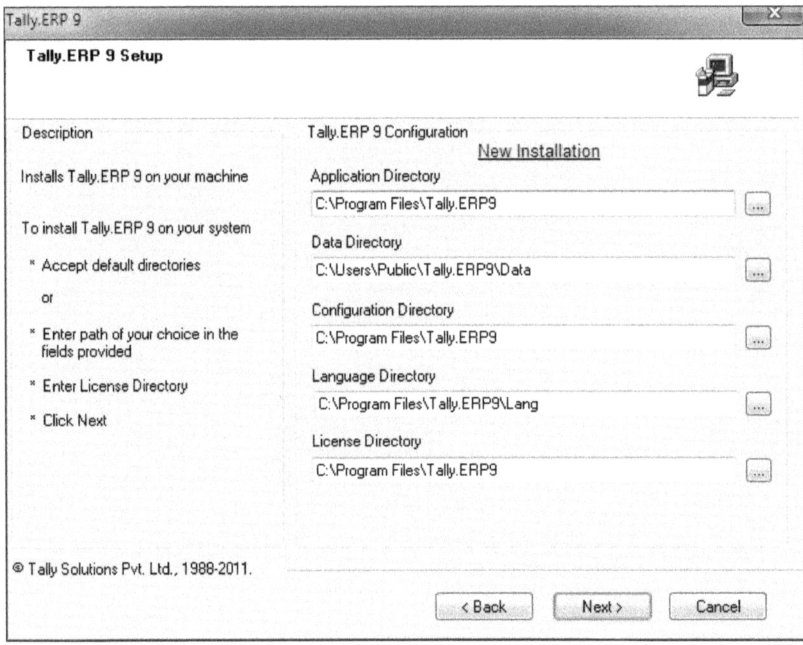

Figure 3.6 Tally.ERP 9 Setup

10. The **Tally.ERP 9 Setup** screen appears. In **Tally.ERP 9 Configuration** section accept the default directories or click on the buttons provided to change the path of **Application Directory**, **Data Directory**, **Configuration Directory**, **Language Directory** or **License Directory** respectively.

   - **Application Directory**: **Tally.ERP 9** program files reside in this directory.
   - **Data Directory**: **Tally.ERP 9** data resides in this directory.
   - **Configuration Directory**: **Tally.ERP 9** configuration file reside in this directory.
   - **Language Directory**: **Tally.ERP 9** language files (.dct) reside in this directory.
   - **License Directory**: **Tally.ERP 9** license file (.lic) resides in this directory.

11. Click **Next**.

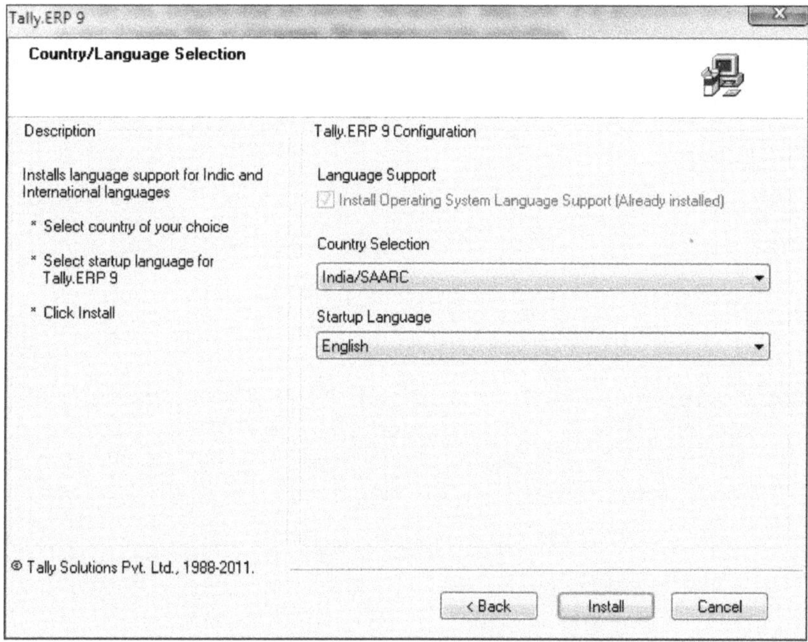

Figure 3.7 Country/Language Selection

12. In the **Country/Language Selection** screen, check **Install Operating System Language Support** to install **Tally.ERP 9** with multi-lingual support.

13. In **Country Selection** choose **India/SAARC** when you are residing in **India** or **SAARC** countries else choose **Others**.

   - *To use **Tally.ERP 9** in **English** only, uncheck **Install Operating Systems Language Support***
   - *In **Country Selection** choose **India/SAARC**, if you are residing in India or SAARC countries, else choose **Others***

14. Click **Install**

The **Setup Status** screen is displayed as shown.

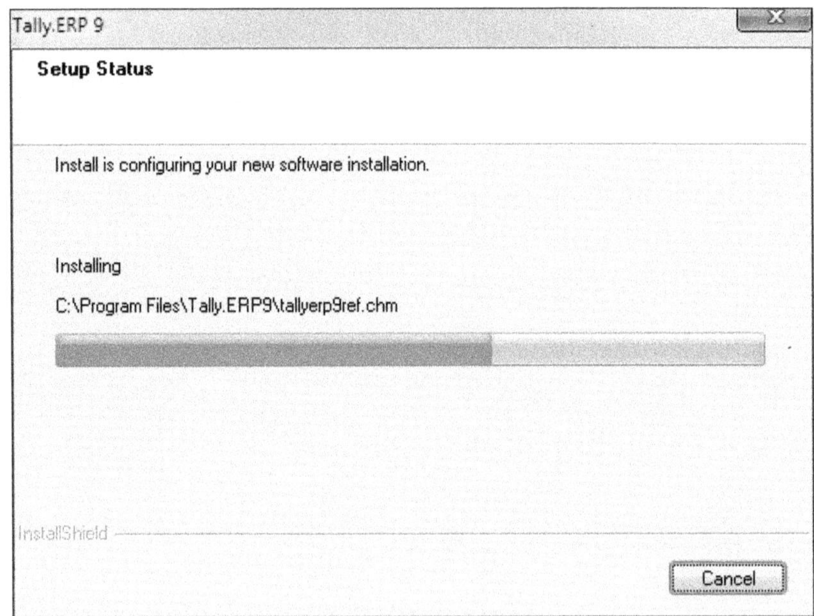

Figure 3.8 Setup Status

□ *When language support files are not available, installer prompts for language support files in the **Files Needed** screen. Insert operating systems CD in the drive or click **Browse** and select the i386 folder where the required language support files reside on your computer.*

□ *Click **OK** to install **Language Support**.*

□ *Click **Cancel** when do not have the operating system CD.*

On detecting an active Windows firewall on the license server, the installer displays the following message.

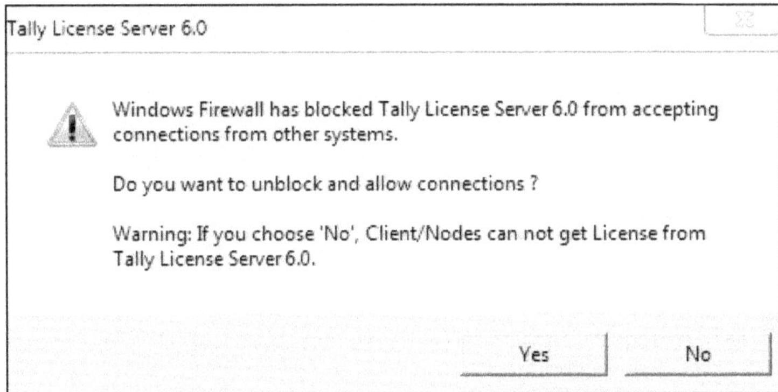

Figure 3.9 Unblock License Server

15. Click **Yes** to allow the Tally License Server accept connections from its clients
16. On successful installation of **Tally.ERP 9**, the **Tally.ERP 9 Installed Successfully** screen will be displayed as shown.

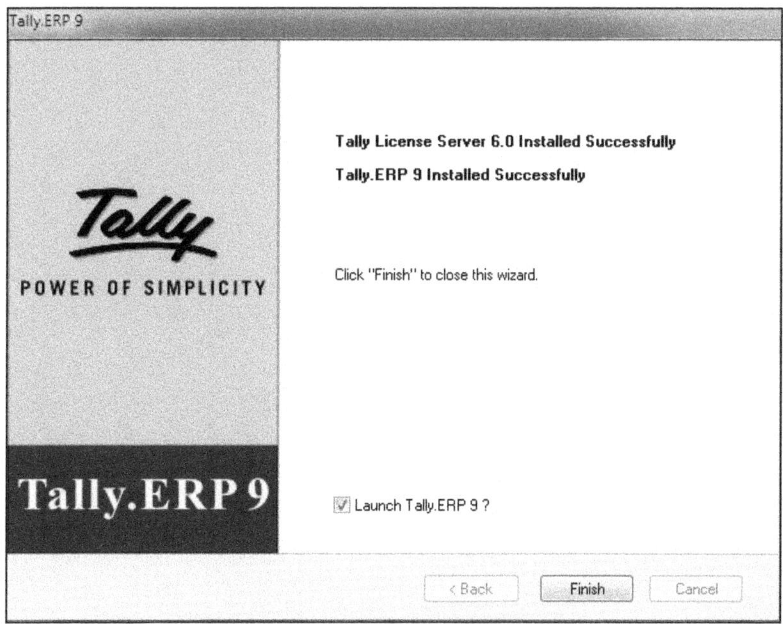

Figure 3.10 Tally.ERP 9 Installed Successfully

3.1.2 Share the Data Folder

Share the **Tally.ERP 9** Data folder located on the computer where you installed the **Tally.ERP 9** program with full read and write permissions so that users on the network can access **Tally.ERP 9** data.

Note the following details:

- **Name/IP address** of this system.
- **Share Name** for the shared Data folder.

3.1.3 Installing Tally.ERP 9 on Client

Method 1

- Double click the **INSTALL.EXE** icon available on the CD.

Or

Method 2

- Click **START** from Windows.
- Select **RUN.**
- TYPE **<CD drive>:\INSTALL.**
- Press **ENTER.**

Follow the instructions displayed on your screen to proceed with the Installation of **Tally.ERP 9**. The **Tally.ERP 9 Setup Wizard** is displayed as shown.

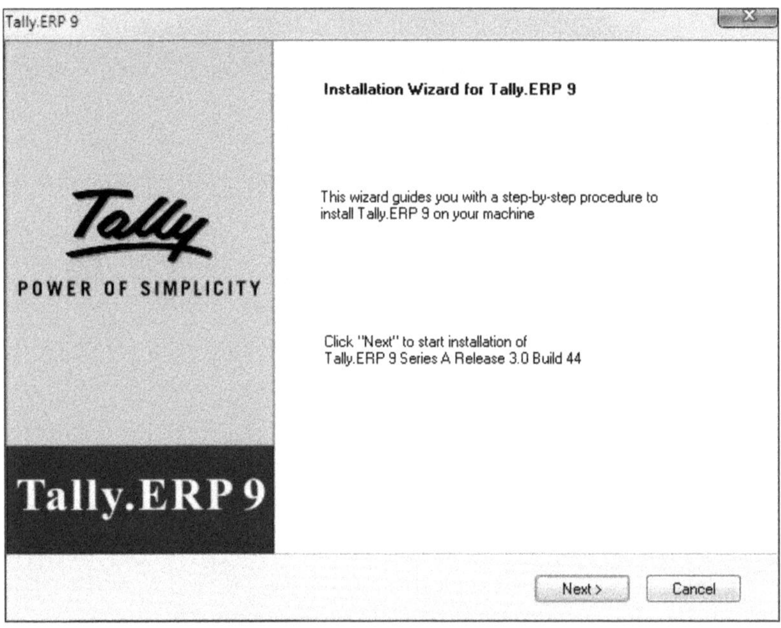

Figure 3.11 Tally.ERP 9 Setup Wizard

1. Click **Next** to continue with Installation.

The **Tally.ERP 9 Setup** screen is displayed as shown

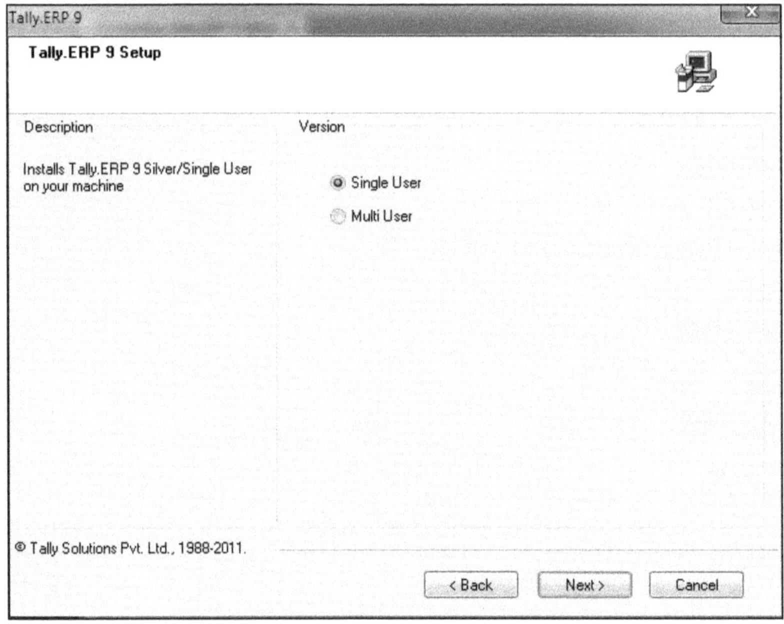

Figure 3.12 Tally.ERP 9 Setup

2. Select **Multi User**

3. Select **Client Machine**
4. Click **Next**
5. The **Tally.ERP 9 Setup** screen is displayed as shown.

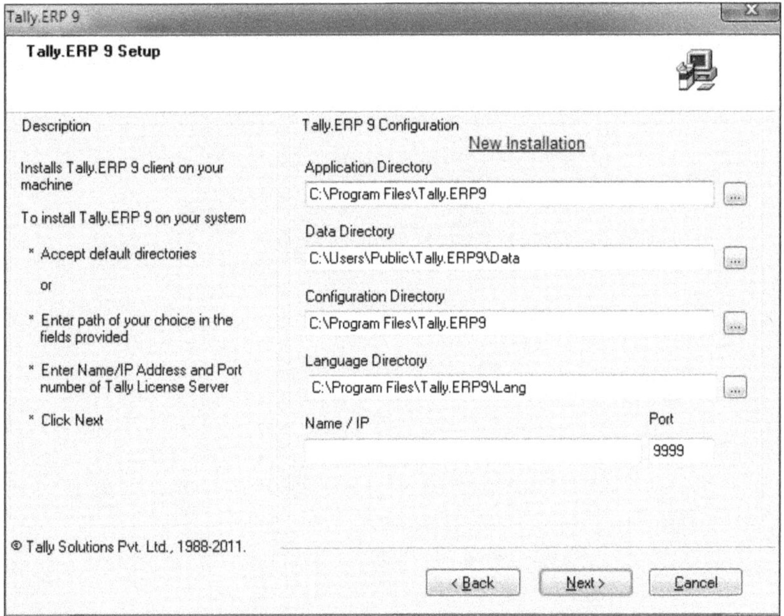

Figure 3.13 Tally.ERP 9 Setup

6. In **Tally.ERP 9 Configuration** section accept the default Application, Data, Configuration Language directories and enter the server's Name/IP address and Port number.

   □ **Application Directory**: **Tally.ERP 9** program files reside in this directory.

   □ **Data Directory**: Enter the **Name/IP Address** of the computer and the name of the shared data folder noted earlier.

   □ **Configuration Directory**: **Tally.ERP 9** configuration file reside in this directory.

   □ **Language Directory**: **Tally.ERP 9** Language files (.dct) reside in this directory.

   □ Enter the **Name/IP address** of the computer where **License Server** is installed in **Name / IP** field and enter the port number, you had noted earlier, in the **Port** field.

7. Click **Next**

The **Country/Language Selection** screen is displayed as shown

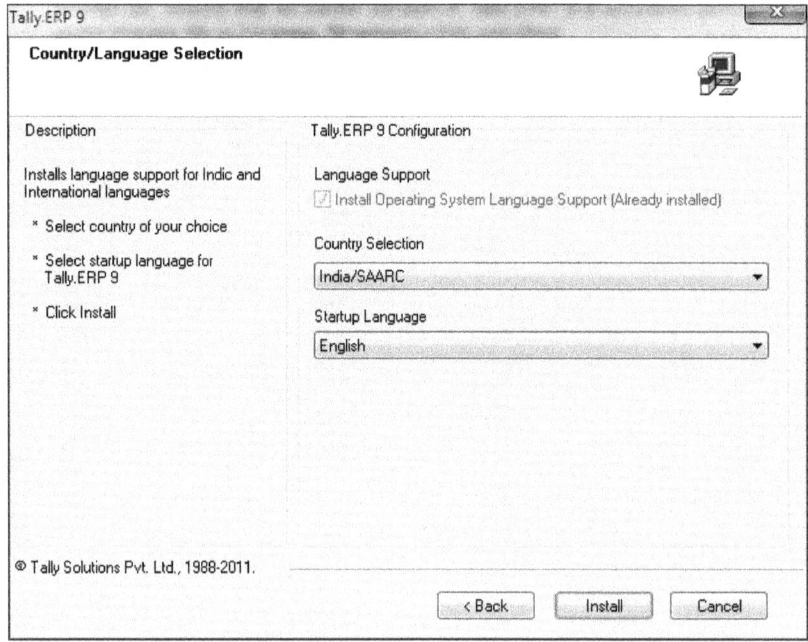

Figure 3.14 Country/Language Selection

8. Check **Install Operating System Language Support** to install **Tally.ERP 9** with multi-lingual support.

9. In **Country Selection** choose **India/SAARC** when you are residing in **India** or **SAARC** countries else choose **Others**.

□ *To use* ***Tally.ERP 9*** *in* ***English*** *only, uncheck* ***Install Operating Systems Language Support***

□ *In* ***Country Selection*** *choose* ***India/SAARC,*** *if you are residing in India or SAARC countries, else choose* ***Others***

10. Click **Install**

11. The **Tally.ERP 9 Installed Successfully** screen appears as shown

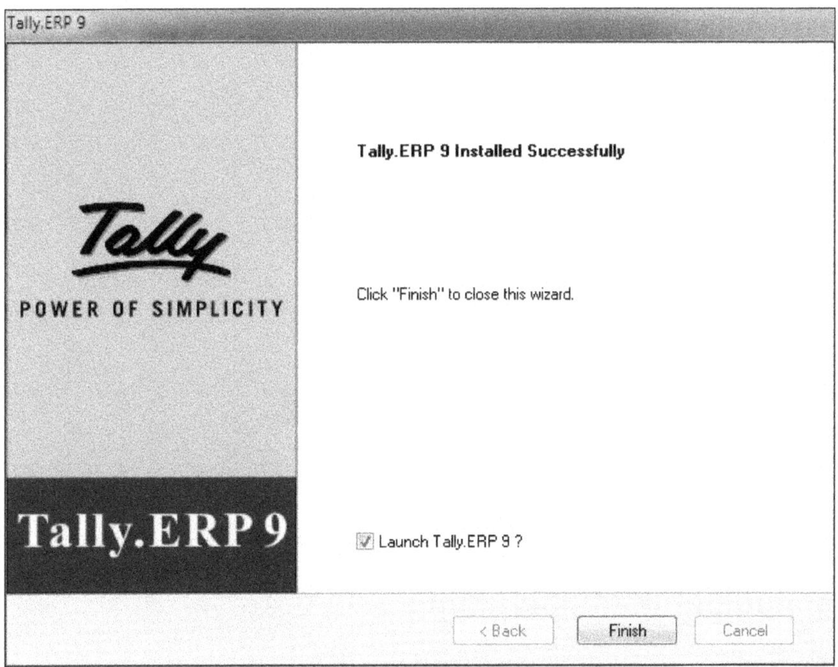

Figure 3.15 Tally.ERP 9 Installed Successfully

12. Click **Finish**

Lesson 4:   Installing Tally.ERP 9 Auditors' Edition

The installer will assist you in the installation of **Tally.ERP 9** and **License Server** on one system or on different systems.

4.1 Installing Tally.ERP 9 - Gold

Installing Tally.ERP 9 Multi-User/Gold is broadly classified into the following:

- **Installing Tally.ERP 9 on Server:** Installs the **License Service** and **Tally.ERP 9** on the computer designated as **License Server**.
- **Installing Tally.ERP 9 on Client**: Installs **Tally.ERP 9** only on a computer in the **LAN**. The user needs to provide the license server's **Name** or **IP Address** and **Port Number**.

We will first look at installing both components License Server and Tally.ERP 9 on the server followed by installing Tally.ERP 9 on the client.

*To install **Tally.ERP 9** on a computer with Windows XXXX operating system, it is essential that the user has administrator rights (create, write, update, modify & delete) for Application, Data, Configuration, License and Language Directories.*

4.1.1 Installing Tally.ERP 9 on Server

You can install both **Tally.ERP 9** and **License Server** by using any one of the following methods:

Method 1

- Double click the INSTALL.EXE icon available on the CD

Or

Method 2

- Click **START** from Windows
- Select **RUN**
- TYPE **<CD drive>:\INSTALL**
- Press **ENTER**

Follow the instructions displayed on your screen to proceed with the Installation of **Tally.ERP 9**. The **Tally.ERP 9 Setup Wizard** is displayed as shown.

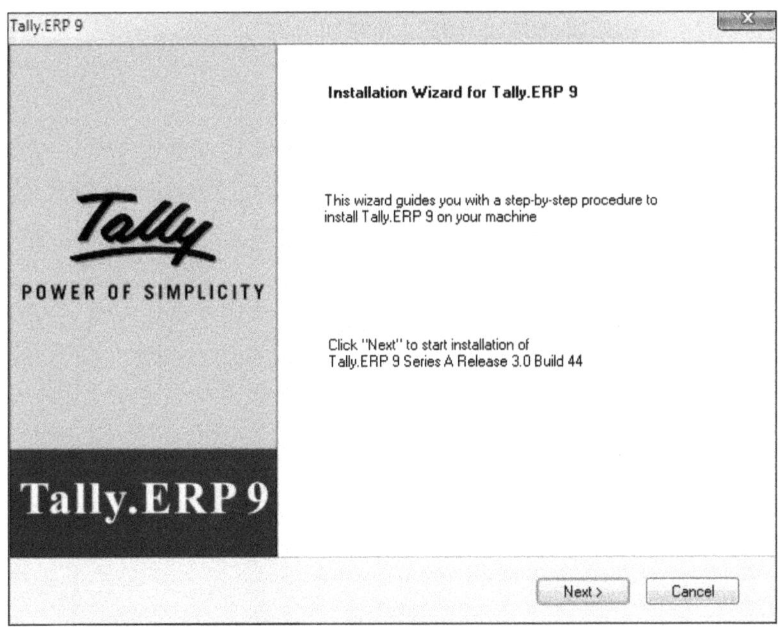

Figure 3.1 Tally.ERP 9 Setup Wizard

1.   Click **Next** to continue with Installation.

The **Tally.ERP 9 Setup** screen is displayed as shown

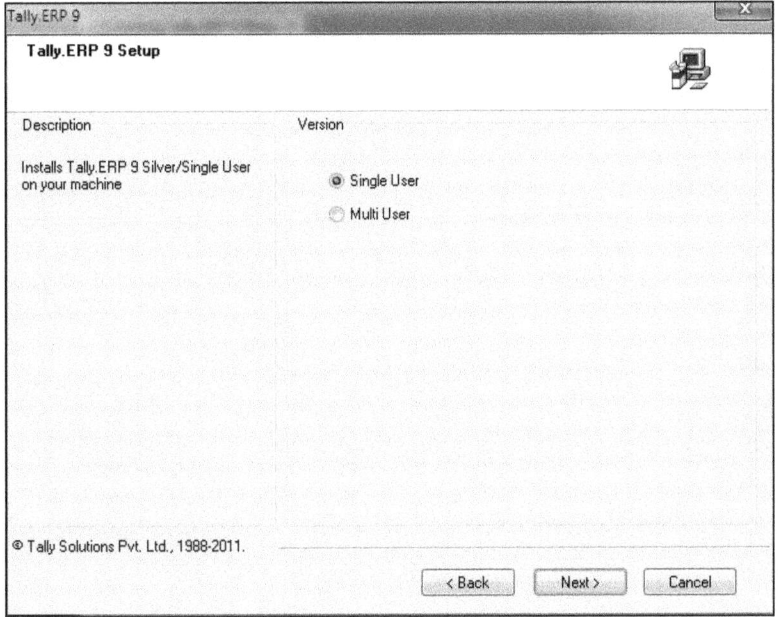

Figure 3.2 Tally.ERP 9 Setup

2.   Select **Multi User**

3. Select **Server Machine**

The **Tally.ERP 9 Setup** screen is displayed as shown

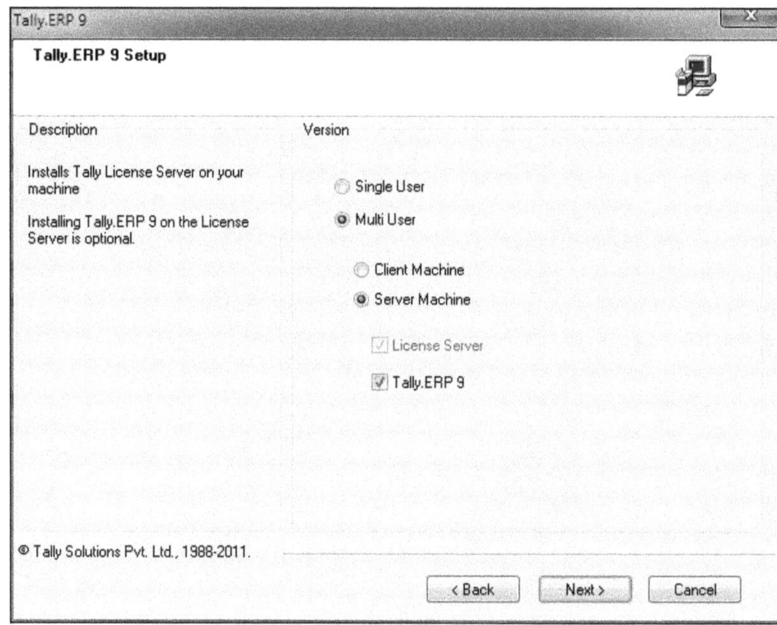

Figure 3.3 License Server Installation

*To install **License Service** only uncheck the option **Tally.ERP 9**.*

4. Click **Next**

The **Tally.ERP 9 Setup** screen is displayed as shown

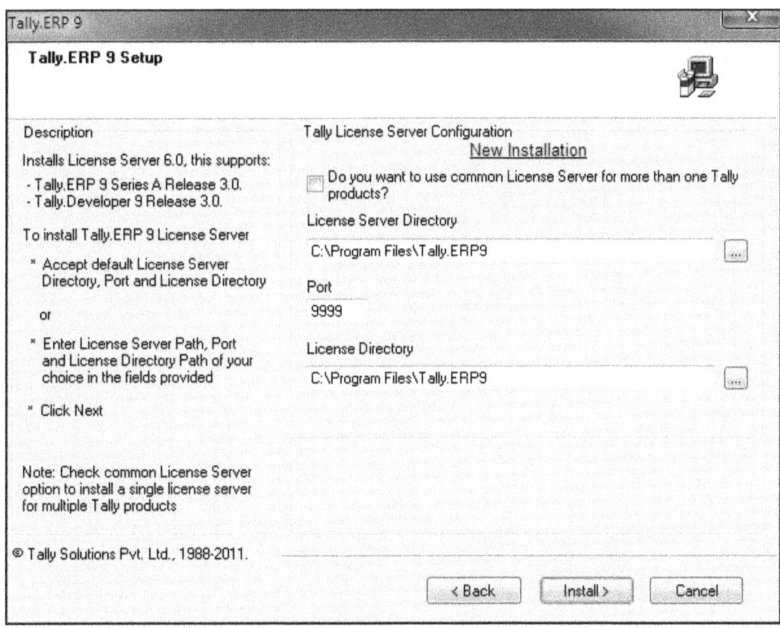

Figure 3.4 License Server Installation

5. In the **Tally License Server Configuration** section accept the default **License Server Directory**, **Port** number and **License Directory** or specify the **License Server Directory**, **Port** and **License Directory** of your choice.

6. Click **Install**

7. On detecting earlier version(s) of License Server installed on your computer. The installer displays LicenseServers Installed.

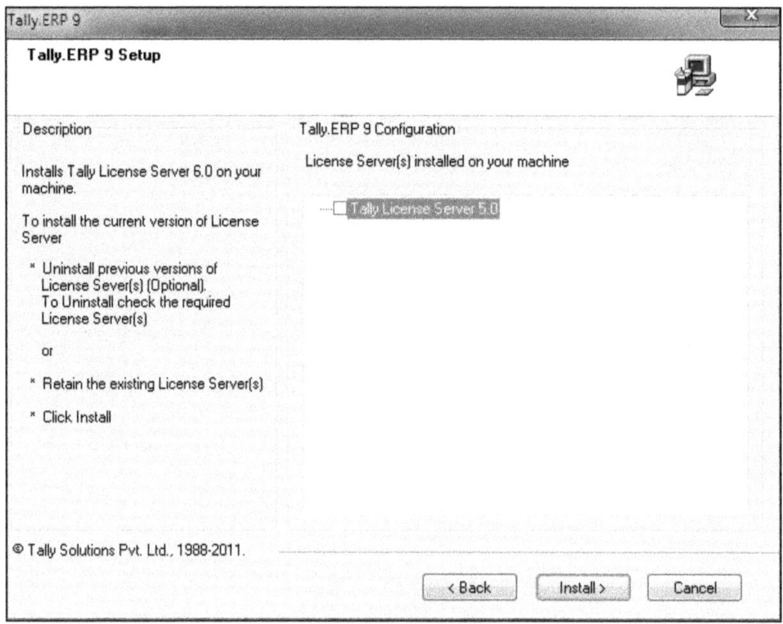

Figure 3.5 Earlier License Servers

8. Check the required version(s) of license server that needs to be uninstalled.
9. Click **Install**

The **Tally.ERP 9 Setup** screen is displayed as shown.

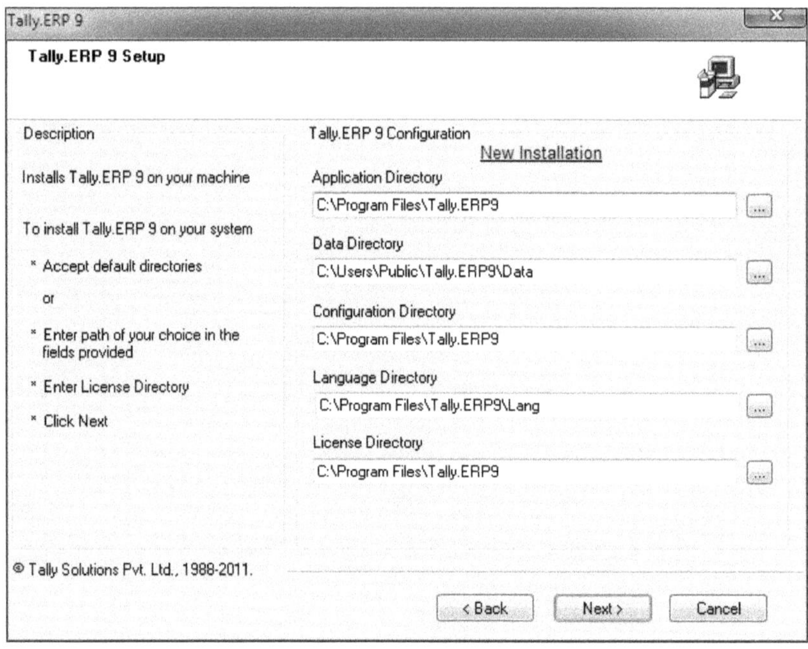

Figure 3.6 Tally.ERP 9 Setup

10. The **Tally.ERP 9 Setup** screen appears. In **Tally.ERP 9 Configuration** section accept the default directories or click on the buttons provided to change the path of **Application Directory**, **Data Directory**, **Configuration Directory**, **Language Directory** or **License Directory** respectively.

- **Application Directory**: **Tally.ERP 9** program files reside in this directory.
- **Data Directory**: **Tally.ERP 9** data resides in this directory.
- **Configuration Directory**: **Tally.ERP 9** configuration file reside in this directory.
- **Language Directory**: **Tally.ERP 9** language files (.dct) reside in this directory.
- **License Directory**: Tally.ERP 9 license file (.lic) resides in this directory.

11. Click **Next**.

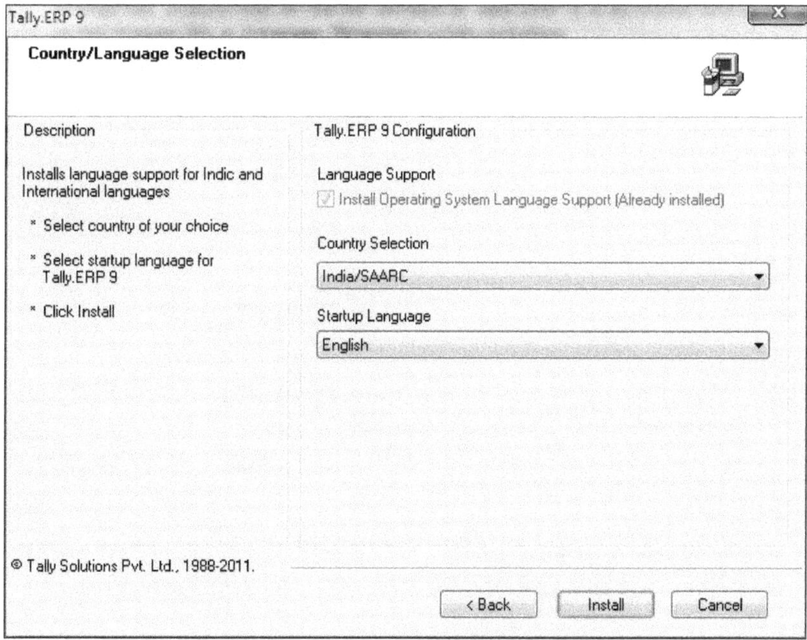

Figure 3.7 Country/Language Selection

12. In the **Country/Language Selection** screen, check **Install Operating System Language Support** to install **Tally.ERP 9** with multi-lingual support.

13. In **Country Selection** choose **India/SAARC** when you are residing in **India** or **SAARC** countries else choose **Others**.

- *To use **Tally.ERP 9** in **English** only, uncheck **Install Operating Systems Language Support***
- *In **Country Selection** choose **India/SAARC,** if you are residing in India or SAARC countries, else choose **Others***

14. Click **Install**

The **Setup Status** screen is displayed as shown.

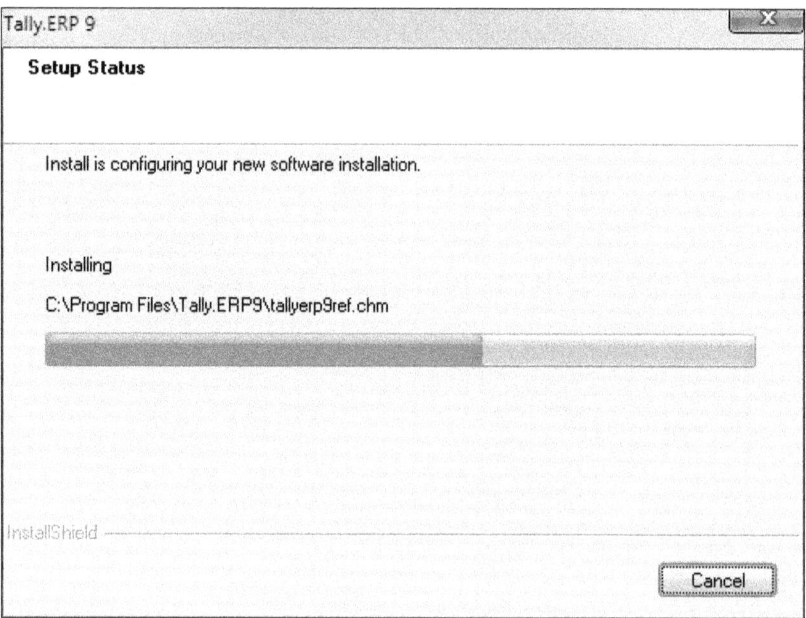

Figure 3.8 Setup Status

□ *When language support files are not available, installer prompts for language support files in the **Files Needed** screen. Insert operating systems CD in the drive or click **Browse** and select the i386 folder where the required language support files reside on your computer.*

□ *Click **OK** to install **Language Support**.*

□ *Click **Cancel** when do not have the operating system CD.*

On detecting an active Windows firewall on the license server, the installer displays the following message.

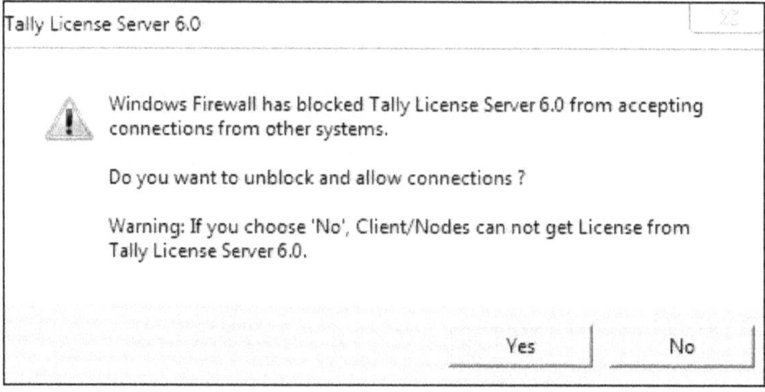

Figure 3.9 Unblock License Server

15. Click **Yes** to allow the Tally License Server accept connections from its clients
16. On successful installation of **Tally.ERP 9**, the **Tally.ERP 9 Installed Successfully** screen will be displayed as shown.

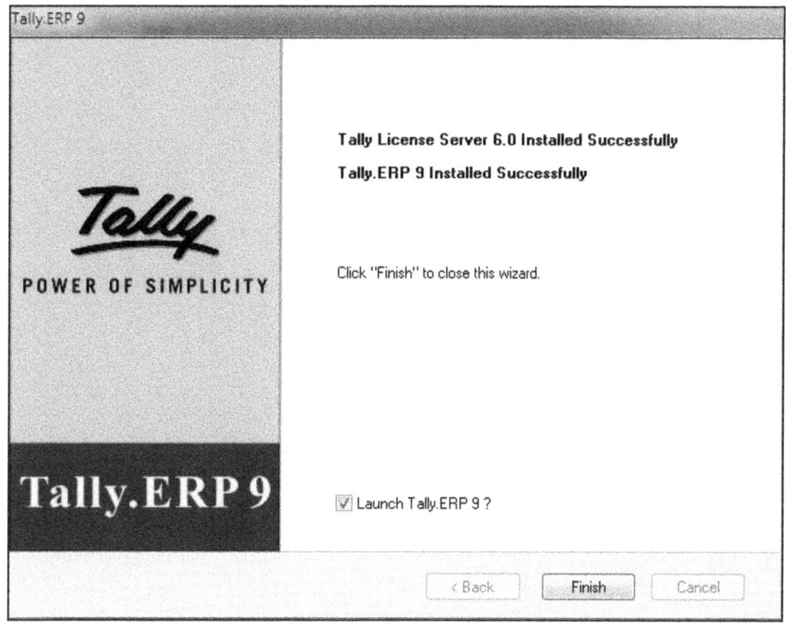

Figure 3.10 Tally.ERP 9 Installed Successfully

4.1.2 Share the Data Folder

Share the **Tally.ERP 9** Data folder located on the computer where you installed the **Tally.ERP 9** program with full read and write permissions so that users on the network can access **Tally.ERP 9** data.

Note the following details:

- **Name/IP address** of this system.
- **Share Name** for the shared Data folder.

4.1.3 Installing Tally.ERP 9 on Client

Method 1

- Double click the **INSTALL.EXE** icon available on the CD.

Or

Method 2

- Click **START** from Windows.
- Select **RUN.**
- TYPE **<CD drive>:\INSTALL.**
- Press **ENTER.**

Follow the instructions displayed on your screen to proceed with the Installation of **Tally.ERP 9**. The **Tally.ERP 9 Setup Wizard** is displayed as shown.

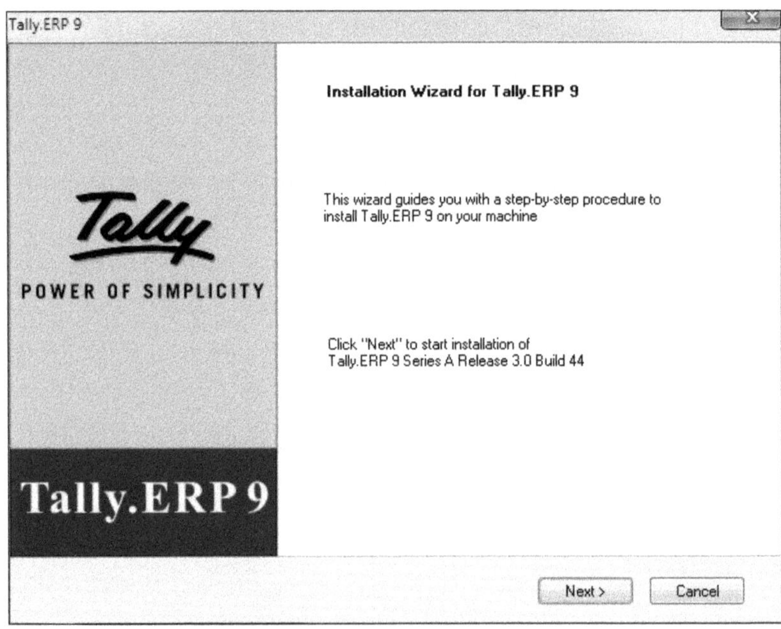

Figure 3.11 Tally.ERP 9 Setup Wizard

1. Click **Next** to continue with Installation.

The **Tally.ERP 9 Setup** screen is displayed as shown

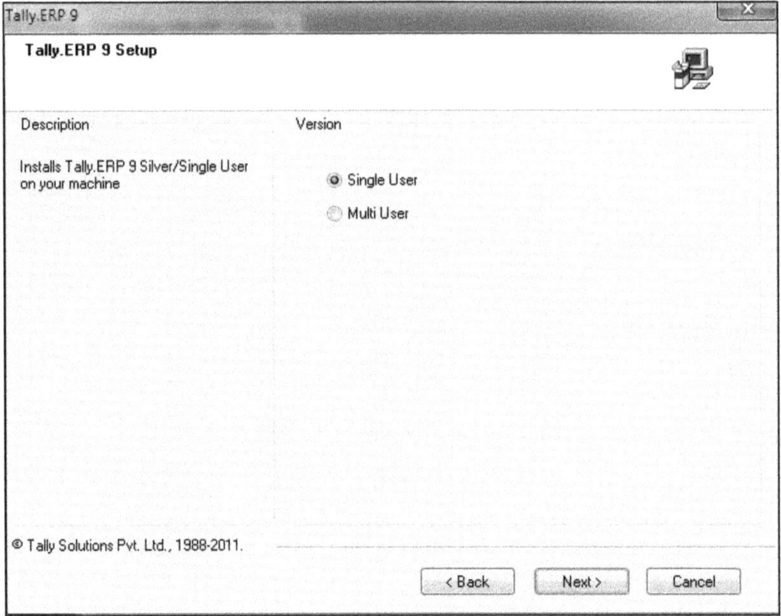

Figure 3.12 Tally.ERP 9 Setup

2. Select **Multi User**

3. Select **Client Machine**
4. Click **Next**
5. The **Tally.ERP 9 Setup** screen is displayed as shown.

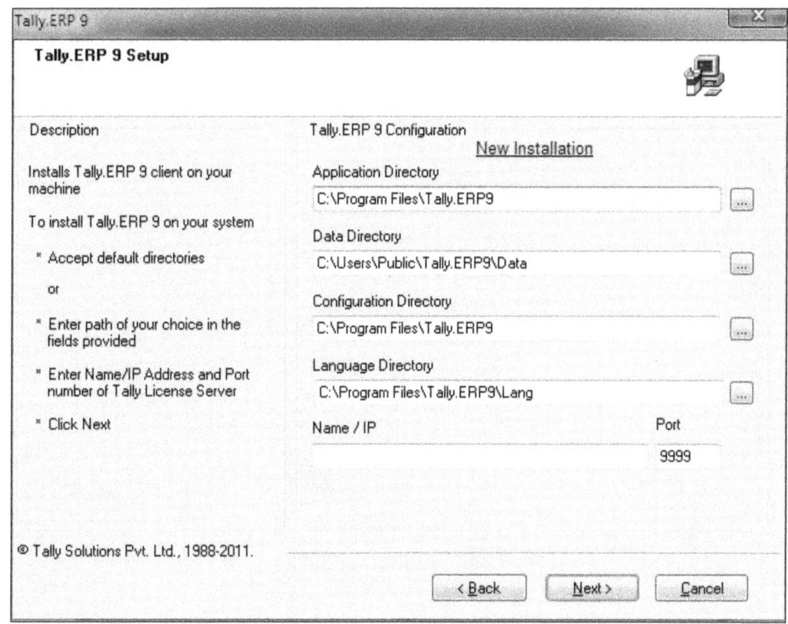

Figure 3.13 Tally.ERP 9 Setup

6. In **Tally.ERP 9 Configuration** section accept the default Application, Data, Configuration Language directories and enter the server's Name/IP address and Port number.
   - **Application Directory**: **Tally.ERP 9** program files reside in this directory.
   - **Data Directory**: Enter the **Name/IP Address** of the computer and the name of the shared data folder noted earlier.
   - **Configuration Directory**: **Tally.ERP 9** configuration file reside in this directory.
   - **Language Directory**: **Tally.ERP 9** Language files (.dct) reside in this directory.
   - Enter the **Name/IP address** of the computer where **License Server** is installed in **Name / IP** field and enter the port number, you had noted earlier, in the **Port** field.
7. Click **Next**

The **Country/Language Selection** screen is displayed as shown

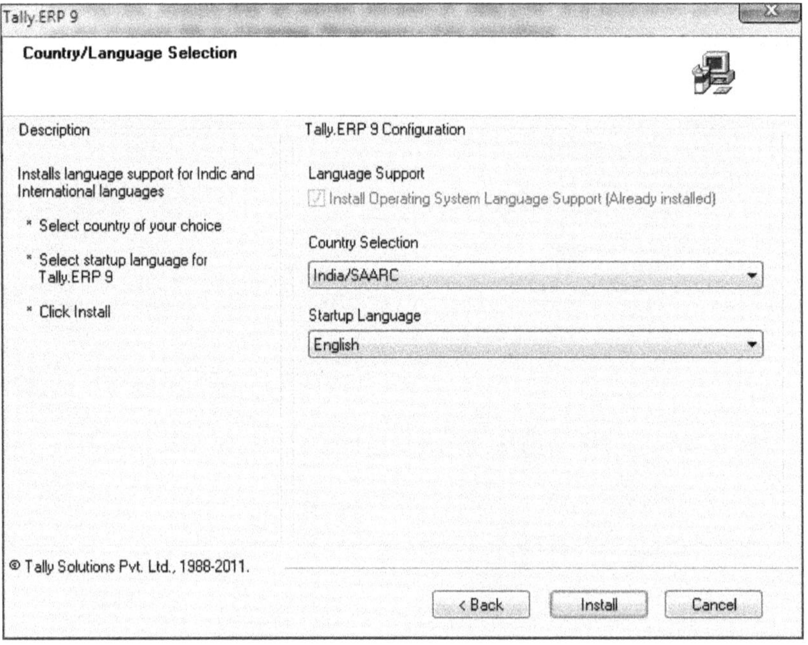

Figure 3.14 Country/Language Selection

8.   Check **Install Operating System Language Support** to install **Tally.ERP 9** with multi-lingual support.

9.   In **Country Selection** choose **India/SAARC** when you are residing in **India** or **SAARC** countries else choose **Others**.

□   *To use **Tally.ERP 9** in **English** only, uncheck **Install Operating Systems Language Support***

□   *In **Country Selection** choose **India/SAARC,** if you are residing in India or SAARC countries, else choose **Others***

10.   Click **Install**

11.   The **Tally.ERP 9 Installed Successfully** screen appears as shown

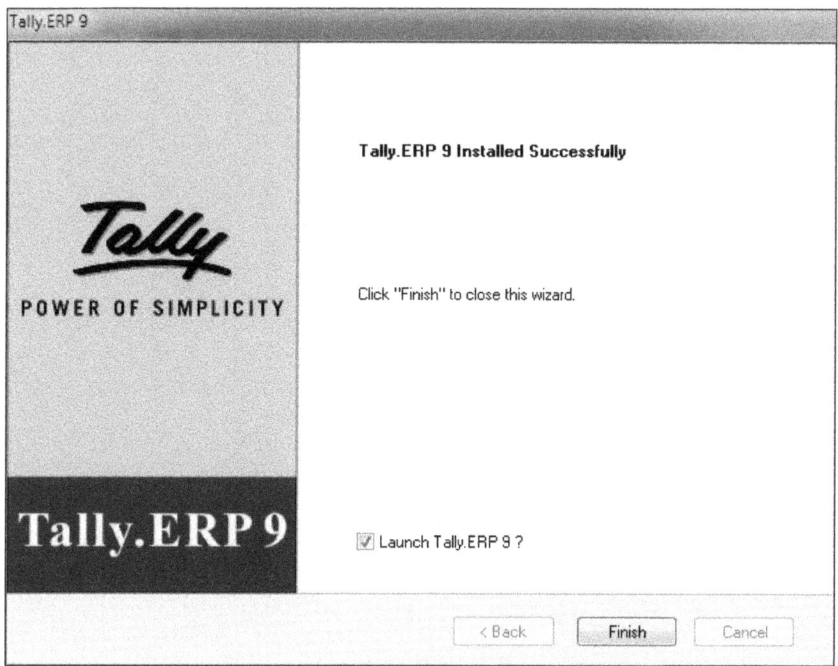

Figure 3.15 Tally.ERP 9 Installed Successfully

12. Click **Finish**

Lesson 5:   Installing Tally.ERP 9 for Rental License

The installer will assist you in the installation of **Tally.ERP 9** and **License Server** on one system or on different systems.

5.1 Installing Tally.ERP 9 - Gold

Installing Tally.ERP 9 Multi-User/Gold is broadly classified into the following:

- **Installing Tally.ERP 9 on Server:** Installs the **License Service** and **Tally.ERP 9** on the computer designated as **License Server**.
- **Installing Tally.ERP 9 on Client**: Installs **Tally.ERP 9** only on a computer in the **LAN**. The user needs to provide the license server's **Name** or **IP Address** and **Port Number**.

We will first look at installing both components License Server and Tally.ERP 9 on the server followed by installing Tally.ERP 9 on the client.

*To install **Tally.ERP 9** on a computer with Windows XXXX operating system, it is essential that the user has administrator rights (create, write, update, modify & delete) for Application, Data, Configuration, License and Language Directories.*

5.1.1 Installing Tally.ERP 9 on Server

You can install both **Tally.ERP 9** and **License Server** by using any one of the following methods:

Method 1

- Double click the INSTALL.EXE icon available on the CD

Or

Method 2

- Click **START** from Windows
- Select **RUN**
- TYPE **<CD drive>:\INSTALL**
- Press **ENTER**

Follow the instructions displayed on your screen to proceed with the Installation of **Tally.ERP 9**. The **Tally.ERP 9 Setup Wizard** is displayed as shown.

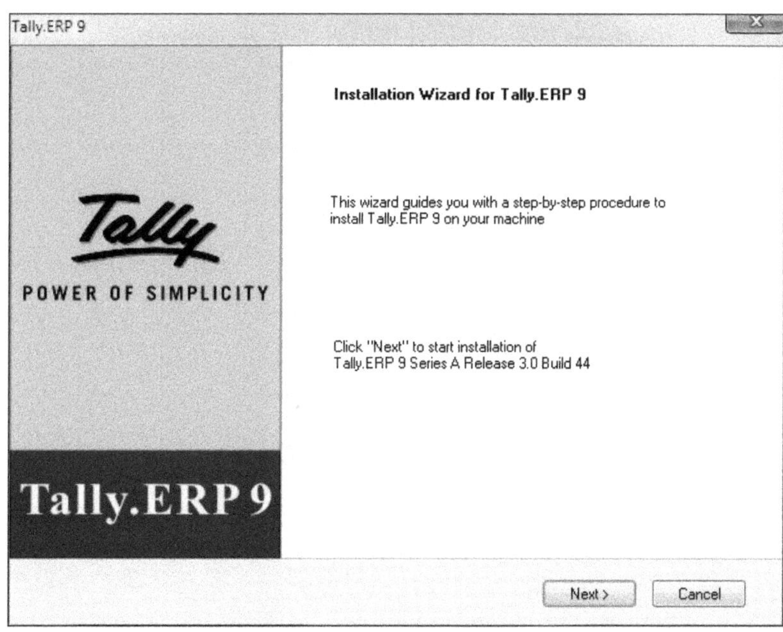

Figure 3.1 Tally.ERP 9 Setup Wizard

1. Click **Next** to continue with Installation.

The **Tally.ERP 9 Setup** screen is displayed as shown

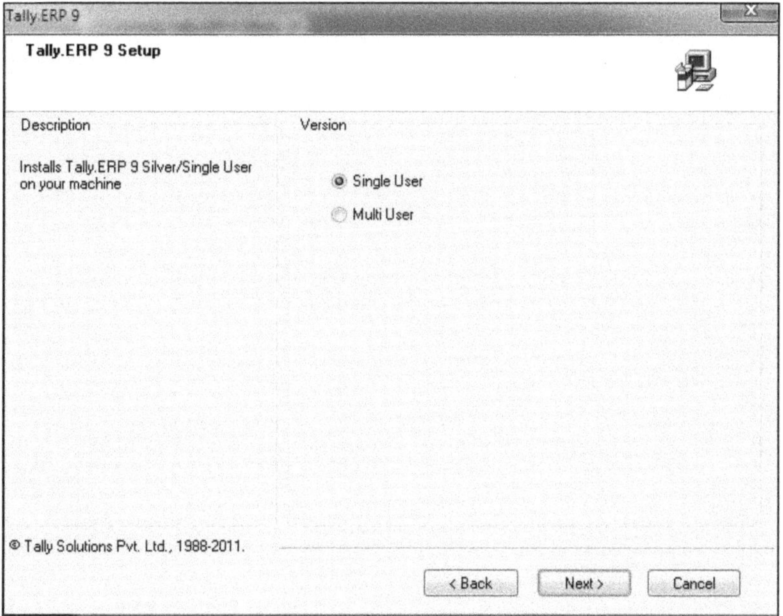

Figure 3.2 Tally.ERP 9 Setup

2. Select **Multi User**

3. Select **Server Machine**

The **Tally.ERP 9 Setup** screen is displayed as shown

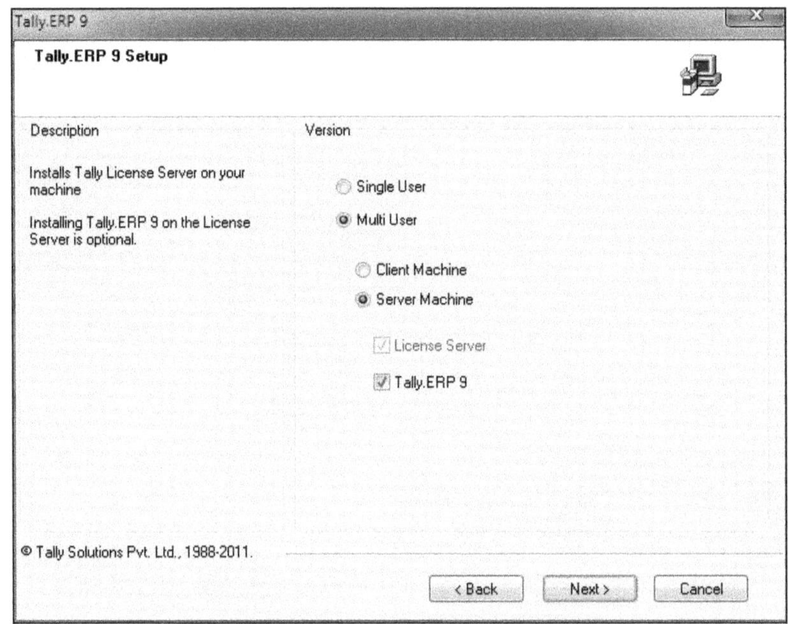

Figure 3.3 License Server Installation

*To install **License Service** only uncheck the option **Tally.ERP 9**.*

4. Click **Next**

The **Tally.ERP 9 Setup** screen is displayed as shown

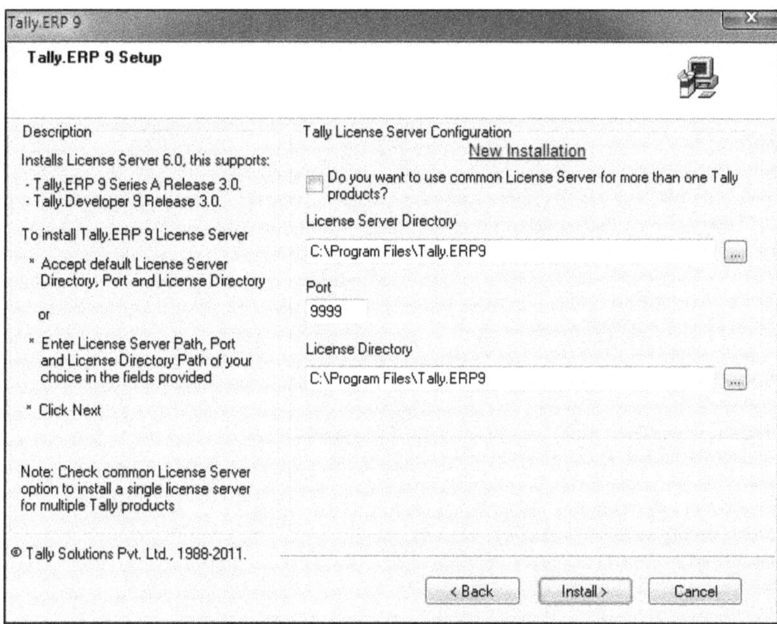

Figure 3.4 License Server Installation

5. In the **Tally License Server Configuration** section accept the default **License Server Directory**, **Port** number and **License Directory** or specify the **License Server Directory**, **Port** and **License Directory** of your choice.
6. Click **Install**

7. On detecting earlier version(s) of License Server installed on your computer. The installer displays LicenseServers Installed.

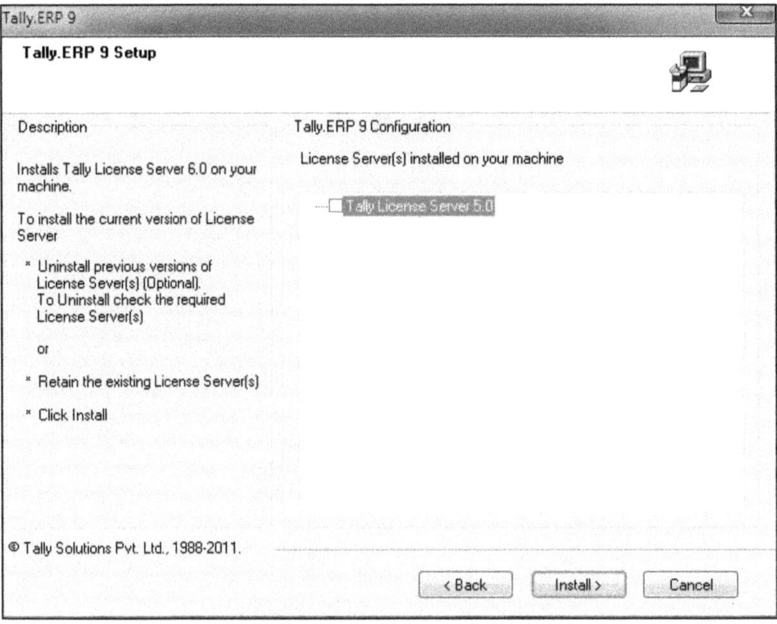

Figure 3.5 Earlier License Servers

8. Check the required version(s) of license server that needs to be uninstalled.
9. Click **Install**

The **Tally.ERP 9 Setup** screen is displayed as shown.

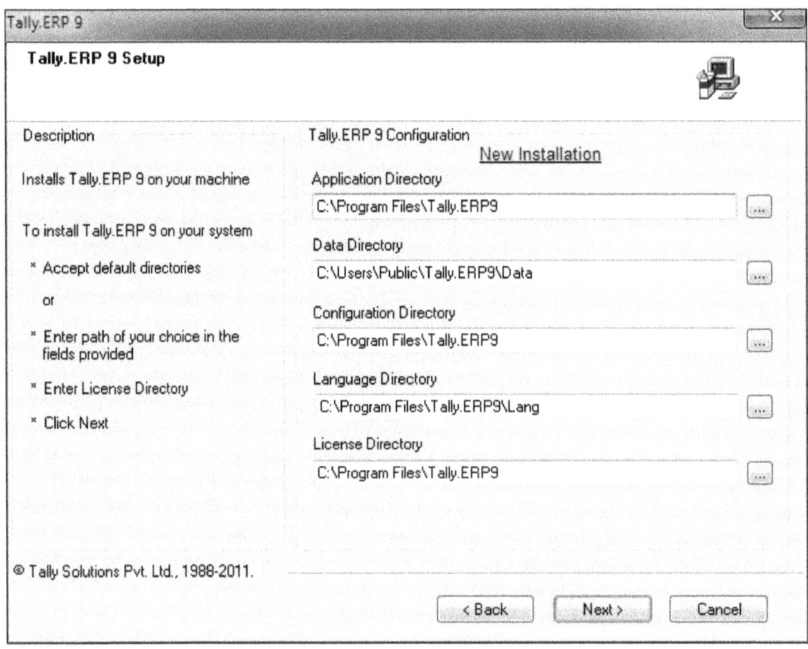

Figure 3.6 Tally.ERP 9 Setup

10. The **Tally.ERP 9 Setup** screen appears. In **Tally.ERP 9 Configuration** section accept the default directories or click on the buttons provided to change the path of **Application Directory**, **Data Directory**, **Configuration Directory**, **Language Directory** or **License Directory** respectively.

- **Application Directory**: **Tally.ERP 9** program files reside in this directory.
- **Data Directory**: **Tally.ERP 9** data resides in this directory.
- **Configuration Directory**: **Tally.ERP 9** configuration file reside in this directory.
- **Language Directory**: **Tally.ERP 9** language files (.dct) reside in this directory.
- **License Directory**: Tally.ERP 9 license file (.lic) resides in this directory.

11. Click **Next**.

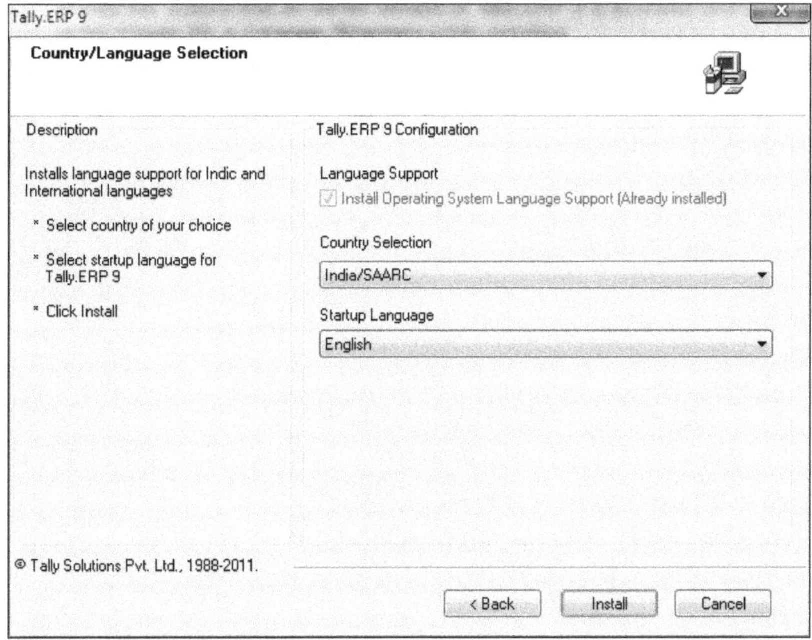

Figure 3.7 Country/Language Selection

12. In the **Country/Language Selection** screen, check **Install Operating System Language Support** to install **Tally.ERP 9** with multi-lingual support.

13. In **Country Selection** choose **India/SAARC** when you are residing in **India** or **SAARC** countries else choose **Others**.

- *To use **Tally.ERP 9** in **English** only, uncheck **Install Operating Systems Language Support***
- *In **Country Selection** choose **India/SAARC,** if you are residing in India or SAARC countries, else choose **Others***

14. Click **Install**

The **Setup Status** screen is displayed as shown.

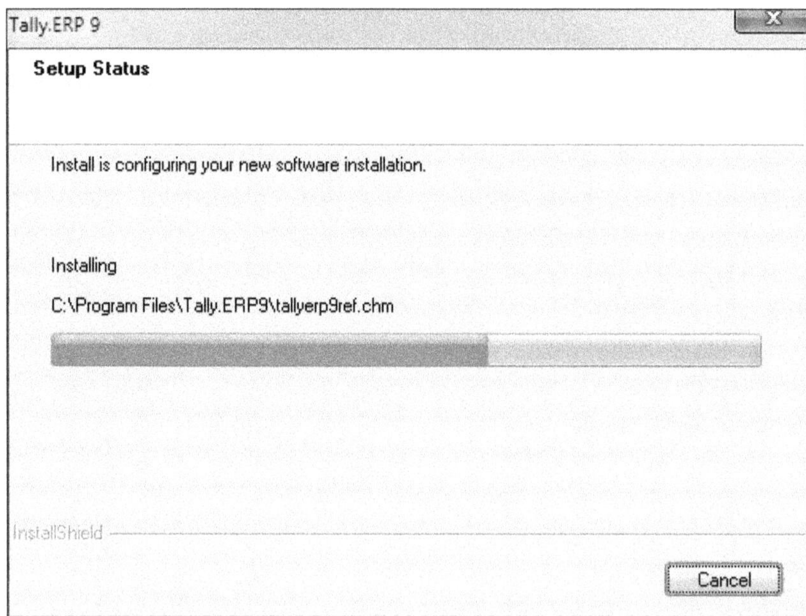

Figure 3.8 Setup Status

> □ *When language support files are not available, installer prompts for language support files in the **Files Needed** screen. Insert operating systems CD in the drive or click **Browse** and select the i386 folder where the required language support files reside on your computer.*
>
> □ *Click **OK** to install **Language Support**.*
>
> □ *Click **Cancel** when do not have the operating system CD.*

On detecting an active Windows firewall on the license server, the installer displays the following message.

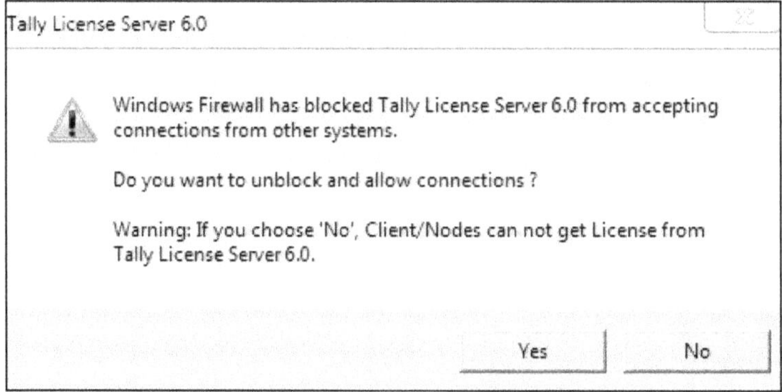

Figure 3.9 Unblock License Server

15. Click **Yes** to allow the Tally License Server accept connections from its clients
16. On successful installation of **Tally.ERP 9**, the **Tally.ERP 9 Installed Successfully** screen will be displayed as shown.

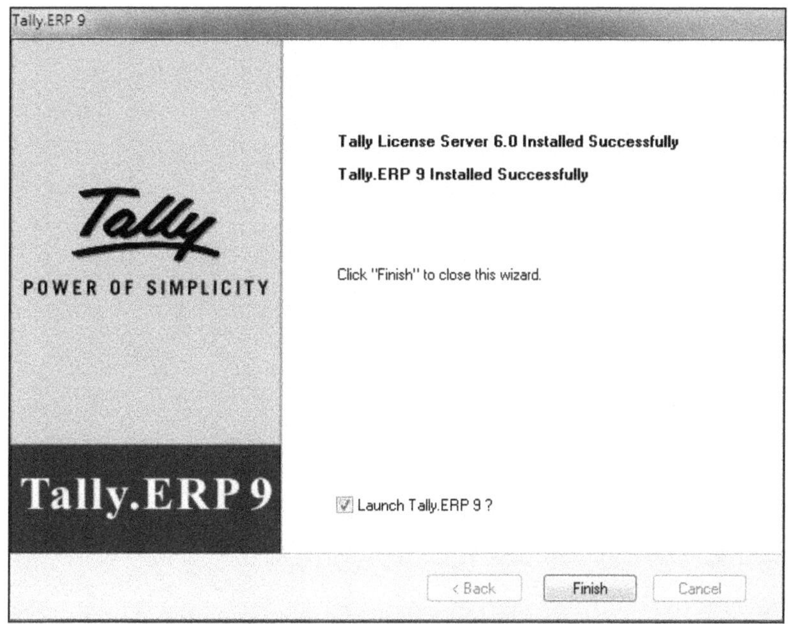

Figure 3.10 Tally.ERP 9 Installed Successfully

5.1.2 Share the Data Folder

Share the **Tally.ERP 9** Data folder located on the computer where you installed the **Tally.ERP 9** program with full read and write permissions so that users on the network can access **Tally.ERP 9** data.

Note the following details:

- **Name/IP address** of this system.
- **Share Name** for the shared Data folder.

5.1.3 Installing Tally.ERP 9 on Client

Method 1

- Double click the **INSTALL.EXE** icon available on the CD.

Or

Method 2

- Click **START** from Windows.
- Select **RUN.**
- TYPE **<CD drive>:\INSTALL.**
- Press **ENTER.**

Follow the instructions displayed on your screen to proceed with the Installation of **Tally.ERP 9**.
The **Tally.ERP 9 Setup Wizard** is displayed as shown.

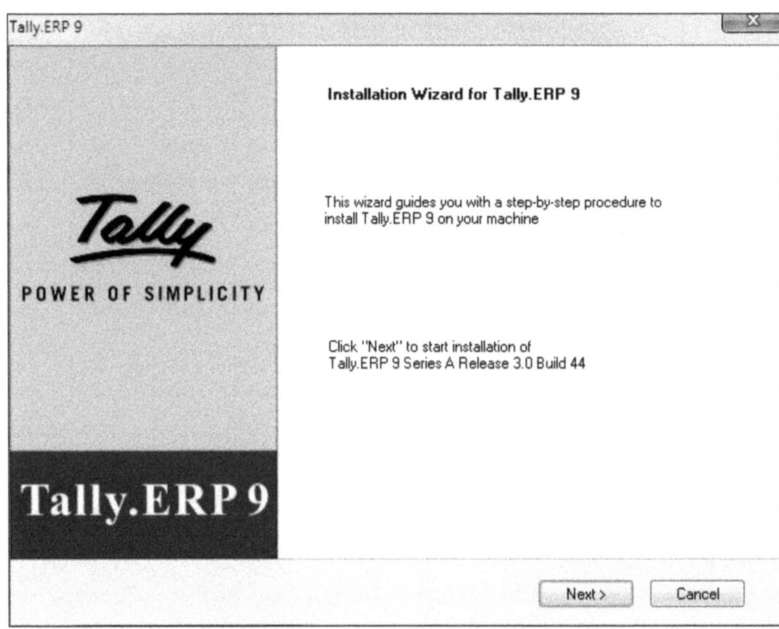

Figure 3.11 Tally.ERP 9 Setup Wizard

1. Click **Next** to continue with Installation.

The **Tally.ERP 9 Setup** screen is displayed as shown

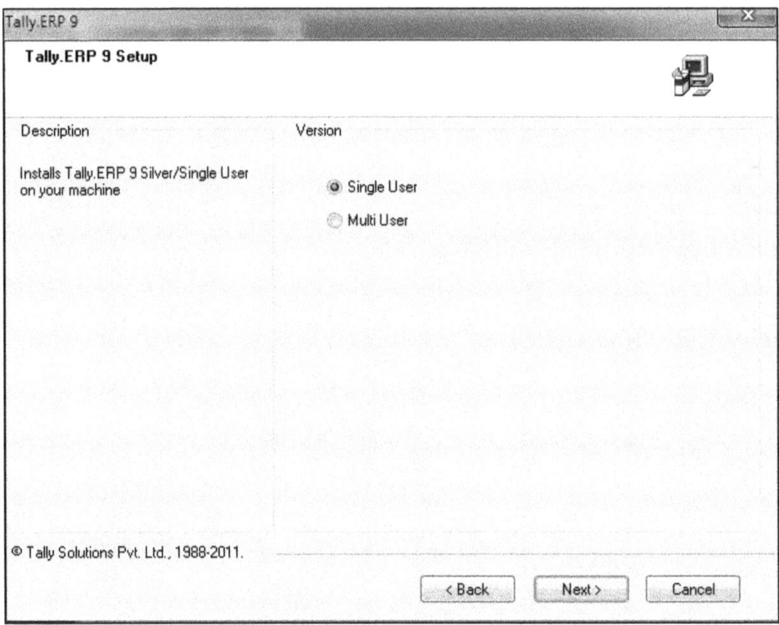

Figure 3.12 Tally.ERP 9 Setup

2. Select **Multi User**

3. Select **Client Machine**
4. Click **Next**
5. The **Tally.ERP 9 Setup** screen is displayed as shown.

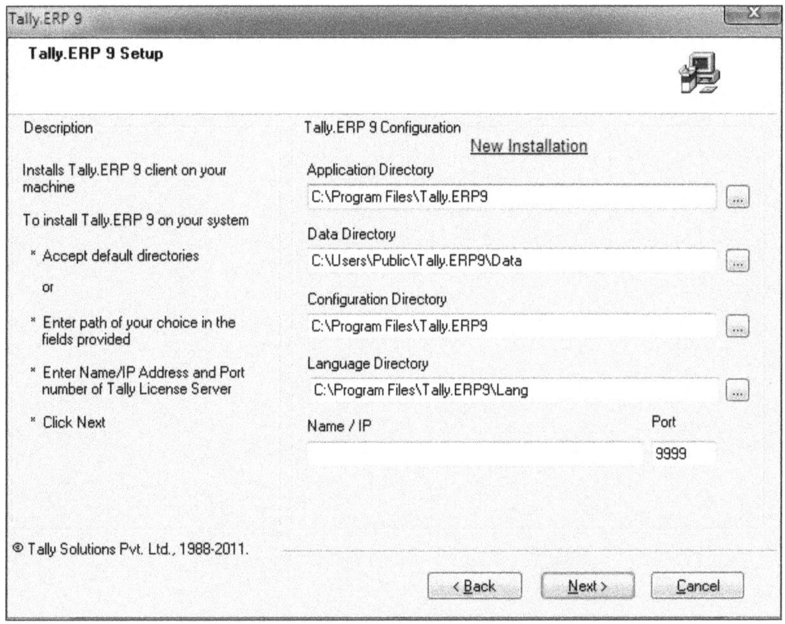

Figure 3.13 Tally.ERP 9 Setup

6. In **Tally.ERP 9 Configuration** section accept the default Application, Data, Configuration Language directories and enter the server's Name/IP address and Port number.
   - **Application Directory**: **Tally.ERP 9** program files reside in this directory.
   - **Data Directory**: Enter the **Name/IP Address** of the computer and the name of the shared data folder noted earlier.
   - **Configuration Directory**: **Tally.ERP 9** configuration file reside in this directory.
   - **Language Directory**: **Tally.ERP 9** Language files (.dct) reside in this directory.
   - Enter the **Name/IP address** of the computer where **License Server** is installed in **Name / IP** field and enter the port number, you had noted earlier, in the **Port** field.
7. Click **Next**

The **Country/Language Selection** screen is displayed as shown

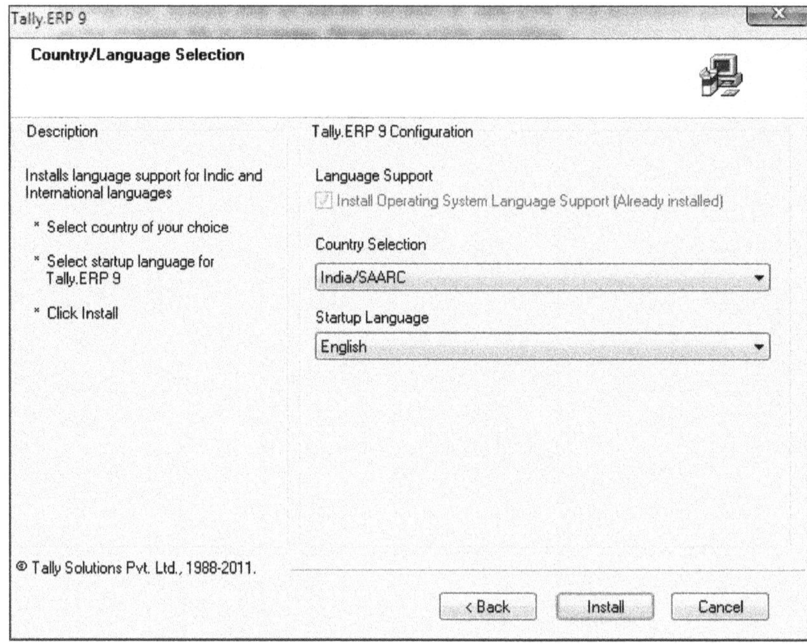

Figure 3.14 Country/Language Selection

8. Check **Install Operating System Language Support** to install **Tally.ERP 9** with multi-lingual support.

9. In **Country Selection** choose **India/SAARC** when you are residing in **India** or **SAARC** countries else choose **Others**.

□ *To use **Tally.ERP 9** in **English** only, uncheck **Install Operating Systems Language Support***

□ *In **Country Selection** choose **India/SAARC**, if you are residing in India or SAARC countries, else choose **Others***

10. Click **Install**

11. The **Tally.ERP 9 Installed Successfully** screen appears as shown

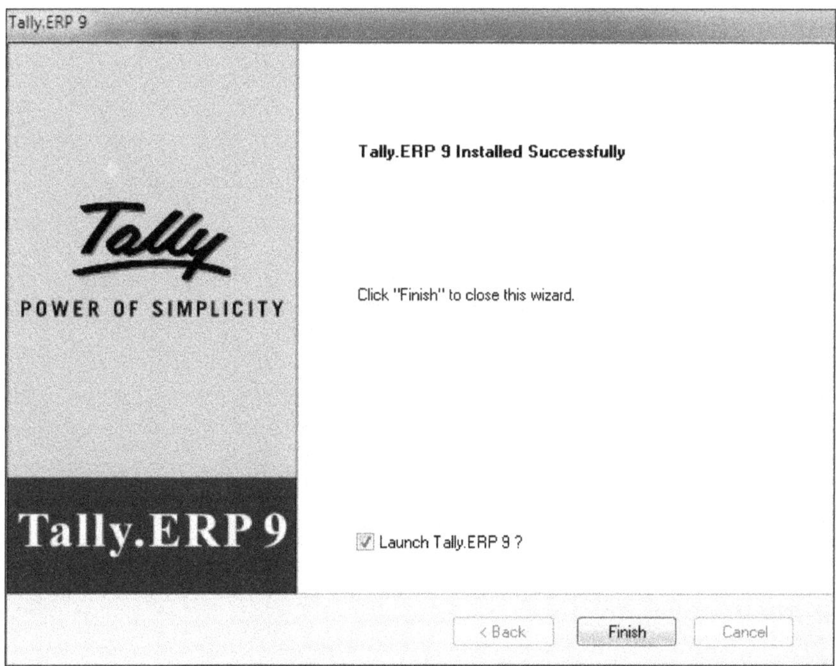

Figure 3.15 Tally.ERP 9 Installed Successfully

12.   Click **Finish**

Lesson 6: Installing Tally.ERP 9 in Silent Mode (for Advanced Users)

Users from large enterprises who install Tally.ERP 9 frequently do not have to repeat the task of providing the same information for each installation, instead, these users can now record the complete installation procedure in a script file and store it at the specified location for later use.

The installer uses the script file for subsequent installations and does not prompt the user for the required parameters to complete the installation; this process is called **Silent Installation.**

6.1 Record the Installation

To record the installation of **Tally.ERP 9**, type the following command at the command prompt

install /r /f1 "<Path\Filename>"

Where:

/r - record the installation

/f1 - specify the path and filename.

Path - specify the path where the file has to be stored

Filename - name of the file to save the installation parameters

Example

Install /r /f1 "C:\SilentInstall\InstalParamts.iss"

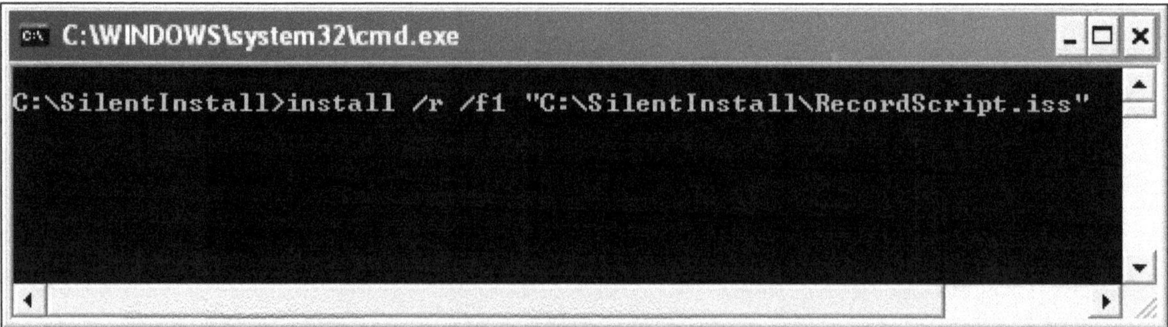

Figure 6.1 Recording an Installation

Notes

□ *Follow the normal installation procedure to record it in a script file.*

□ *Install.exe must be present in the folder/drive from where the command is given.*

□ *Ensure that the path and filename are enclosed within double quotes.*

□ *Ensure that you do not to have blank space between /f1, path and filename.*

□ *In case the user does not specify the path and script filename, by default the installer creates Setup.iss file in the default Windows folder*

On recording the installation, the script file will appears as shown below:

```
RecordScript.iss - Notepad
File  Edit  Format  View  Help
[InstallShield Silent]
Version=v7.00
File=Response File
[File Transfer]
OverwrittenReadOnly=NoToAll
[{4AA1FE2E-373C-447E-9995-BAA7E4FD0E24}-DlgOrder]
Dlg0={4AA1FE2E-373C-447E-9995-BAA7E4FD0E24}-DIRECTORY_SELECTION_DIALOG-22003
Count=5
Dlg1={4AA1FE2E-373C-447E-9995-BAA7E4FD0E24}-LANGUAGE_SELECTION_DIALOG-22005
Dlg2={4AA1FE2E-373C-447E-9995-BAA7E4FD0E24}-CONT.CONTINUE_FINISH_DIALOG-12032
Dlg3={4AA1FE2E-373C-447E-9995-BAA7E4FD0E24}-CONT.DIRECTORY_SELECTION_DIALOG-22003
Dlg4={4AA1FE2E-373C-447E-9995-BAA7E4FD0E24}-CONTINUE_FINISH_DIALOG-12032
[{4AA1FE2E-373C-447E-9995-BAA7E4FD0E24}-DIRECTORY_SELECTION_DIALOG-22003]
InstallProgram=Tally.ERP9
ApplicationDirectory=C:\Tally.ERP9
DataDirectory=C:\Tally.ERP9\Data
ConfigurationDirectory=C:\Tally.ERP9
LanguageDirectory=C:\Tally.ERP9\Lang
UseLicenseServer=0
LicenseDirectory=C:\Tally.ERP9
[{4AA1FE2E-373C-447E-9995-BAA7E4FD0E24}-LANGUAGE_SELECTION_DIALOG-22005]
Country=India/SAARC
StartupLanguage=English
InstallOSLanguageSupport=1
[Application]
Name=Install
Version=1.000.00000
Company=©Tally Solutions Pvt. Ltd., 1988-2009.
Lang=0009
[{4AA1FE2E-373C-447E-9995-BAA7E4FD0E24}-CONT.CONTINUE_FINISH_DIALOG-12032]
CONT.ContinueOrFinish=Continue
[{4AA1FE2E-373C-447E-9995-BAA7E4FD0E24}-CONT.DIRECTORY_SELECTION_DIALOG-22003]
CONT.InstallProgram=LicenseServer
CONT.LicenseServerDirectory=C:\TallyLicenseServer
CONT.LicenseServerPort=9927
CONT.OvewriteExistingLicenseServer=No
[{4AA1FE2E-373C-447E-9995-BAA7E4FD0E24}-CONTINUE_FINISH_DIALOG-12032]
ContinueOrFinish=Finish
```

Figure 6.2 Recorded Script file

6.2 Installing in Silent Mode

To install **Tally.ERP 9** in **Silent Mode**, type the following command at the command prompt:

Install /s /f1 "<path\filename>"

Where:

/s - install in Silent Mode

/f1 - specify the path and filename.

path - specify the path where the file has to be stored

filename - name of the file to read the installation parameters

Example

Install /s /f1 "C:\SilentInstall\InstalParamts.iss"

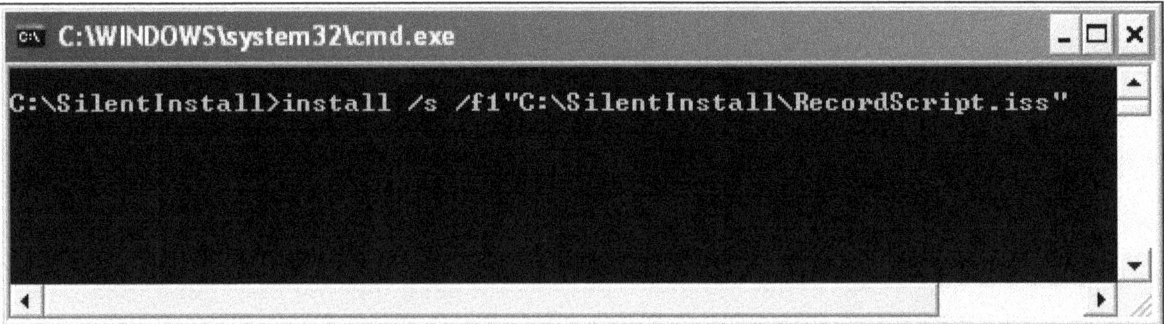

Figure 6.3 Play a recorded script

Lesson 7:   Launching Tally.ERP 9

You can start **Tally.ERP 9** by using any one of the methods shown below:

- Go to **Start** > **Programs** > **Tally.ERP 9**
- The **Tally.ERP 9** sub-menu is displayed as shown.

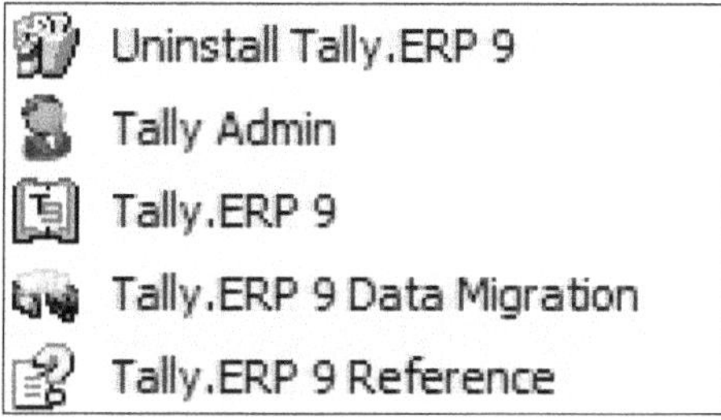

Figure 7.1 Tally.ERP 9

- Select **Tally.ERP 9**.

Or

- Double click the **Tally.ERP 9** shortcut displayed on the desktop.

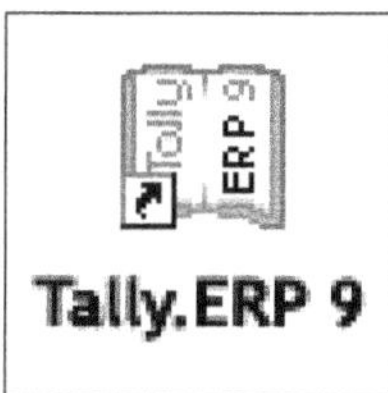

Figure 7.2 Tally Shortcut Icon

Or

- Click the **Tally.ERP 9** icon in the Quick Launch bar if enabled.

Lesson 8:   Activating Tally.ERP 9 Single Site

8.1 Introduction

Licensing mechanism in Tally.ERP 9 is revamped. It's made simple, faster and comes with a host of enhancements which includes improved user experience and troubleshooting connectivity issues.

The enhancements introduced are as follows

- User Experience
    - Single menu option for License Activation and Reactivation
    - Additional fields for multi-site activation available at the click of a button
    - Reactivate without Unlock Key - Just provide the Account/Site Administrator's ID
    - and password, Tally.ERP 9 works in permanent mode immediately after reactivation
    - On detecting that the administrator is attached to more than a site or an account, the resolution screen appears and helps in solving the site reactivation.
    - On attempting to activate the surrendered license or reactivate an un-activated serial number the user is redirected to the reactivation form or to the activation form respectively.
- Troubleshooting
    - **Connectivity issues**: The system automatically detects any problems on the network during license Activation and Reactivation and provides you with the possible resolutions.
    - **Client in Educational Mode**: While attempting to establish a connection with the license server, the system detects and lists the problems along with the possible solutions and actions.

8.2 Activating Tally.ERP 9

In **Tally.ERP 9,** licensing works on the concept of sites. A site is a single instance of **Tally.ERP 9 Silver** or **Gold** installed and activated. The License Activation is shown in two simple steps:

8.2.1 Step 1: Activate Tally.ERP 9

When you start **Tally.ERP 9** for the first time, the **Startup** screen is displayed as shown.

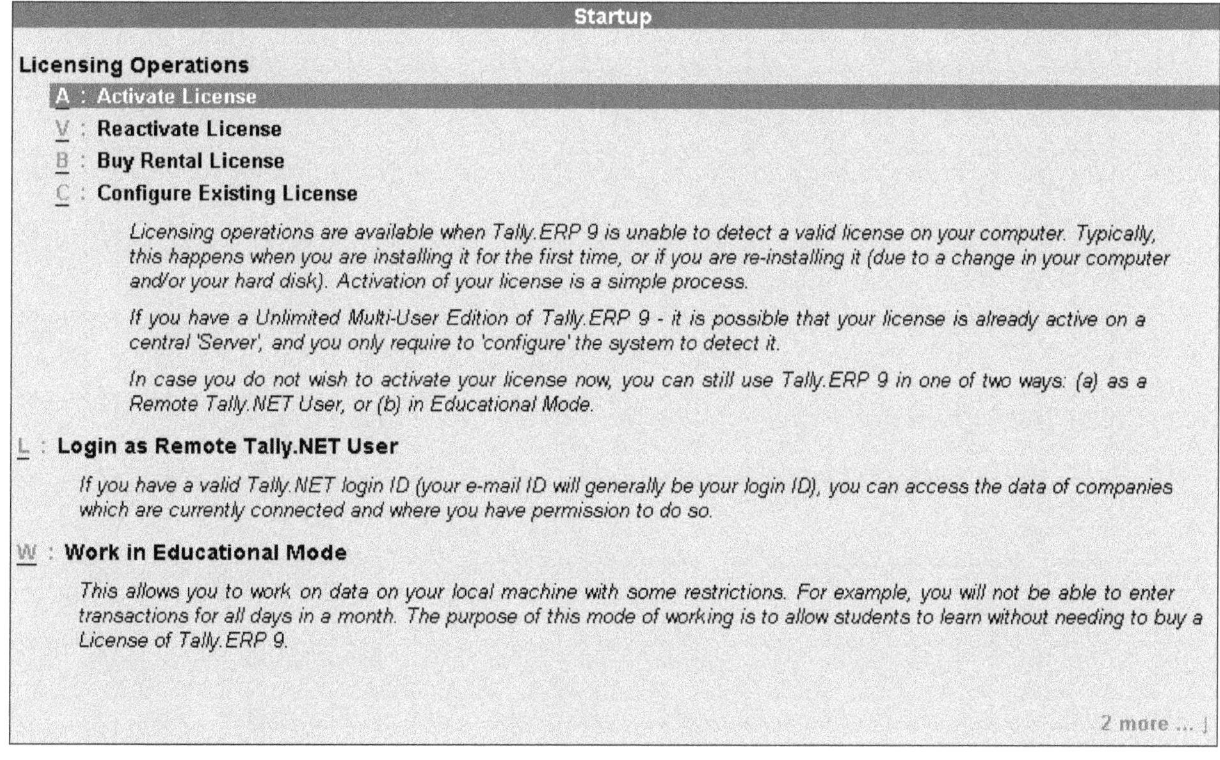

Figure 8.1   Startup Screen

❑   Select **Activate License** and press **Enter**.

❑ The **Activate License** form appears as shown:

<table>
<tr><td align="center">

Activate License

Serial Number / Promotional Code: ███████████████████

(Enter 'Serial Number' to activate Regular License or 'Promotional Code' to activate Promotional Rental License.)

Activation Key :

E-Mail ID of Administrator :
Repeat (E-Mail ID of Administrator) :

Account Name :
(Easy identification of your Account. It could be organization name or individual name.)

Activating your License is a simple two-step process. Once your Serial Number and Activation Key combinataion or Promotional Code is confirmed, you will receive an E-Mail giving you some important details:

1. Your Tally.NET Account ID (which you may later modify)
2. An Unlock License Key (which you will require to complete the Activation process)
3. Details on how to access your Tally.NET Account and use it effectively for your organization.

Please remember that the Activation process can be completed only with the 'Unlock License Key' which is sent in the E-Mail to the Administrator. It is important, therefore, that a valid E-Mail is given.

Note: In case you have multiple copies of Tally.ERP 9 (because of multiple locations of your offices), you may already have a Tally.NET Account. In such case, press F2 (Multi Site) to activate additional site for your organization.

</td></tr>
</table>

Figure 8.2 Single Site Activation form

❑ Enter the **Serial** Number printed on the *Installation Guide* in **Serial Number / Promotional Code** field.

❑ Enter the Activation **Key** printed on the *Installation Guide* in the **Activation Key** field.

❑ *Serial Number and Activation Key need to be provided in combination to activate a regular license only. Where as enter the promotional key only to activate the promotional rental. The promotional key Is a unique alpha-numeric string provided to the each Tally Partner.*

❑ *Press F2 or click F2: Multi-Site available on the vertical toolbar for a Multi-Site activation form.*

□ Enter a your **email address** in the **Email ID of Administrator** field. An account is created using the email address provided, the serial number is linked to the account. The **Unlock Key, Account Information** and Account **Password** will be emailed separately to the email-id provided.

□ For the purpose of confirmation enter the same email address in **Repeat (E-mail ID of Administrator)** field.

□ Enter the name of the account in **Account Name** field, an account is created using the name provided.

*The **E-Mail ID of Administrator** and **Repeat (Email ID of Administrator)** fields are case insensitive.*

The completed License Activation form appears as shown

Activate License

Serial Number / Promotional Code: 730003086
(Enter 'Serial Number' to activate Regular License or 'Promotional Code' to activate Promotional Rental License.)

Activation Key : PTX7MH2U

E-Mail ID of Administrator : tallyuser@tallysolutions.com
Repeat (E-Mail ID of Administrator) : tallyuser@tallysolutions.com

Account Name : tallyuser_
(Easy identification of your Account. It could be organization name or individual name.)

Activating your License is a simple two-step process. Once your Serial Number and Activation Key combinataion or Promotional Code is confirmed, you will receive an E -Mail giving you some important details:

1. Your Tally.NET Account ID (which you may later modify)
2. An Unlock License Key (which you will require to complete the Activation process)
3. Details on how to access your Tally.NET Account and use it effectively for your organization.

Please remember that the Activation process can be completed only with the 'Unlock License Key' which is sent in the E-Mail to the Administrator. It is important, therefore, that a valid E-Mail is given.

Note: In case you have multiple copies of Tally.ERP 9 (because of multiple locations of your offices), you may already have a Tally.NET Account. In such case, press F2 (Multi Site) to activate additional site for your organization.

Figure 8.3 Activation Form

□ Press **Enter.**

Tally.ERP 9 searches for the availability of Internet Connectivity on your computer. On success-fully finding the internet connection the system proceeds to activate the license online which is explained in Online Activation section.

Or

While searching for an Internet connection on your computer, in case the system detects any one of the issues/errors shown below. The resolution screen appears providing the possible solutions for the issues/errors. The user needs to resolve the issue/error and activate the license online. In case the issue or error remain unresolved, the user needs to activate the license offline. .

- Internet connectivity is not established/not working/unavailable.
- Outbound connectivity is blocked
- Invalid entry in the hosts file
- Connection Time Out
- Connection Refused
- Network is disabled
- Could not find the IP Address
- Sending / Receiving failed

Online Activation

- Tally.ERP 9 displays the message **Congratulations! Your Activation Request has been Processed. An encrypted file is now on your machine**.
- Press **Enter** to continue.
- Proceed to section **Step 2: Procedure to Unlock License File**.

Offline Activation

- **Tally.ERP 9** displays a **Connection Error** screen containing the **Error Code** and **System Error Code** along with the **Reasons for Failure**, **Possible Solutions** and **What to do now? (Actions)**.

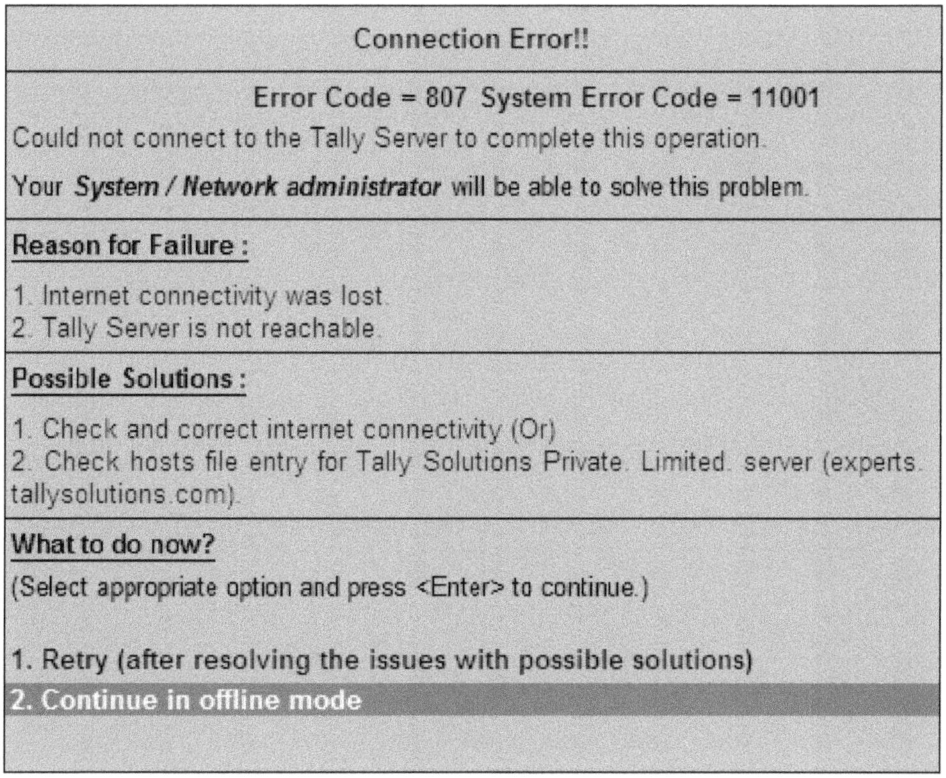

Connection Error!!

Error Code = 807 System Error Code = 11001

Could not connect to the Tally Server to complete this operation.

Your *System / Network administrator* will be able to solve this problem.

Reason for Failure :

1. Internet connectivity was lost.
2. Tally Server is not reachable.

Possible Solutions :

1. Check and correct internet connectivity (Or)
2. Check hosts file entry for Tally Solutions Private. Limited. server (experts.tallysolutions.com).

What to do now?

(Select appropriate option and press <Enter> to continue.)

1. Retry (after resolving the issues with possible solutions)
2. Continue in offline mode

Figure 8.4 Offline Activation Message

- Select **Continue in offline mode**
- **Tally.ERP 9** displays a message **Your Offline Activation Request file has been Created Successfully**. A license request file named **tally_req.lic** is generated and stored in the default **Tally.ERP 9** folder.
- Copy the **tally_req.lic** onto a pen drive/CD and paste the file into the **Tally.ERP9** folder. This computer must be connected to the Internet and Tally.ERP 9 could be running in **Licensed** or **Educational** mode.

*In case Tally.ERP 9 is running in Licensed mode: Go to **Gateway of Tally** > **F12: Configure** > **Licensing** > **Send External Request***

- Start **Tally.ERP 9**

The **Startup** screen appears as shown:

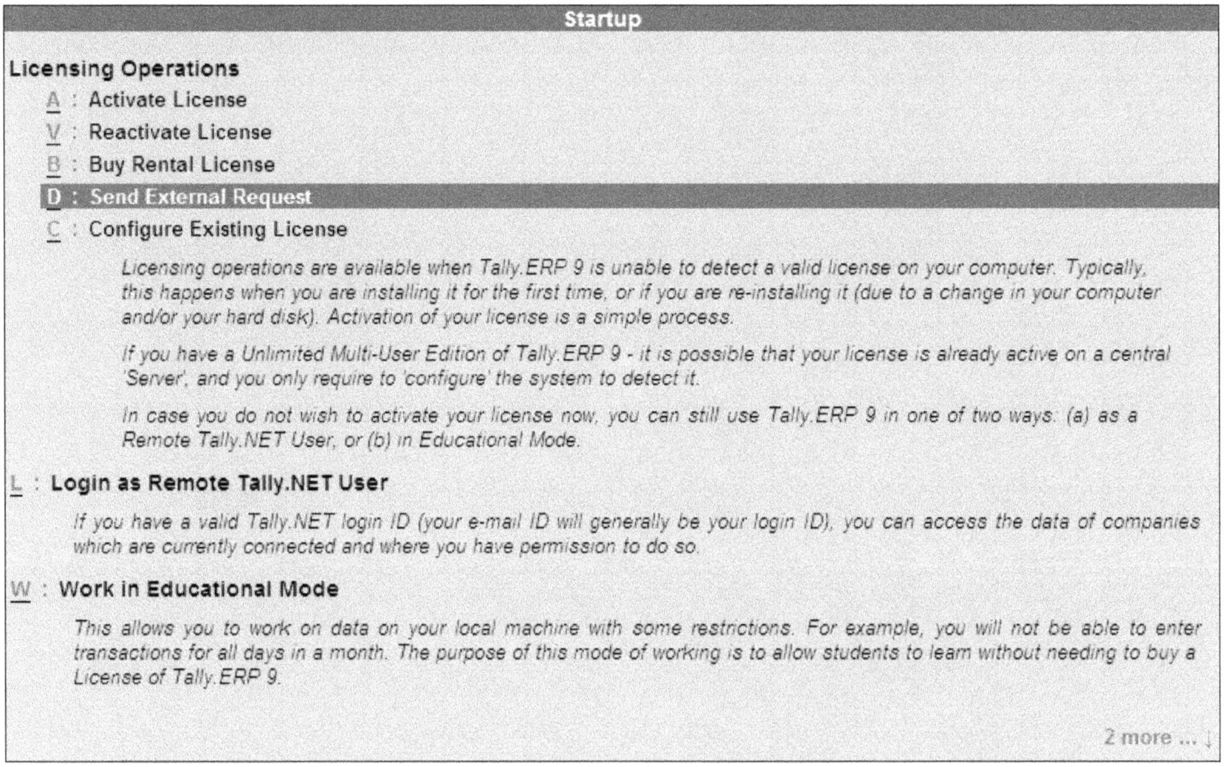

Startup

Licensing Operations

A : Activate License
V : Reactivate License
B : Buy Rental License
D : Send External Request
C : Configure Existing License

Licensing operations are available when Tally.ERP 9 is unable to detect a valid license on your computer. Typically, this happens when you are installing it for the first time, or if you are re-installing it (due to a change in your computer and/or your hard disk). Activation of your license is a simple process.

If you have a Unlimited Multi-User Edition of Tally.ERP 9 - it is possible that your license is already active on a central 'Server', and you only require to 'configure' the system to detect it.

In case you do not wish to activate your license now, you can still use Tally.ERP 9 in one of two ways: (a) as a Remote Tally.NET User, or (b) in Educational Mode.

L : **Login as Remote Tally.NET User**

If you have a valid Tally.NET login ID (your e-mail ID will generally be your login ID), you can access the data of companies which are currently connected and where you have permission to do so.

W : **Work in Educational Mode**

This allows you to work on data on your local machine with some restrictions. For example, you will not be able to enter transactions for all days in a month. The purpose of this mode of working is to allow students to learn without needing to buy a License of Tally.ERP 9.

2 more ... ↓

Figure 8.5 Startup

❑   Select **Send External Request**

❑   **Tally.ERP 9** displays the following message

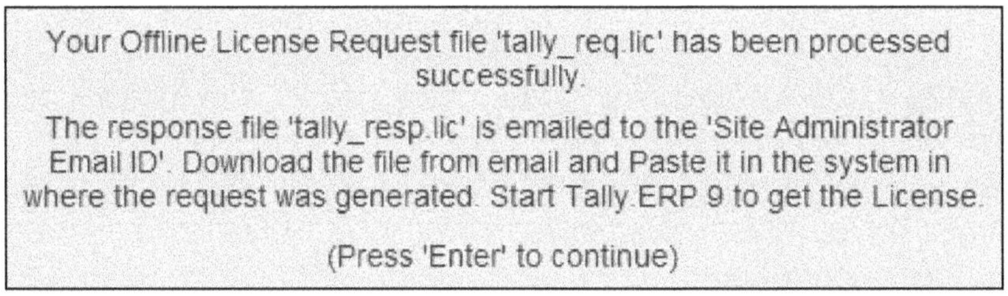

Your Offline License Request file 'tally_req.lic' has been processed successfully.

The response file 'tally_resp.lic' is emailed to the 'Site Administrator Email ID'. Download the file from email and Paste it in the system in where the request was generated. Start Tally.ERP 9 to get the License.

(Press 'Enter' to continue)

❑   Start **Tally.ERP 9**.

❑   Proceed to section **Step 2: Procedure to Unlock License File**

- *The offline request file is emailed to the account administrator of a single site or the respective site administrator of a multi-site account.*

- *When there is a delay in receiving the **Unlock Key**, select **Work in Temporary License Mode** to continue working with a temporary license for a stipulated period displayed in the Information Panel. Further, if you do not receive the **Unlock Key** within the stipulated duration, activate **Tally.ERP 9** and continue working with a temporary license thrice additionally. This facility is also extended for Reactivation of license.*

- *In the temporary license mode you will not be able to migrate the data from earlier versions of Tally.*

Or

- Try to resolve the issue shown with **Possible Solutions** and continue activating the license in online mode

8.2.2 Step 2: Procedure to Unlock License File

Access your email and retrieve the unlock key before proceeding to unlock the license file.

The **Unlock License** screen appears

- Type the unlock key retrieved in **Unlock Key** field and press **Enter.**

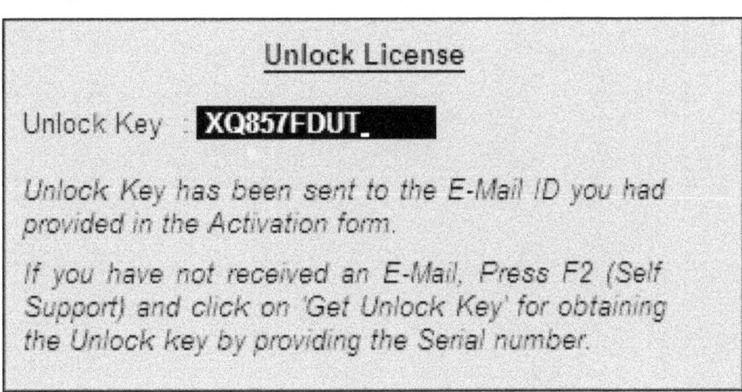

Figure 8.6 Unlock License

Access your email and retrieve the unlock key before proceeding to unlock the license file.

On successfully unlocking the license, **Tally.ERP 9** displays a message as shown.

> Congratulations ! Your license is successfully activated!
>
> Welcome to the world of Tally.ERP 9 !
>
> (Press 'Enter' to Continue)

Figure 8.7 License Succesfully Activated

*A request to activate the license can be made from the server or client machine while activating **Tally.ERP 9 Gold** or **Auditors' Edition**.*

❑ Press **Enter** to continue

❑ The **Gateway of Tally** appears displaying the **Company Info** menu. The information related to the product **Edition** and number of **Users** allowed appear under **Version** block

where as the **License Serial Number** and **Account ID** appear under **License** block of the Information panel. .

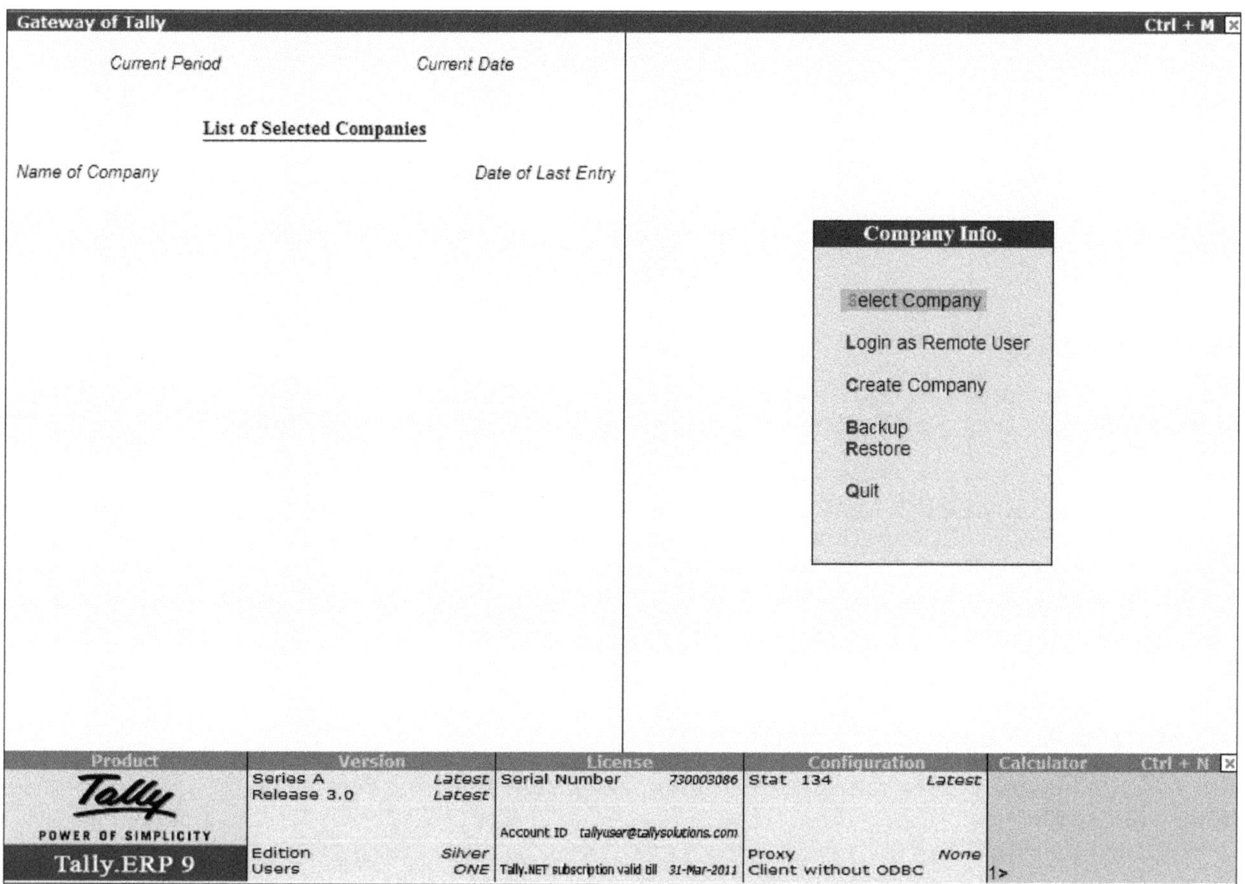

Figure 8.8   Tally.ERP 9 License Details for Single User

Similarly, you can also activate **Tally.ERP 9 Gold or Tally.ERP 9 Auditors' Edition** Single Site License.

Lesson 9:   Activating Tally.ERP 9 Multi Site

Introduction

A Multi-Site has more than one **Tally.ERP 9 Silver** or **Gold** licenses active on different machines or locations under a single account comprising of same or different serial numbers.

On purchase of **Tally.ERP 9** Multi Site License, the associated Tally Partner creates an **Account ID** using your E-Mail ID, the Multi Site License Serial Numbers are associated to the account created. You need to provide the **Account ID** and **Password** to access the account information, or reactivate **Tally.ERP 9** license.

The Multi Site Activation is shown in two simple steps

9.1 Step1: Activate Tally.ERP 9

After the successful installation when you start **Tally.ERP 9** for the first time, the **Startup** screen appears as shown.

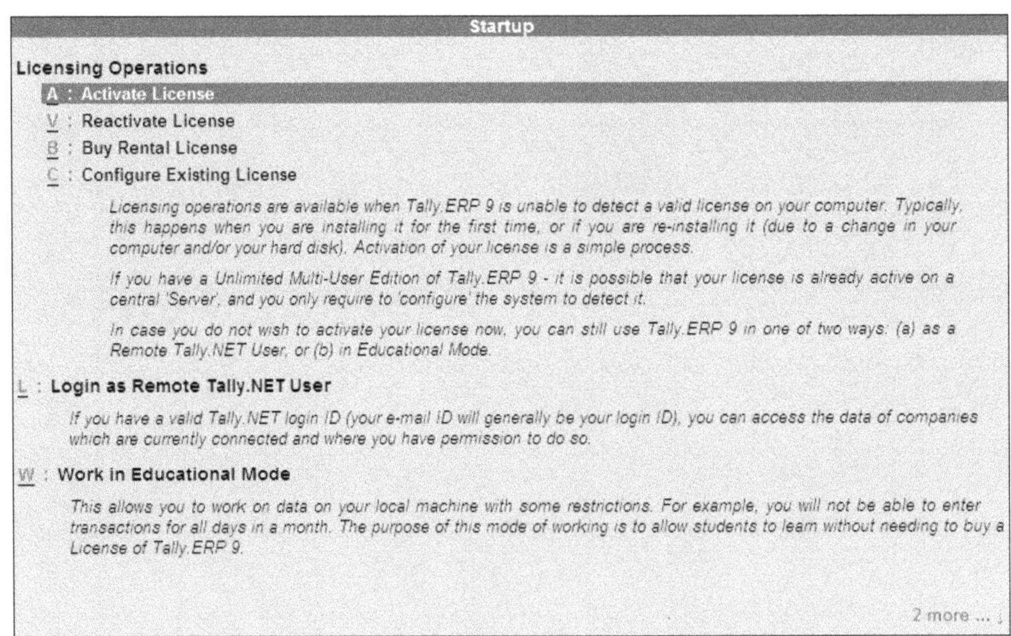

Figure 9.1 Startup

- Select **Activate License** and press **Enter**.

The **Activate License** form appears

- Press **F2** or click **F2: Multi Site**

The **Activate Site License** form appears as shown

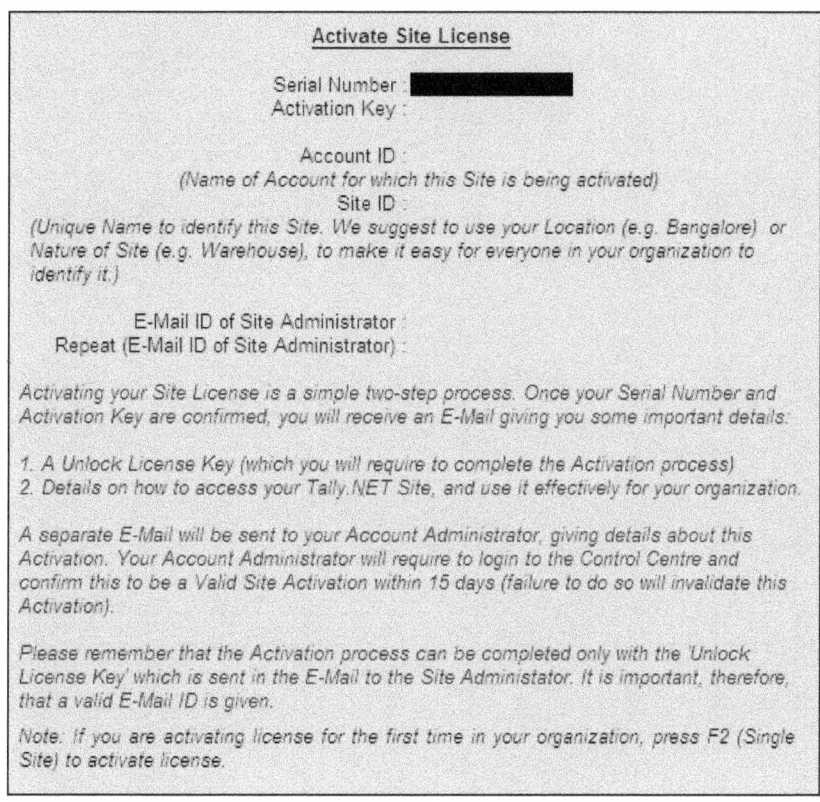

Figure 9.2 Activate Site License

- Enter the **Serial Number** printed on the *Installation Guide* in the **Serial Number** field
- Enter the **Activation Key** printed on the *Installation Guide* in the **Activation Key** field.
- Enter the Account ID in the **Account ID** field
- Enter the **Site Name** in **Site ID** field. An account can have one or more active sites.
- Enter your **E-mail ID** in **E-mail ID of Site Administrator** field. The **Unlock key**, **Password** and account information is mailed to the E-Mail ID provided.
- For the purpose of confirmation re-enter the email address in the **Repeat (E-mail ID of Site Administrator)** field.

*The **E-Mail ID of Administrator** and **Repeat (Email ID of Administrator)** fields are case insensitive.*

The completed **Activate Site License** form appears as shown:

<table>
<tr><td>

Activate Site License

Serial Number : 720003186
Activation Key : **DXY2ACX7M**

Account ID : **tallyuser@tallysolutions.com**
(Existing ID of the account for which this Site is being activated)
Site ID : **Site A**
(Unique Name to identify this Site. We suggest to use your Location (e.g. Bangalore) or Nature of Site (e.g. Warehouse), to make it easy for everyone in your organization to identify it.)

E-Mail ID of Site Administrator : **tallyuser@tallysolutions.com**
Repeat (E-Mail ID of Site Administrator) : **tallyuser@tallysolutions.com**

Activating your Site License is a simple two-step process. Once your Serial Number and Activation Key are confirmed, you will receive an E-Mail giving you some important details:

1. A Unlock License Key (which you will require to complete the Activation process)
2. Details on how to access your Tally.NET Site, and use it effectively for your organization.

A separate E-Mail will be sent to your Account Administrator, giving details about this Activation. Your Account Administrator will require to login to the Control Centre and confirm this to be a Valid Site Activation within 15 days (failure to do so will invalidate this Activation).

Please remember that the Activation process can be completed only with the 'Unlock License Key' which is sent in the E-Mail to the Site Administator. It is important, therefore, that a valid E-Mail ID is given.

Note: If you are activating license for the first time in your organization, press F2 (Single Site) to activate license.

</td></tr>
</table>

Figure 9.3 Multi Site Activation Form

❑ Press **Enter**.

Tally.ERP 9 searches for the availability of Internet Connectivity on your computer. On successfully finding the internet connection the system proceeds to activate the license online which is explained in **Online Activation** section.

Or

While searching for an Internet connection on your computer, in case the system detects any one of the issues/errors shown below. The resolution screen appears providing the possible solutions for the issues/errors. The user needs to resolve the issue/error and activate the license online. In case the issue or error remain unresolved, the user needs to activate the license offline. .

❑ Internet connectivity is not established/not working/unavailable.

❑ Outbound connectivity is blocked

❑ Invalid entry in the hosts file

❑ Connection Time Out

❑ Connection Refused

❑ Network is disabled

❑ Could not find the IP Address

❑ Sending / Receiving failed

Online Activation

- **Tally.ERP 9** displays a message **Congratulations! Your activation Request has been processed**. An encrypted file is now on your machine.
- Press **Enter** to continue.
- Proceed to section **Step 2: Procedure to Unlock License File**.

Offline Activation

- **Tally.ERP 9** displays a **Connection Error** screen containing the **Error Code** and **System Error Code** along with the **Reasons for Failure**, **Possible Solutions** and **What to do now? (Actions)**.

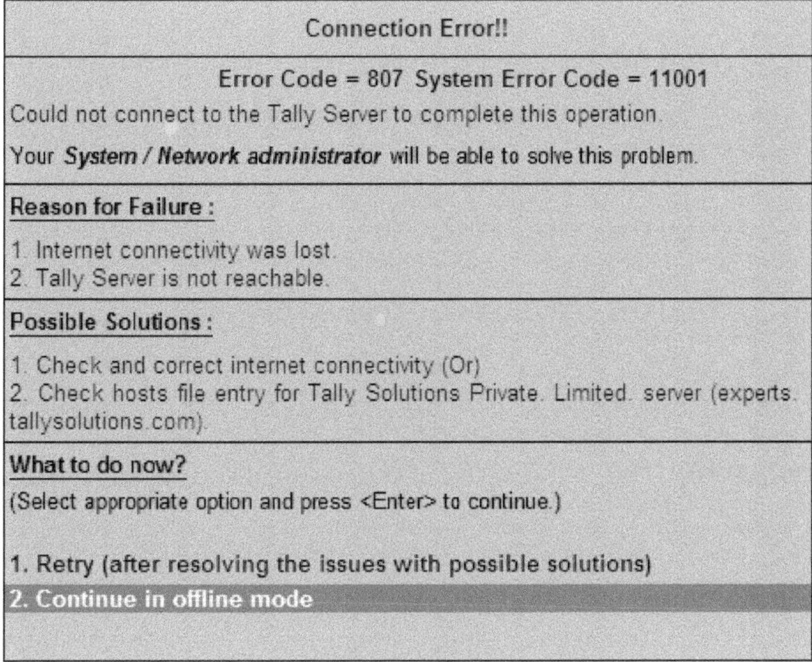

Figure 9.4 Offline Activation Message

- Select Continue in offline mode
- **Tally.ERP 9** displays a message **Your Offline Activation Request file has been Created Successfully**. A license request file named **tally_req.lic** is generated and stored in the default **Tally.ERP 9** folder.
- Copy the **tally_req.lic** onto a pen drive/CD and paste the file into the **Tally.ERP9** folder. This computer must be connected to the Internet and Tally.ERP 9 coule be running in **Licensed** or **Educational** mode.

In case Tally.ERP 9 is running in Licensed mode: Go to **Gateway of Tally** > **F12: Configure** > **Licensing** > **Send External Request**

❑ Start **Tally.ERP 9**

The **Startup** screen appears as shown:

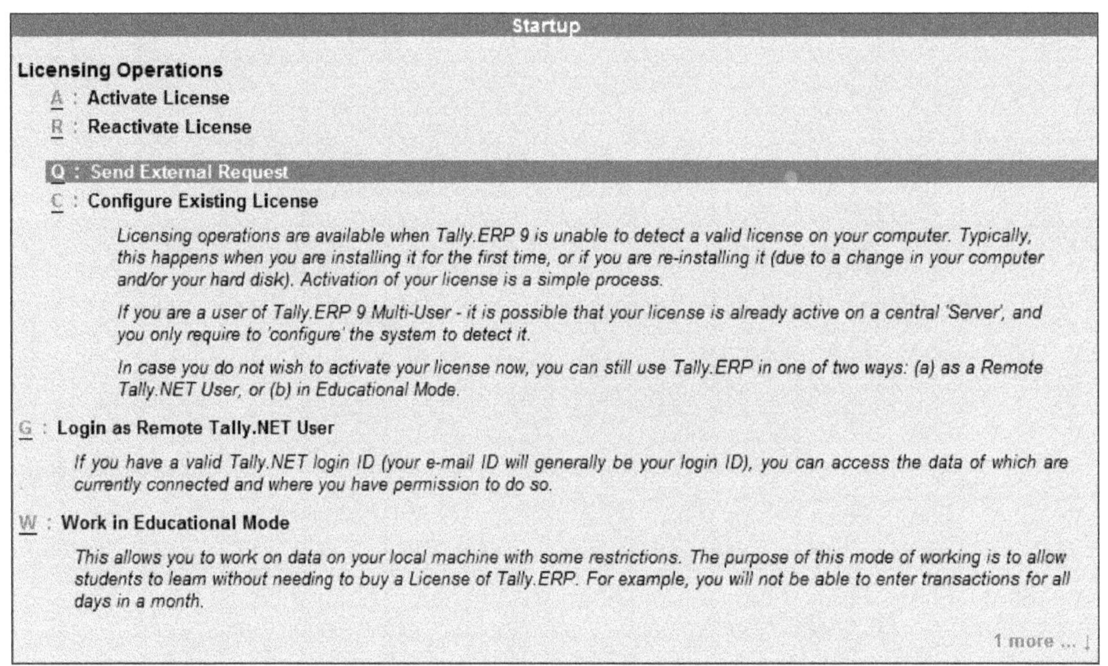

Figure 9.5 Startup

❑ Select **Send External Request** and press **Enter**

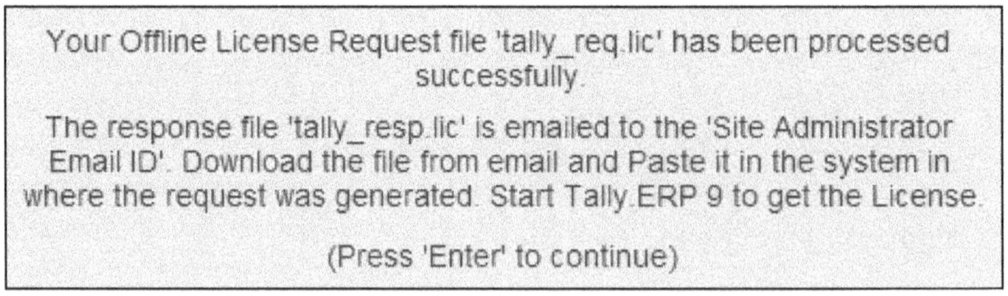

Figure 9.6 Offline Request License Message

- Start **Tally.ERP 9**.
- Proceed to the section **Step 2: Procedure to Unlock License File**.

- *When there is a delay in receiving the **Unlock Key**, select **Work in Temporary License Mode** to continue working with a temporary license for a stipulated period displayed in the Information Panel. Further, if you do not receive the **Unlock Key** within the stipulated period, you may activate and continue working with a temporary license thrice additionally. This facility is also extended for Reactivation of license.*

- *In the temporary license mode you will not be able to migrate the data from earlier versions of Tally.*

- *The offline request file is emailed to the account administrator of a single site or the respective site administrator of a multi-site account.*

Or

- Try to resolve the issue shown with **Possible Solutions** and continue activating the license in online mode

9.2 Step 2: Procedure to Unlock the License File

Access your email and retrieve the unlock key before proceeding to unlock the license file.

The **Unlock License** screen appears.

- Enter the **Unlock Key** emailed in the **Unlock Key** field and press **Enter.**

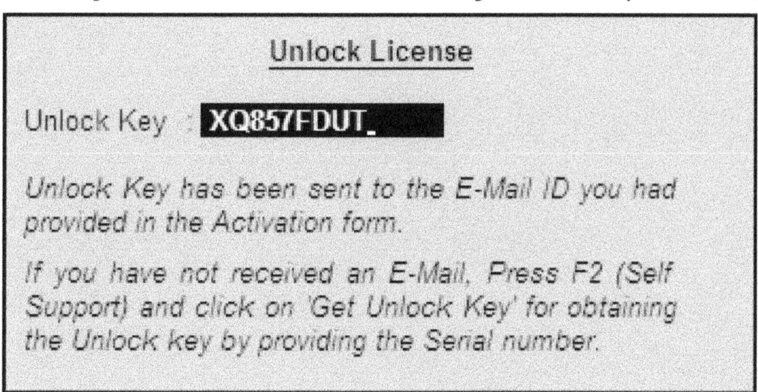

Figure 9.7 Unlock License

Access your email and retrieve the unlock key before proceeding to unlock the license file.

On successfully unlocking the license file, a message is displayed as shown.

> Congratulations ! Your license is successfully activated!
>
> Welcome to the world of Tally.ERP 9 !
>
> (Press 'Enter' to Continue)

Figure 9.8 License Activates Successfully

On starting **Tally.ERP 9,** the **Edition** and **User** information is displayed under **Version** block, the License **Serial Number**, **Site ID** and **Account ID** are displayed under the **License** block of the information panel.

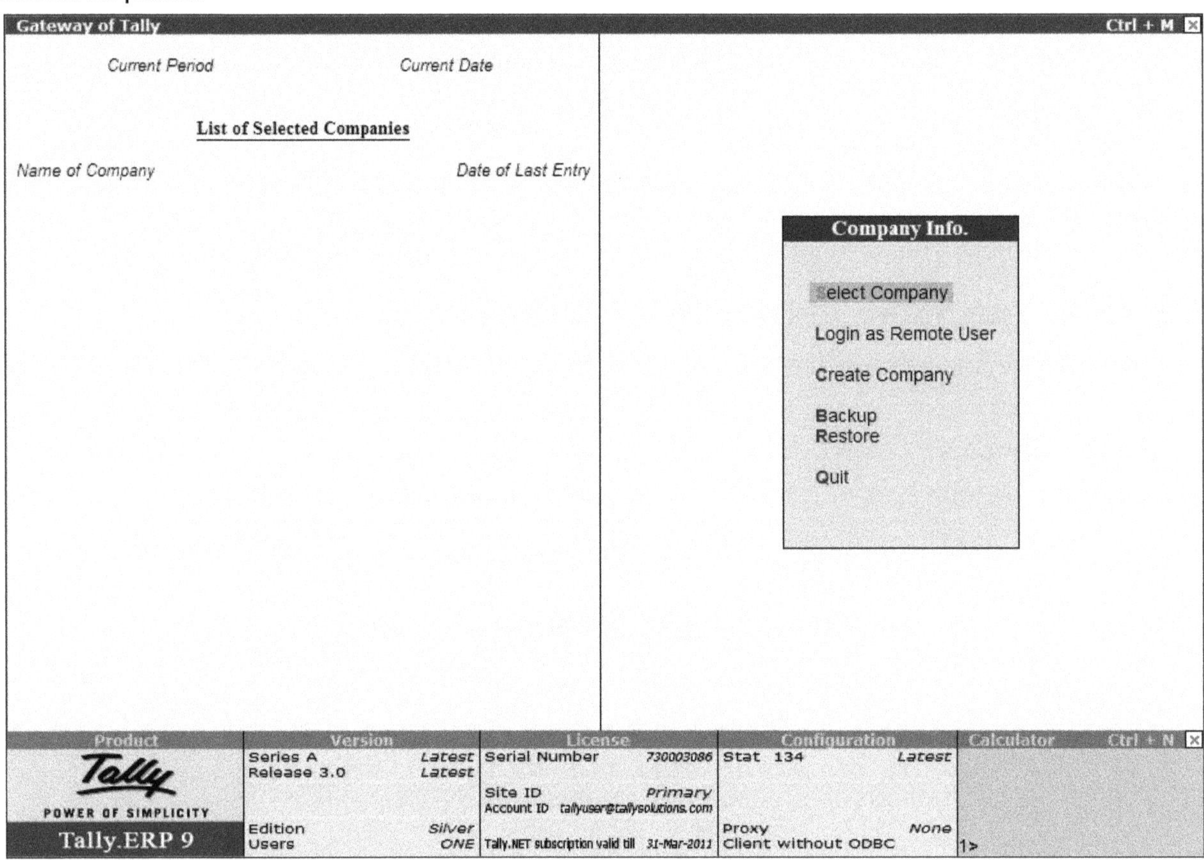

Figure 9.9 License Details

On successful activation of a **Site** belonging to an **Account**, the **Account Administrator** is informed by E-mail about the activation. The **Account Administrator** in turn has to **Confirm** the activation within a span of **15** days from the date of activating the Site.

Any licensing operation performed for a Site is logged in the **Support Centre** and by default the status is displayed as **Closed**.

Similarly, you can also activate **Tally.ERP 9 Gold** or **Tally.ERP 9 Auditors' Edition** for Multi Site Licenses.

Lesson 10:   Licensing Resolution

10.1 Licensing Resolution

Licensing resolutions occur when the systems encounters a conflict with the Site/Account Administrator's E-Mail ID or a Site ID while activating a license. This system has a built-in capability that detects duplicate Email Id or Site Id within an account or across accounts and proceeds to resolve the conflict through the licensing mechanism available separately for Single Site and Multi - Site license activations

10.1.1 License Resolution - Single Site

When the user provides an E-Mail ID that already exist within an account or across accounts. Tally.ERP 9 prompts the user with the resolution. You can select the required option ë screen shown below:

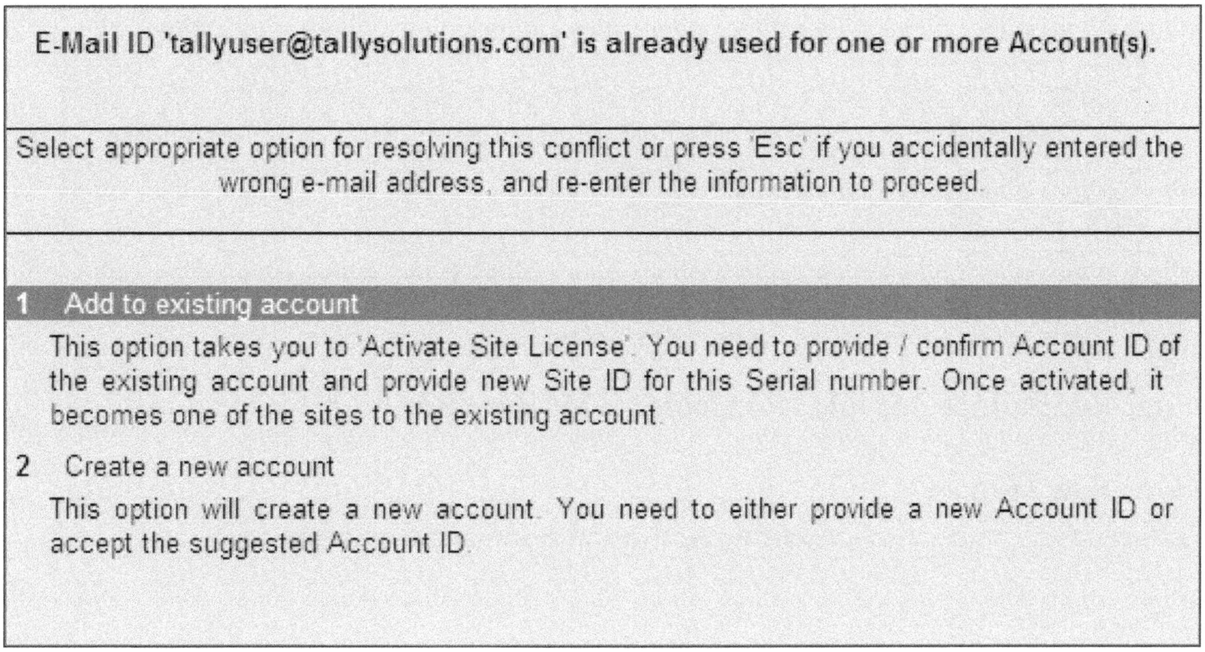

E-Mail ID 'tallyuser@tallysolutions.com' is already used for one or more Account(s).

Select appropriate option for resolving this conflict or press 'Esc' if you accidentally entered the wrong e-mail address, and re-enter the information to proceed.

1   Add to existing account

This option takes you to 'Activate Site License'. You need to provide / confirm Account ID of the existing account and provide new Site ID for this Serial number. Once activated, it becomes one of the sites to the existing account.

2   Create a new account

This option will create a new account. You need to either provide a new Account ID or accept the suggested Account ID.

Figure 10.1 User Resolution

Add to an existing Account

On selectting this option the **Activate Site License** screen appears as Shown :

Activate Site License

Serial Number : 745000056
Activation Key : tally999

Account ID : tallyuser@tallysolutions.com
(Existing ID of the account for which this Site is being activated)
Site ID : **Ware House 1**
(Unique Name to identify this Site. We suggest to use your Location (e.g. Bangalore) or Nature of Site (e.g. Warehouse), to make it easy for everyone in your organization to identify it.)

E-Mail ID of Site Administrator : **user@tallysolutions.com**
Repeat (E-Mail ID of Site Administrator) : **user@tallysolutions.com**

Activating your Site License is a simple two-step process. Once your Serial Number and Activation Key are confirmed, you will receive an E-Mail giving you some important details:

1. A Unlock License Key (which you will require to complete the Activation process)
2. Details on how to access your Tally.NET Site, and use it effectively for your organization.

A separate E-Mail will be sent to your Account Administrator, giving details about this Activation. Your Account Administrator will require to login to the Control Centre and confirm this to be a Valid Site Activation within 15 days (failure to do so will invalidate this Activation).

Please remember that the Activation process can be completed only with the 'Unlock License Key' which is sent in the E-Mail to the Site Administator. It is important, therefore, that a valid E-Mail ID is given.

Note: If you are activating license for the first time in your organization, press F2 (Single Site) to activate license.

Figure 10.2 Activate Site License

You can now follow the Site Activation process to activate a Site.

Create a New Account

On selecting this option the **Supporting Activation Form** appears as shown

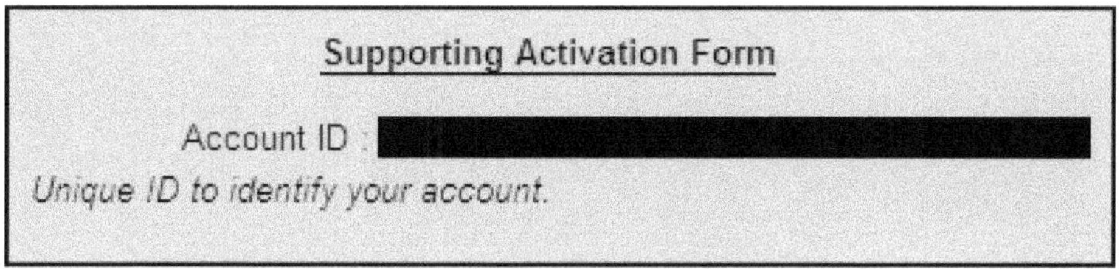

Supporting Activation Form

Account ID :

Unique ID to identify your account.

Figure 10.3 Supporting Activation Form

- Enter the required E-Mail ID to create a new account.

The license serial number provided will be activated in the newly created account.

10.1.2 License Resolution - Multi-Site

When the user provides an E-Mail ID which is already existing within the same or different account or when the Site ID is duplicated within the same account, Tally.ERP 9 detects the duplicate email id or Account ID as a conflict and provides the option to resolve it.

The conflict of a duplicate Account/Site Administrators E-Mail ID or Site ID can either be resolved by providing a new E-Mail ID or Site ID to activate the license serial number. In case the license serial number was surrendered earlier, the user can opt to reactivate the same.

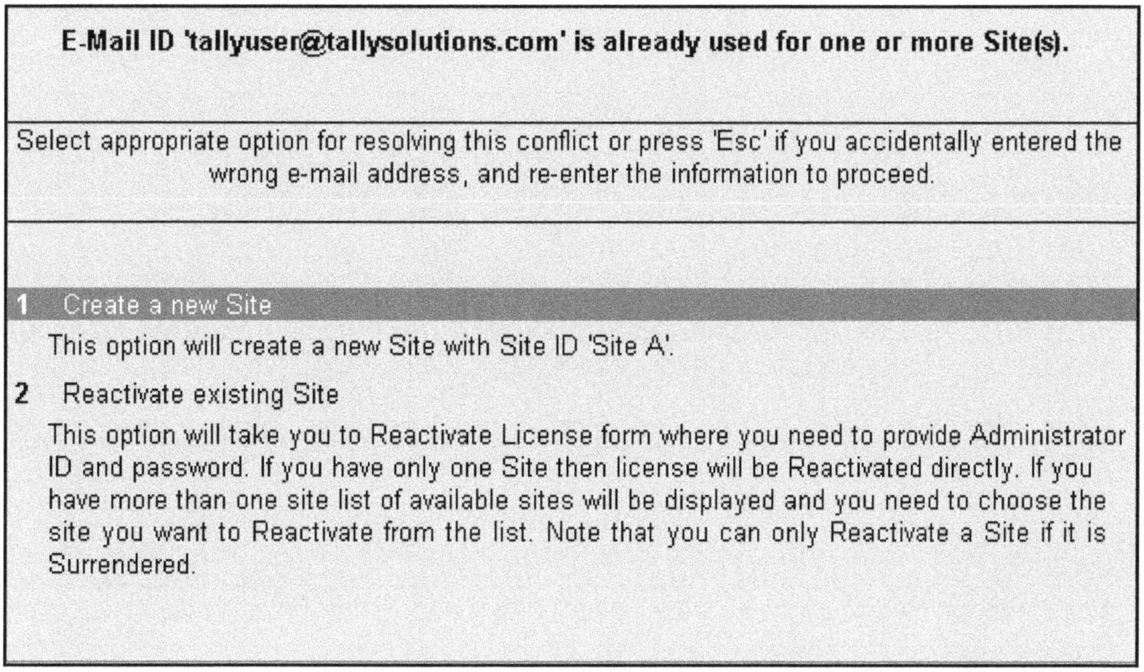

E-Mail ID 'tallyuser@tallysolutions.com' is already used for one or more Site(s).

Select appropriate option for resolving this conflict or press 'Esc' if you accidentally entered the wrong e-mail address, and re-enter the information to proceed.

1 Create a new Site

This option will create a new Site with Site ID 'Site A'.

2 Reactivate existing Site

This option will take you to Reactivate License form where you need to provide Administrator ID and password. If you have only one Site then license will be Reactivated directly. If you have more than one site list of available sites will be displayed and you need to choose the site you want to Reactivate from the list. Note that you can only Reactivate a Site if it is Surrendered.

Figure 10.4 Supporting Activation Form

      ❑ Select **Create a New Site**

Tally.ERP 9 dipslays the message **Congratulations! Your Activation Request has been Processed. An encrypted file is now on your machine**.

      ❑ Provide the unlock license file in **Unlock License** field to activate the license.

Reactivate Existing Site

Provide E-Mail ID of the Administrator and password to reactivate the site by following the steps shown:

Figure 10.5 Reactivate License

      ❑ Enter the password for the Email ID provided

The **Reactivate License** screen appears, based on the availability of the Internet connection the user can opt to activate the license in Online or Offline mode.

Online Re-activation

      ❑ Tally.ERP 9 displays the message **Congratulations! Your Activation Request has been Processed. An encrypted file is now on your machine**.

      ❑ Press **Enter** to continue.

      ❑ Proceed to section **Step 2: Procedure to Unlock License File**.

Offline Re-activation

Tally.ERP 9 displays a **Connection Error** screen containing the **Error Code** and **System Error Code** along with the **Reasons for Failure**, **Possible Solutions** and **What to do now? (Actions)**

      ❑ Select **Continue in offline mode**

      ❑ **Tally.ERP 9** displays a message **Your Offline Activation Request file has been Created Successfully**. A license request file named **tally_req.lic** is generated and stored in the default **Tally.ERP 9** folder.

- Copy the **tally_req.lic** onto a pen drive/CD and paste the file into the **Tally.ERP9** folder. This computer must be connected to the Internet and Tally.ERP 9 could be running in **Licensed** or **Educational** mode.
- Start **Tally.ERP 9**

The **Startup** screen appears

- Select **Send External Request**
- **Tally.ERP 9** displays a message **Offline Response File Generated Successfully**.
- Copy **tally_resp.lic** file to a pendrive/CD and paste this file to the **Tally.ERP9** folder of the computer where **Tally.ERP 9** is to be activated

The **Reactivation Successful** message appears.

- Press **Enter**

The **Gateway of Tally** appears displaying the **Info Panel** which contains information on the **Release**, **Edition** and **Users** under **Version** block, the **Serial Number**, **Account ID** and validity **of Tally.NET Subscription** under **License** block and various configuration details under the **Configuration** block.

Lesson 11:   Configuring Tally.ERP 9

The user can locally configure the Tally.ini using the configuration options available. You can add or modify parameters to the Tally.ini file without actually opening the file.

To configure **Tally.ERP 9**

Go to **Gateway of Tally** or **Company Info** menu

    ◻ Press **F12:Configure**

The **Configuration** menu appears as shown

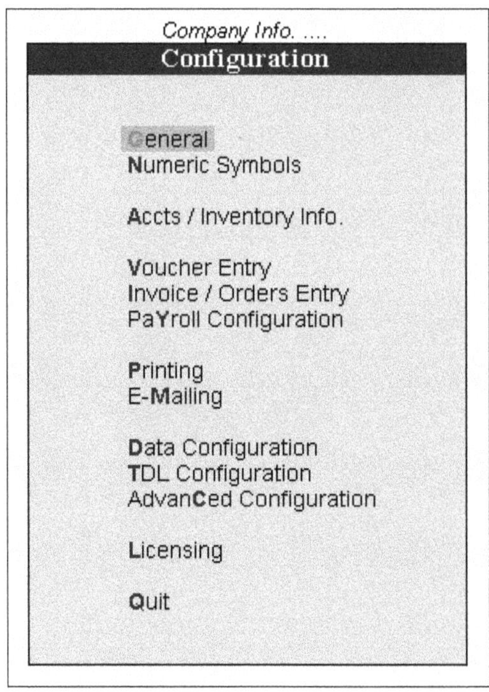

Figure 11.1 Configuration Menu

Here we will be discussing the four categories of the **Configuration** menu

- **Data Configuration**
- **TDL Configuration**
- **Advanced Configuration**
- **Configure Existing Licensing**

11.1 Data Configurations

Tally.ERP 9 allows the user to add or modify the path where the Language, Data and Configuration files reside. To change the required configurations, execute the following steps.

Go to **Gateway of Tally** or **Company Info** menu

- Press **F12:Configure**
- Select **Data Configuration**

The **Data Configuration** screen is displayed.

- By default **C:\Tally.ERP9\Lang** appears in **Location of Language Files** field. Specify the required path, if the language files reside in another folder.
- By default **C:\Tally.ERP9** appears in **Location of Tally Configuration Files** field. Specify the required path, if the configuration file resides in another folder.
- By default **C:\Tally.ERP9\Data** appears in **Location of Export Files** field. You can specify the additional paths required. The path of the export files can also be changed for individual reports.
- By default **C:\Tally.ERP9\Data** appears in **Location of Data Files** field. You can specify the additional paths required. To deactivate a required path you can commenting it with a #,
- By default **Load Companies on Start-up** is enabled,
- In **Companies to preload on Startup,** select the required companies from the **List of Companies** or select **Specific** and mention the required paths to load the required companies on startup

*In case you do not want **Tally.ERP 9** to load companies on startup, set **Load Companies on Startup** to **No.***

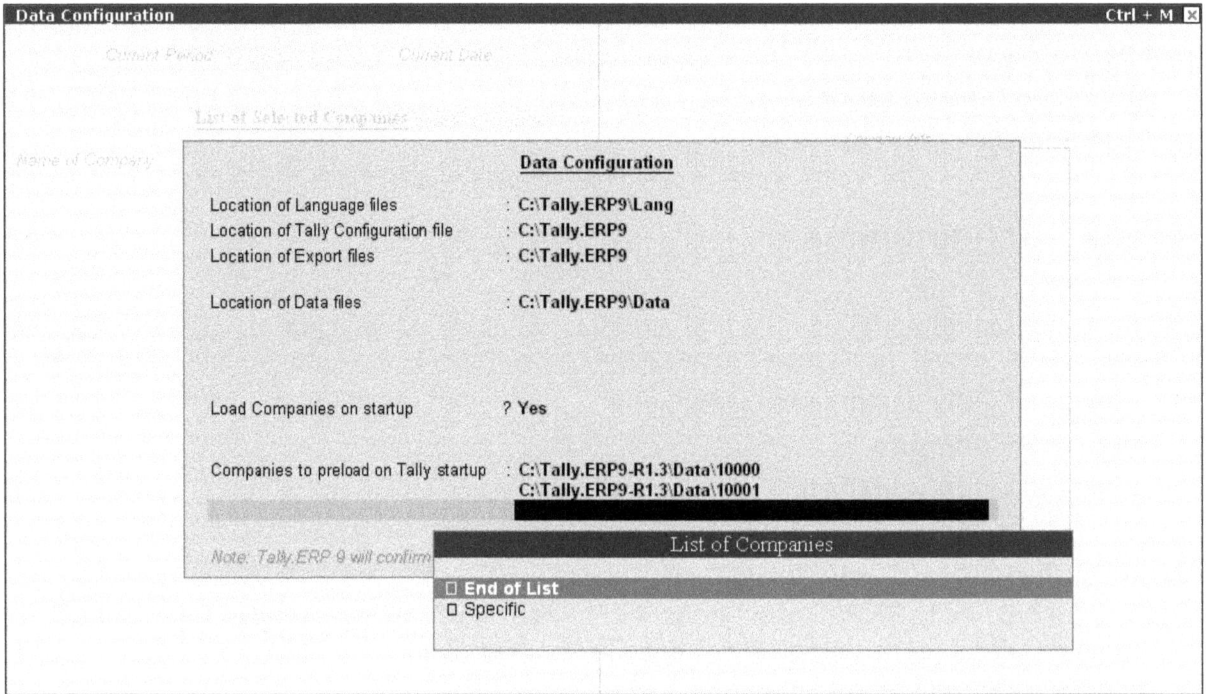

Figure 11.2   Configure Licensing

- ☐ Select **End of List**.
- ☐ **Accept** to save the data configurations.
- ☐ **Tally.ERP 9** displays a message **Do you want to restart Tally.ERP 9 for the changes to have effect?**
- ☐ Press **Y** or click **Yes** to effect changes and restart **Tally.ERP 9**.

11.2 TDL Configuration

The **TDL Configuration** screen shows the details about the TDLs that are active and their origin. In **Tally.ERP 9** with the availability of remote access the application can get TDLs from the following locations:

- ☐ Remote server
- ☐ The owner account and
- ☐ Locally available TDLs

The TDLs are categorized as **Local TDLs**, **Account TDLs** and **Remote TDLs**.

- ☐ Press **F12: Configure**
- ☐ Select **TDL Configuration**.

The **TDL Configuration** screen appears as shown.

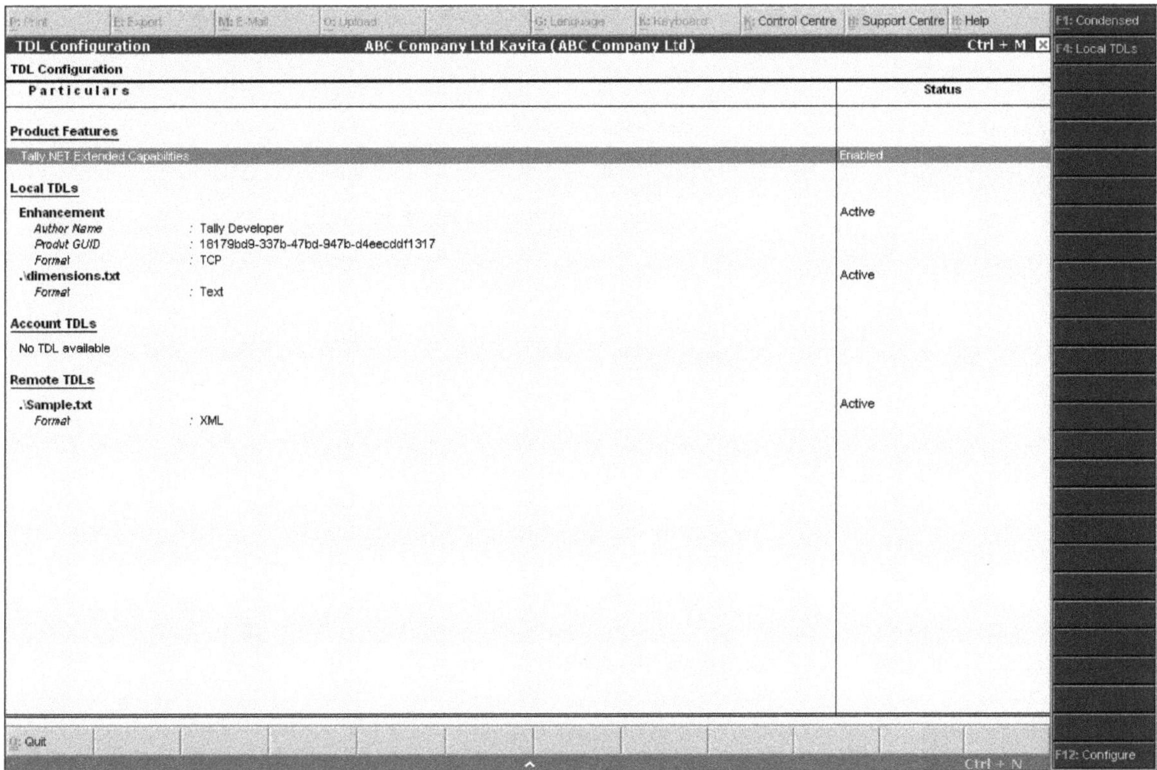

Figure 11.3   TDL Configuration

11.2.1 Local TDLs

Displays the TDLs that are available and their Status as **Active**, **Not Allowed** and **Error**. Select the button **F4: Local TDLs**, it displays the following screen.

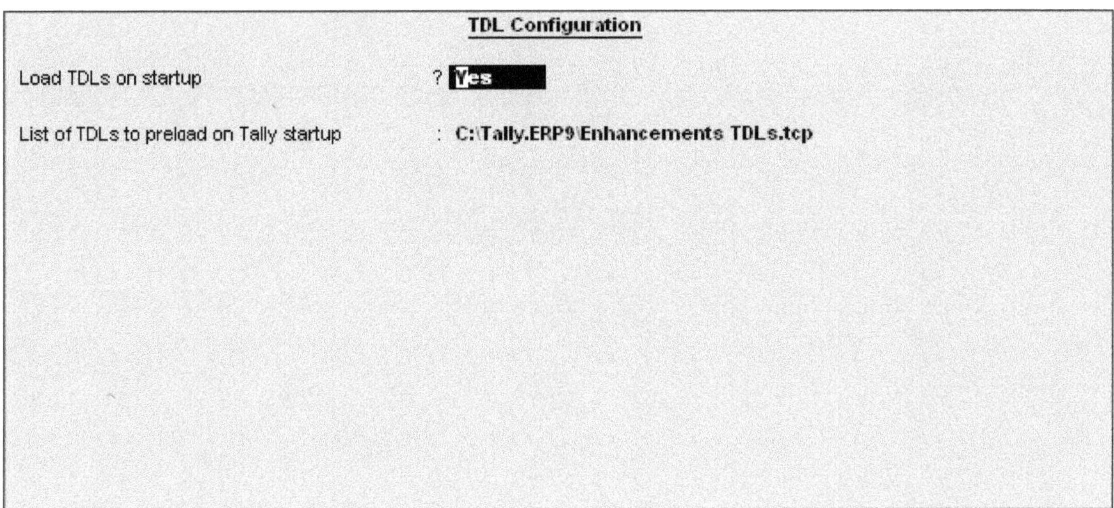

Figure 11.4   TDL Configuration

Multiple TDL files can be specified in this TDL configuration screen as shown.

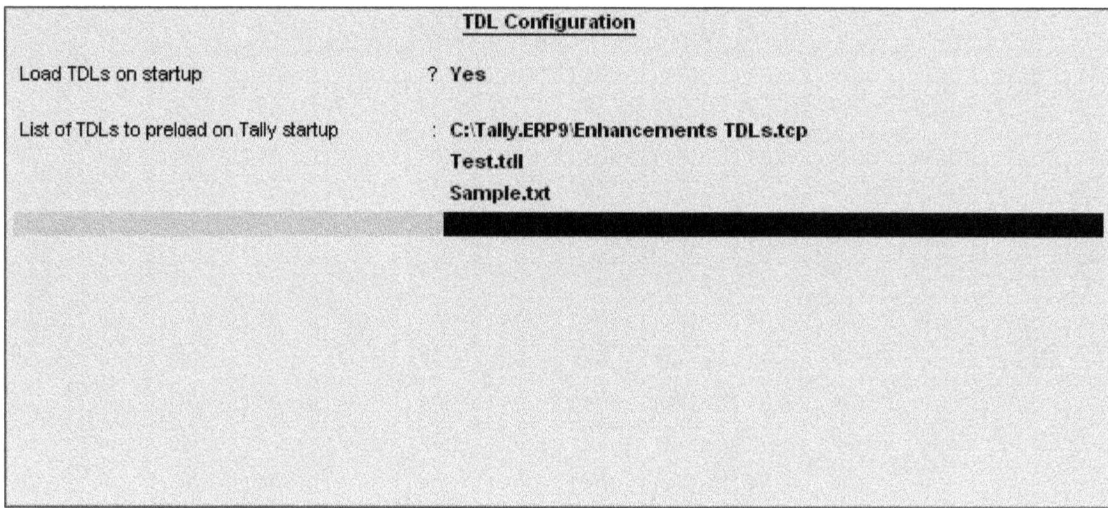

Figure 11.5 Multiple TDL Configuration

Once the **TDLs** are attached, the screen displays the status of each file and when these files are loaded successfully its status is changes to **Active**.

Local TDLs	
Enhancement	Active
C:\Sample.txt	Active
C:\Enhancments.txt	Errors

Figure 11.6   TDL Status

If there is any problem in loading the TDL file then its status is shown as Error. On drill down it displays the details about the error that had occurred.

Local TDLs		
Enhancement		Active
C:\Sample.txt		Active
C:\Enhancments.txt		Errors
Error Message	: error T0001: could not find the file 'C:\Enhancments.txt'	
Format	: Text	

Figure 11.7   Error Status

A **TDL** file can be disabled by prefixing the file name with '#' symbol.

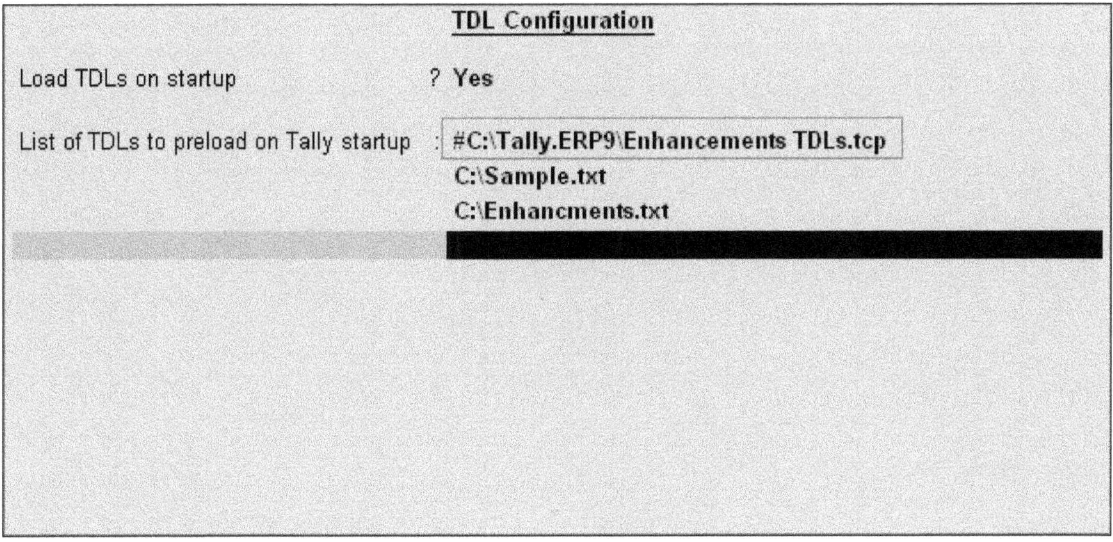

Figure 11.8   TDL Configuraton

The status of the disabled file is then shown as **Not Allowed**.

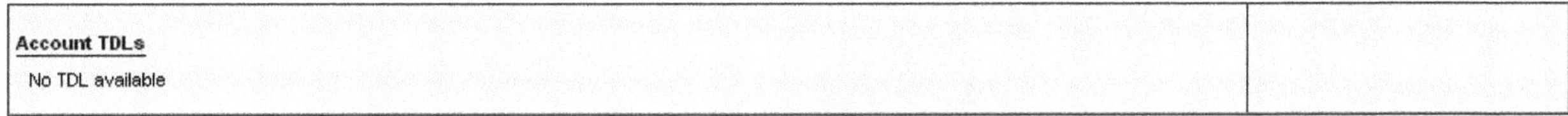

Figure 11.9   Local TDLs

11.2.2 Account TDLs

The list of TDLs are received from the account are displayed under the section Account TDLs. The following screen shows that no TDLs are received from the account:

Figure 11.10   Account TDLs

*For further reading on creating **TDL Configuration** refer to the topic **Control Centre** in **Tally.ERP 9 Reference Manual**.*

11.2.3 Remote TDLs

When a user selects the option to **Login as Remote User**, then the TDLs that are attached on the remote server are also available for the client.

TDLs received from the remote server are listed under the heading **Remote TDLs** as shown:

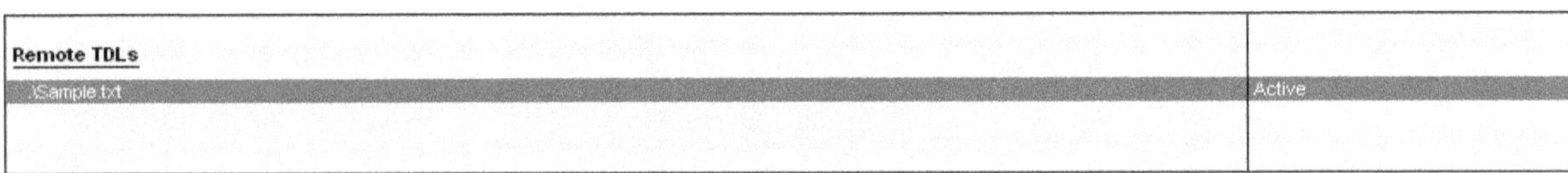

Figure 11.11   Remote TDLs

The List of all the active TDLs on the remote server are displayed.

11.3 Advanced Configuration

The user can add or modify the required parameters required for synchronisation and ODBC. To change the required configurations follow the steps shown:

Go to **Gateway of Tally** or **Company Info** menu

- Press **F12:Configure**
- Select **Advanced Configuration**

The **Client/Server Configuration** screen is displayed.

1. In **Tally is acting** as field select the required type from the list of **Client /Server**.
2. Set **Enable ODBC Server** to **Yes** to start the ODBC connectivity.
3. Enter the required port number in the **Port** field**.**
4. In **Connection Timeout** field set the duration in seconds. The server disconnects from the client when it does not receive any response within the specified duration.
5. Set **Yes** to **Connect to Tally.NET Servers running on Non-HTTP Port** to avoid frequent disconnection from Tally.NET or on receiving **16004 Error Code** frequently.
6. To enable the proxy server communicate the complete URL set **Use absolute URL for HTTP Actions** to **Yes**.
7. Set **Yes** to **Enable Sync Logging** will generate a log file containing information about the synchronised vouchers. By default this file resides in C:\Tally.ERP9 folder or in the folder of your chioce. The information available in this file helps in troubleshooting synchronisation.
8. To overwrite the contents of the previous generated log file set **Truncate previous log before Syncing** to **Yes** .
9. Set **Yes** to **Enable HTTP Log** to login all SOAP and HTTP Post request/response in the filenamed **tallyhttp.log** stored in C:\Tally.ERP9 folder or in the folder of your chioce.
10. Set **Yes** to **Use HTTP Proxy Server** in case you are connected to the Internet through a proxy server
11. Enter the IP Address or the URL and Port in **URL** field
12. Set **Yes** to **Authentication Required** to authenticate before connecting
13. Enter the username and password in **User Name** and **Password** fields respectively.

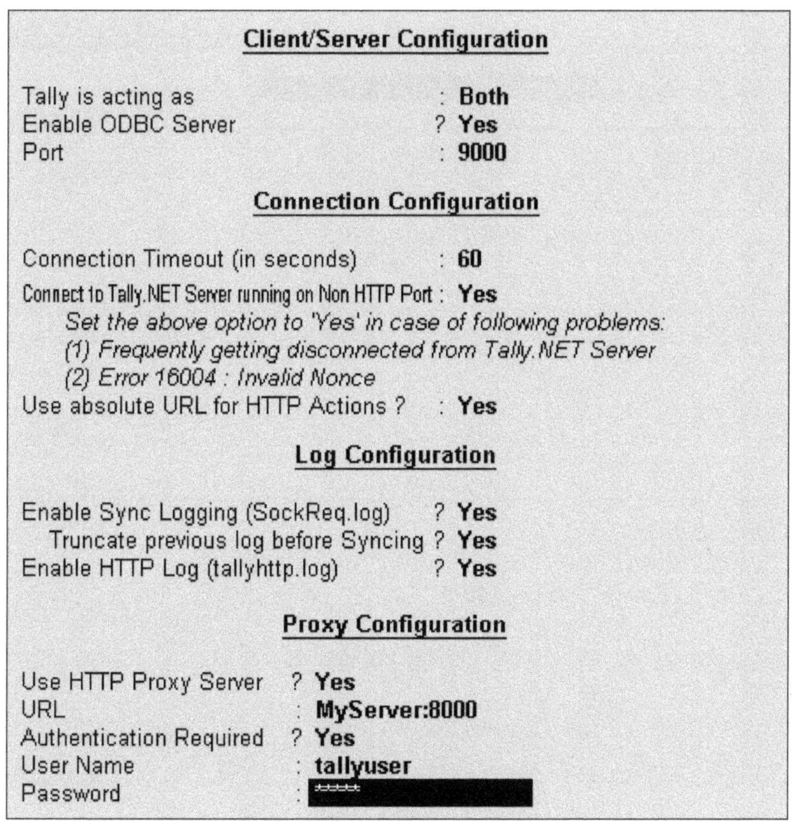

Figure 11.12   Client/Server Configuration

14. **Accept** to save the configurations.
15. **Tally.ERP 9** displays a message **Do you want to restart Tally.ERP 9 for the changes to have effect?**
16. Press **Y** or click **Yes** to effect changes and restart **Tally.ERP 9**.

11.4 Configure Existing License

You can configure the existing license by choosng the license mode, providing the **License Server Name** and **Port Number**. By default, **Tally.ERP 9** uses **9999** port for communication between the license servers and clients, in case you opt for a different port number, please contact the system or network administrator. To configure the existing license following the steps shown.

Go to **Gateway of Tally** or **Company Info** menu

1. Click **F12:Configure** or press **F12** > **Licensing** > **Configure Existing License**.
2. The **Configure Existing License** screen appears.

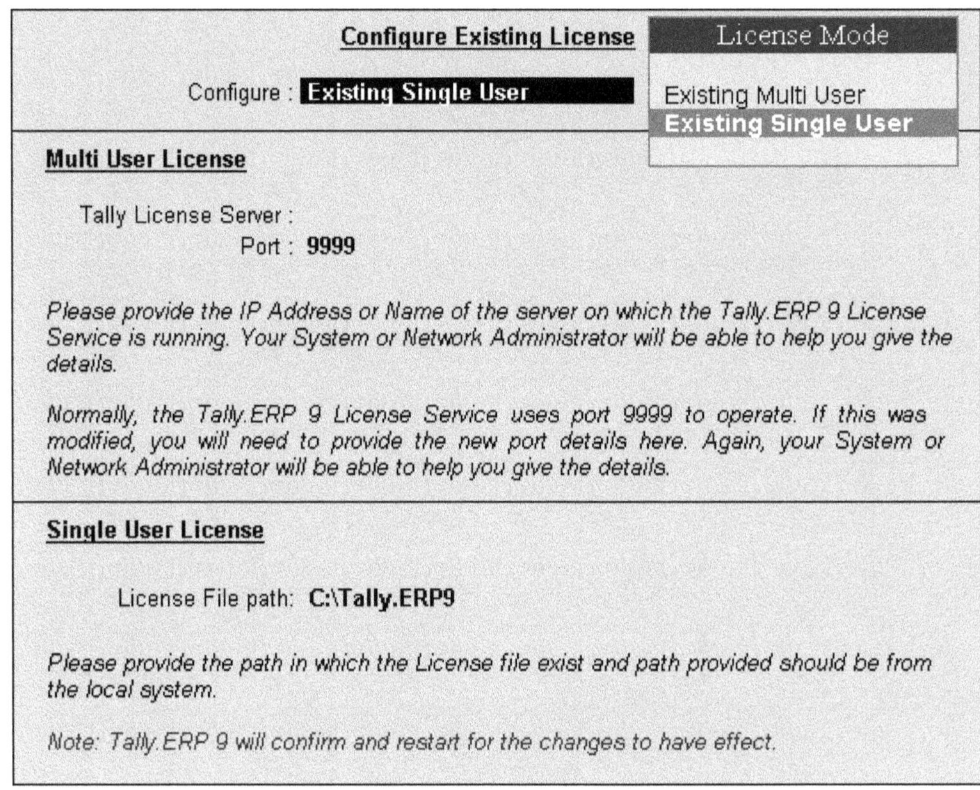

Figure 11.13 Configure existing license

3. Select the license that you want to configure from the list of **License Mode** displayed

Existing Single User License

4. Provide the required path of the license file in **License File Path**

Existing Multi User License

4. Provide the required Name/IP address of the license server in **Tally License Server** field.
5. By default, Tally.ERP 9 License Services uses port **9999** to operate. Provide the required port number, in case you want **Tally.ERP 9** license services to use another port for communication.
6. **Accept** to save the License Configurations.
7. **Tally.ERP 9** displays a message **Do you want to restart Tally.ERP 9 for the changes to have effect?**
8. Press **Y** or click **Yes** to effect changes and restart **Tally.ERP 9**.
9. The remaining options of the Licensing menu, such as, Update License, Surrender License and Reset License are discussed as separate lessons in this book

Lesson 12: Updating License

The procedure to update a **Tally.ERP 9** license for **Single Site** and **Multi Site** is similar. You require to update the license information, when the TDL/General configuration assigned to the account has to be applied to the respective site or when you renew/subscribe for Tally.NET.

Steps for License Updation

From the **Gateway of Tally** or **Company Info** menu

- Press **F12: Configure.**
- Select **Licensing** > **Update License**.
- The **Login as Remote Tally.NET User** screen appears.
- Enter your E-Mail ID in **Your E-Mail ID** field.
- Enter your **Tally.NET Password** in **Your Tally.NET Password**.

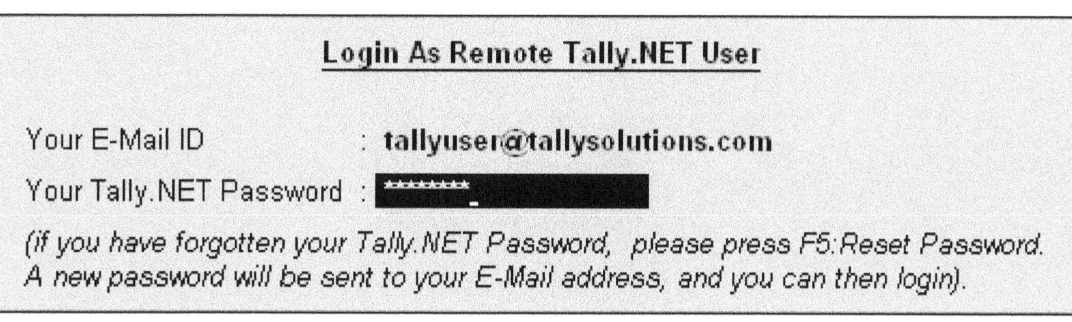

Figure 12.1 Login as Remote User

- **Accept** to update the license
- **Tally.ERP 9** displays the message **License Updated Successfully!**

*On logging in to **Control Centre**, **Support Centre**, **Remote User**, **Surrender License** and **Update License** for the first time after creating the account, Tally.ERP 9 will automatically take you to change the password. To know more on how to change the password read **Change My Password**.*

Lesson 13:   Surrendering License

13.1 Surrendering License

You can surrender the activated **Tally.ERP 9** when:

- Hard Disk has to be formatted
- Reinstalling the Operating System
- Reactivating the license on another computer or site.

To surrender, the user has to execute the following steps:

Go to **Gateway of Tally** or **Company Info** menu

- Press **F12:Configure**.
- Select **Licensing** > **Surrender**.

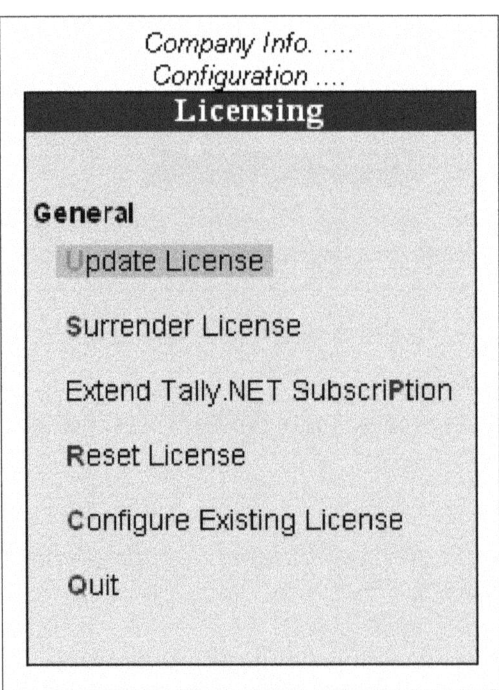

Figure 13.1 Surrender License

- **Tally.ERP 9** displays a message **You are about to Surrender Your License. Continue?**
- Press **Y** or click **Yes** to proceed with surrendering the license.
- The **Login As Remote Tally.NET User** screen is displayed.
- Provide your E-Mail ID in **Your E-Mail ID** field.
- Provide your Tally.NET Password in **Your Tally.NET Password**.

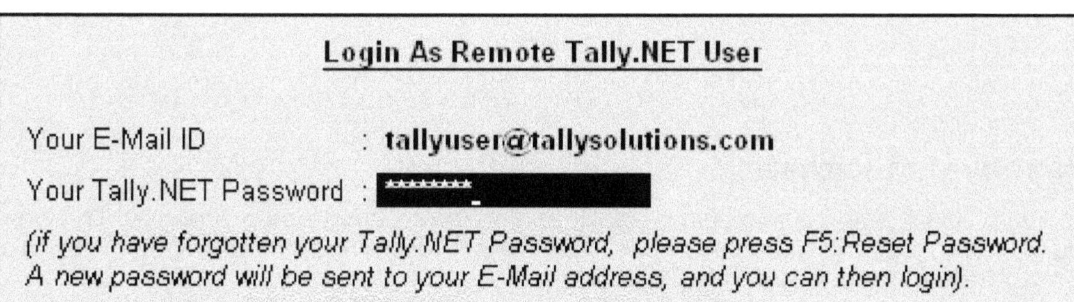

Figure 13.2 Login to Surrender

On logging in to **Control Centre**, **Support Centre**, **Remote User**, **Surrender License** *and* **Update License** *for the first time after creating the account, Tally.ERP 9 will automatically take you to change the password. To know more on how to change the password read* **Change My Password***.*

- Press **Enter**
- **Tally.ERP 9** displays a message as shown.

Figure 13.3 License Surrendered

Lesson 14: Reactivating Tally.ERP 9

14.1 Reactivate License

The process of reactivating a site license is simplified into a single step process. The concept of unlocking the license file is eliminated. The user needs to provide the Email ID of the **Account/ Site Administrator** to reactivate **Tally.ERP 9**

The **Reactivate** License option is used for subsequent activation of **Tally.ERP 9**. After surrendering the **Tally.ERP 9 Single Site** or **Multi-Site** license, when you start **Tally.ERP 9.** It searches for a valid license file in the default folder. When the license file is not available, the user needs to **Reactivate** the license. The process to Reactivate single site or multi site is similar.

The process to Reactivate **Tally.ERP 9** is as follows:

In the **Startup** screen is displayed.

- ❑ Select **Reactivate License** and press **Enter**.

The **Reactivate License** form appears.

- ❑ Enter the Account/Site Administrator's E-mail ID in **E-Mail ID of Administrator**
- ❑ Enter the password in **Password** field..

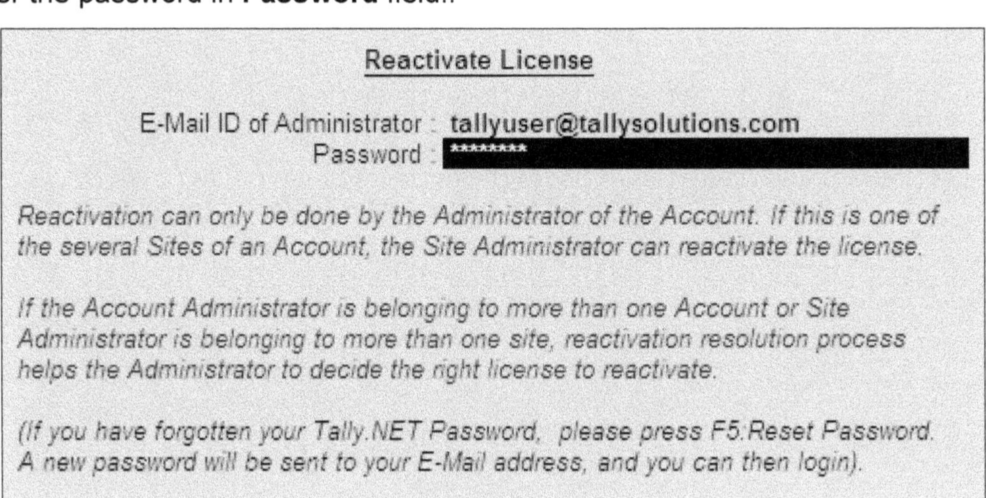

Figure 14.1 Reactivate License Form

- ❑ Press **Enter**

❑ *In case the user is an **Administrator** of more than a one site or an account, the **Reactivate Multisite Resolution** screen appears displaying the list of sites for the respective Administrator. Select a **Surrendered** site to reactivate it.*

❑ *On providing the Account Administrator's E-Mail ID of single site or the Site Administrator's E-Mail ID of the respective site the system proceeds to reactivate the license.*

The **Reactivate License Resolution** screen appears as shown

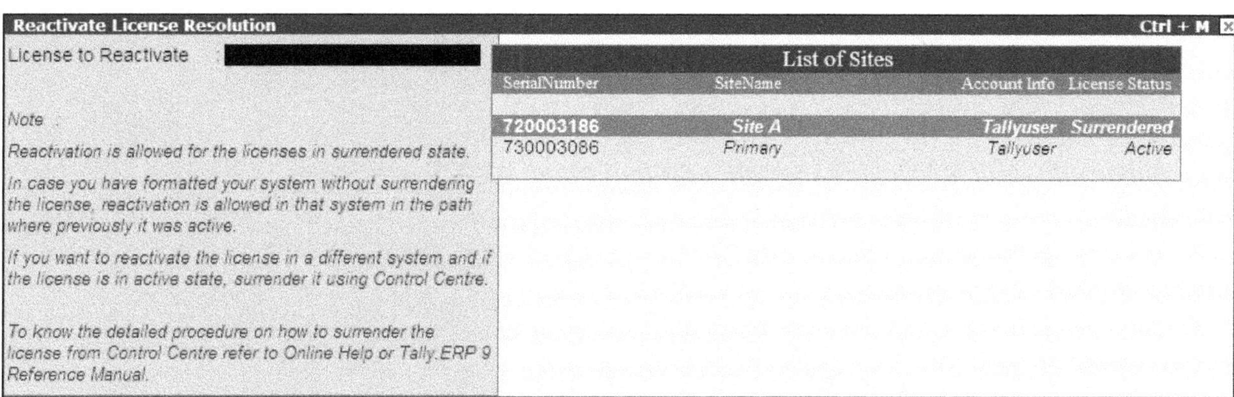

Figure 14.2 Reactivate License Resolution

❑ Select the required Site from the **List of Sites** displayed

*On selecting an **Active** site, Tally.ERP 9 prompts an error message displaying the **System Details**, **License Path** where the license was last activated and suggests the user to surrender the license using the **Control Centre** before reactivating the respective Site.*

Tally.ERP 9 searches for the availability of Internet Connectivity on your computer. On successfully finding the internet connection the system proceeds to activate the license online which is explained in Online Activation section.

Or

While searching for an Internet connection on your computer, in case the system detects any one of the issues/errors shown below. The resolution screen appears providing the possible solutions for the issues/errors. The user needs to resolve the issue/error and activate the license online. In case the issue or error remain unresolved, the user needs to activate the license offline.

❑ Internet connectivity is not established/not working/unavailable.

❑ Outbound connectivity is blocked

❑ Invalid entry in the hosts file

❑ Connection Time Out

- Connection Refused
- Network is disabled
- Could not find the IP Address
- Sending / Receiving failed

Online Activation

- Tally.ERP 9 displays the message **Congratulations! Your Activation Request has been Processed. An encrypted file is now on your machine**.
- Press **Enter** to continue.
- Proceed to section **Step 2: Procedure to Unlock License File**.

Offline Activation

Tally.ERP 9 displays a **Connection Error** screen containing the **Error Code** and **System Error Code** along with the **Reasons for Failure**, **Possible Solutions** and **What to do now? (Actions)**

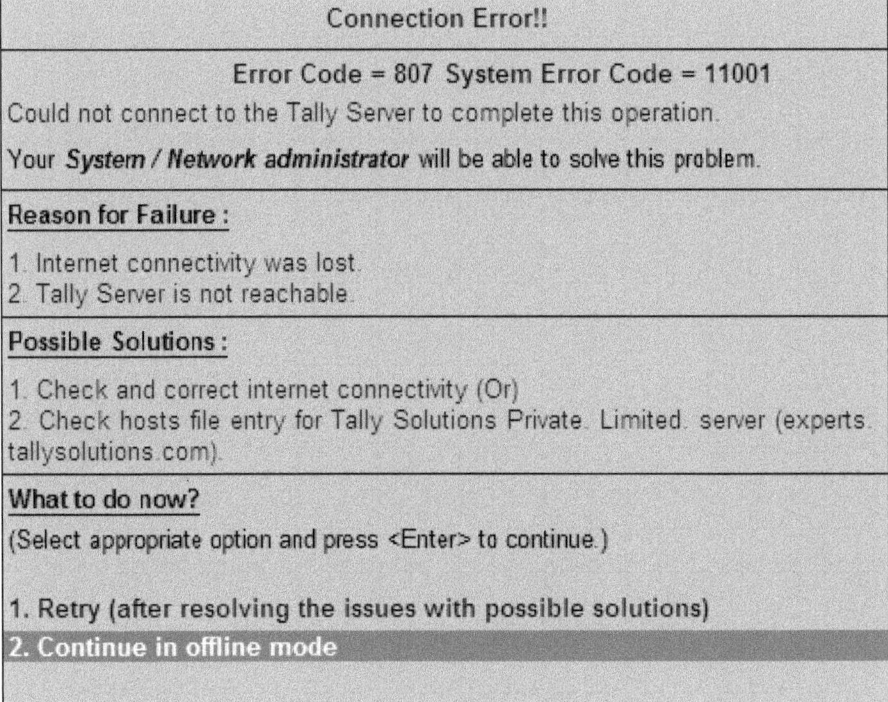

Figure 14.3 Connection Error

- Select **Continue in offline mode**
- **Tally.ERP 9** displays a message **Your Offline Activation Request file has been Created Successfully**. A license request file named **tally_req.lic** is generated and stored in the default **Tally.ERP 9** folder.

- Copy the **tally_req.lic** onto a pen drive/CD and paste the file into the **Tally.ERP9** folder. This computer must be connected to the Internet and Tally.ERP 9 could be running in **Licensed** or **Educational** mode.
- Start **Tally.ERP 9**

The **Startup** screen appears

- Select **Send External Request**
- **Tally.ERP 9** displays a message **Offline Response File Generated Successfully**.
- Copy **tally_lck.lic** file to a pendrive/CD and paste this file to the **Tally.ERP9** folder of the computer where **Tally.ERP 9** is to be activated

The **Reactivation Successful** message appears as shown:

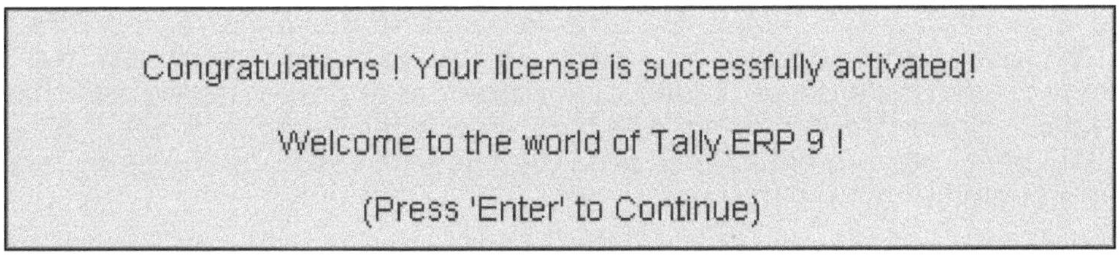

Figure 14.4 Reactivation Successful

- Press **Enter**

The **Gateway of Tally** appears displaying the **Info Panel** which contains information on the **Release**, **Edition** and **Users** under **Version** block, the **Serial Number**, **Account ID** and validity of **Tally.NET Subscription** under **License** block and various configuration details under the **Configuration** block.

Lesson 15: Change Password

15.1 Change Password

The password is emailed to the E-Mail ID of the Account Administrator or the Site Administrator on successfully creating the account. You can use this password to access the account and perform licensing operations such as Reactivate, Surrender and Update license. This password is system generated, alphanumeric string which is nine characters in length. As per the best practices available it is recommended to change the password without any delay even before you log in to perform any other operations.

The task of changing the password is made simple and easy without performing any additional steps. Tally.ERP 9 prompts the user to change the password on attempting to log in to any one of the follwing features for the first time after creating the account.

- Remote Tally.NET User
- Support Centre
- Control Centre
- Surrender License
- Update License

15.1.1 Password Rules

- The password should be a minimum of **5** characters and a maximum of **18** characters in length
- The password can contain alphabets in upper case (A to Z), lower case (a to z) and numbers (0 to 9)
- The password entered is case insensitive, i.e., the password can be entered in either upper case or lower case or both
- Special characters **+,-,*, / ,= ,_ ,comma, full stop,** ~ ,!,@,#,$,%,^,&,(,),[,],{,},|,:,;,',<,>,?,\.
- It is recommended to change the password frequently.

On providing the required Email ID of the **Account Administrator** or the **Site Administrator** and the password in any one of the aforementioned features, the **Change My Password** screen appears as shown:

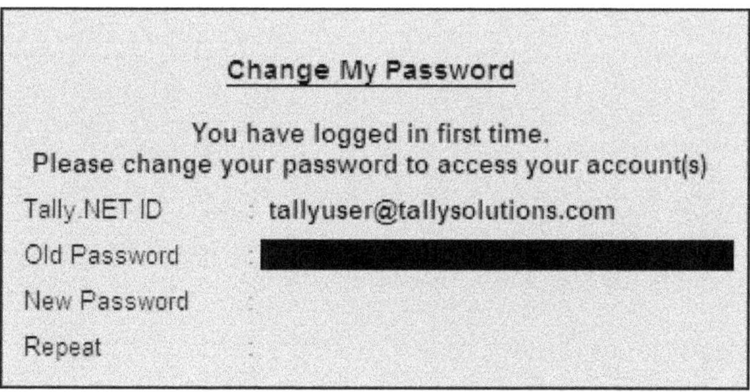

Figure 14.1 Change My Password

- ❑ Enter the previous password in **Old Password** field
- ❑ Enter the new password in **New Password** field
- ❑ Re-enter the password once again in **Repeat** field for the purpose of confirmation

On successfully changing the password the corresponding screen appears.

Provide the new password to subsequently log in to the Control Centre, Support Centre, Remote User, Surrender or Update the license.

To change the password any time later log in to the **Control Centre** and select **My Password**. In case you have forgotten or lost the password you can opt to reset it.

Lesson 16: Reset License

16.1 Reset License

This option enables you to remove all licensing data from the computers. This will bring the user's computer to a state, where **Tally.ERP 9** activation was not done earlier.

To reset **Tally.ERP 9** License, execute the following steps:

Go to **Gateway of Tally** or **Company Info** menu

- ❑   Press **F12:Configure**
- ❑   Select **Licensing > Reset Licensing**

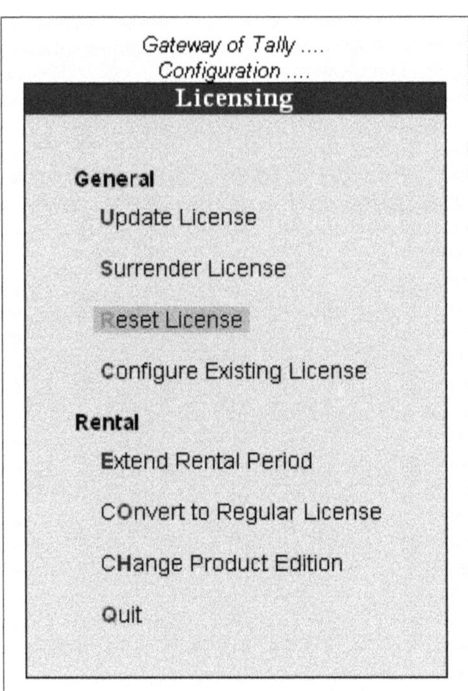

Figure 16.1 Reset License

- ❑   **Tally.ERP 9** displays the message **You are about to Reset Your License. Continue?**
- ❑   Press **Y** or click **Yes** to proceed with surrendering the license.
- ❑   **Tally.ERP 9** displays a message **License Reset Successfully**.

Lesson 17: Work in Educational Mode

Work in **Educational** mode will help you in installing **Tally.ERP 9** on your computers and have a live experience of features and reports available in **Tally.ERP 9**.

Tally.NET User and Tally.NET Auditor can login from a remote location, view reports or scrutinise data while **Tally.ERP 9** works in **Educational** mode.

To experience the features of **Tally.ERP 9** in **Educational** mode, you need to excecute the following steps:

- Start **Tally.ERP 9**.
- The **Startup screen appears**.
- Select **Work in Educational Mode**
- Press **Enter**
- The options **Silver Edition Mode** or **Gold Edition Mode** appear

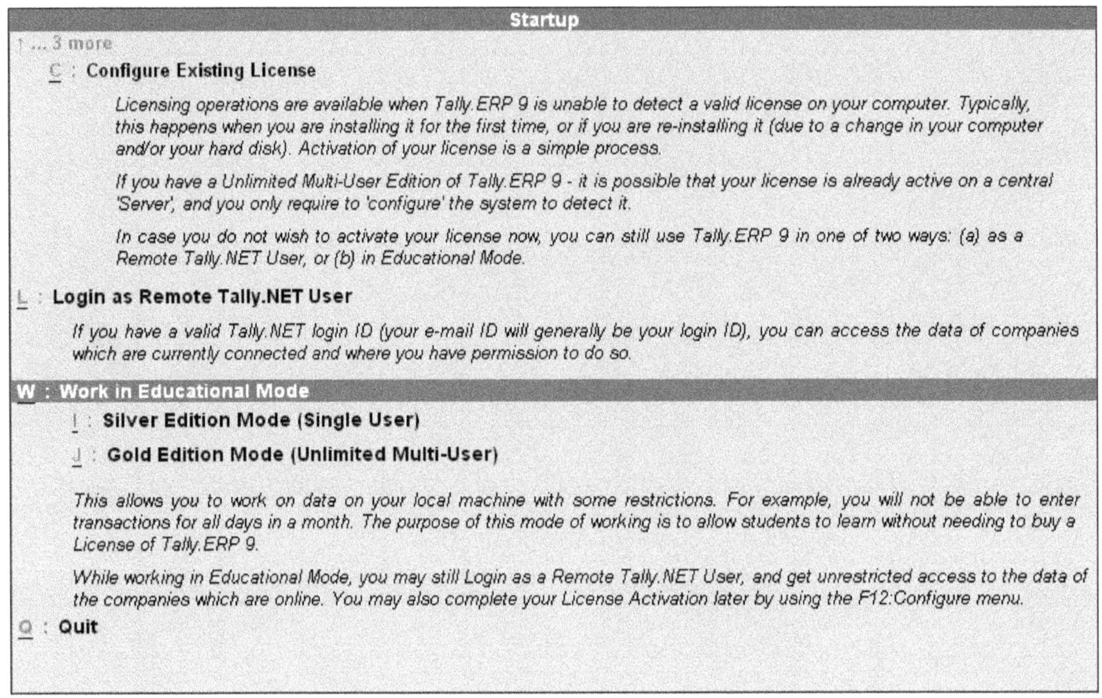

Figure 17.1 Startup

- Select the required option
- Press **Enter**
- Based on the option selected **Tally.ERP 9** will display the **Edition** and number of **Users** in the **Version** block and **Educational Mode** is displayed in **LIcense** block of **Info. Panel.**

□ **Gateway of Tally** screen is displayed as shown.

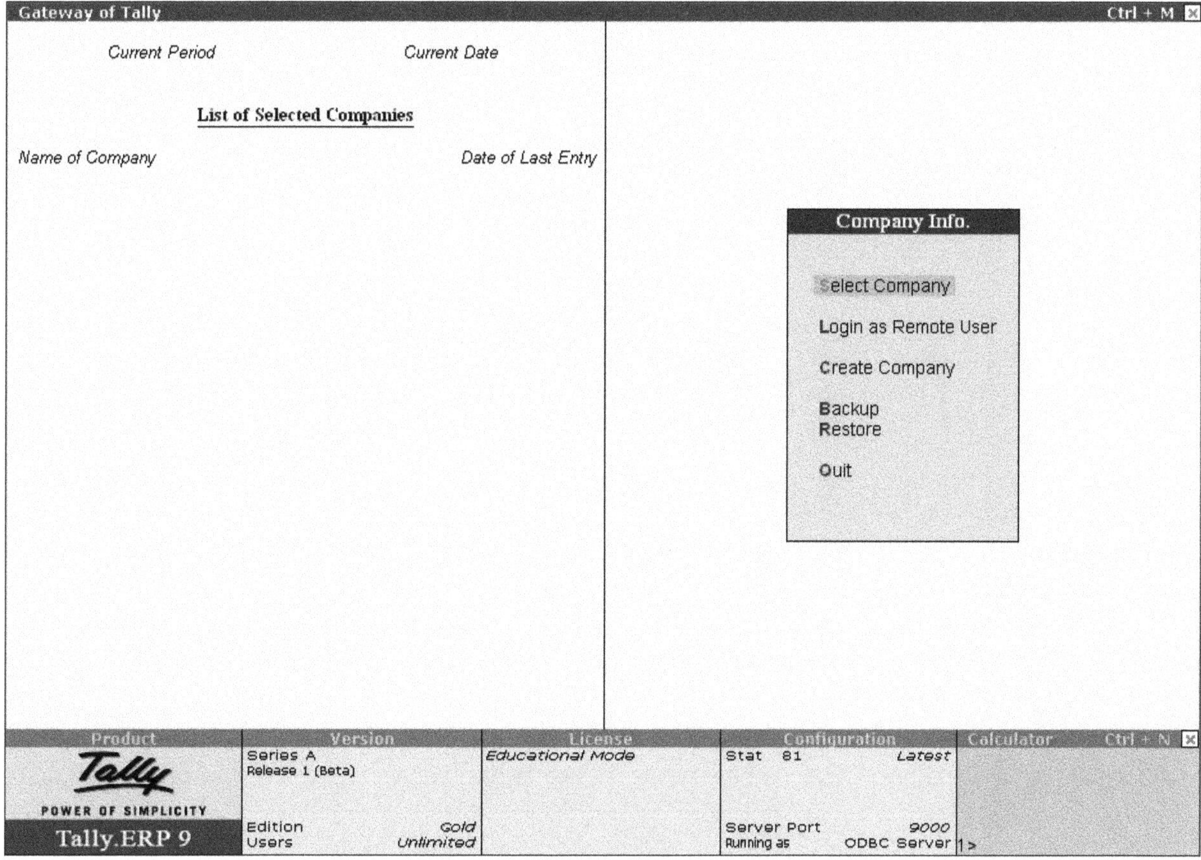

Figure 17.2   Gateway of Tally

Experience the features of **Tally.ERP 9**.

Lesson 18:   Rental Licensing

Rental Licensing in Tally.ERP 9 is provided an objective to facilitate the user to explore, gain an insight and empower themselves with the knowledge of the flagship product **Tally.ERP 9**. The rental licensing enables the users/organisations to activate a **Promotional** license and use all the features of Tally.ERP 9 for a limited period. On expiry of the promotional period, users can opt to extend the license period on payment of requisite charges or purchase a new license from the website, partner or within the product itself.

Rental licenses have been broadly classified into the following categories:

- **Promotional License**: is available for a limited promotional period of 90 days or 3 months from the date of activation. Authorised **Tally Partner** and **Original Equipment Manufacturer** are assigned a **Promotional Code** which is used to activate the **Promotional Rental License**.

- **Rental License**: is renewable on payment of the requisite charges for **Monthly/Quarterly/ Yearly** basis. User can now directly purchase a rental license, activate and use it rather than extending the rental license at the end of the promotional period.

18.1 Activate Rental License

The process to activate a Tally.ERP 9 **Promotional/Rental** license is similar to activating a **Single Site** License, to activate a **Promotional/Rental** license follow the steps shown:

- Start **Tally.ERP 9**

The **Startup** screen appears

- Select **Activate License**

The **Activate License** form appears

- Enter the promotional code in the **Serial Number/Promotional Code** field.

- *The promotional code is provided by an authorised Tally Partner.*

- Enter the Account Administrator's E-Mail Address in **E-Mail ID of the Administrator** field.
- Repeat Account Administrator's E-Mail Address in **Repeat (E-Mail ID of the Administrator)** field

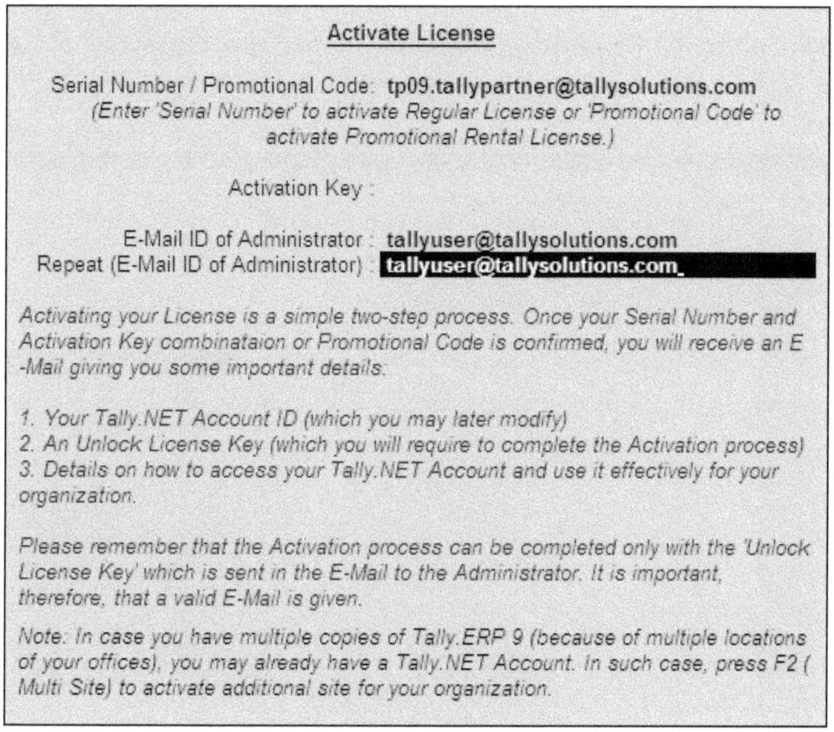

Figure 18.1 Activate License

□ Press **Enter**

The process to activate a Rental License is similar to activating a **Single User** license which is discussed in **Activating Tally.ERP 9 Single Site**.

□ *Promotional Rental License comes with multi user license capability. In order to utilize the complete features of Tally.ERP 9 it is recommended to activate the license through the License Server.*

□ *OEM product dealers cannot activate a rental license using the Offline Mode.*

□ *On activating the rental license using a multi-site account, the resolution screen appears. You can now proceed to activate the license after choosing the required option. To know more, refer to the chapter on Licensing Resolutions.*

□ Tally.ERP 9 displays the message **Congratulations! Your Activation Request has been processed. An encrypted license file is now on your machine.**

□ Press **Enter** to continue

The **Unlock License** screen appears

- Retreive the email and type the unlock key in the **Unlock Key** field
- Press **Enter**

On successful activation of the **Promotional/Rental** license, the **Gateway of Tally** will appear as shown:

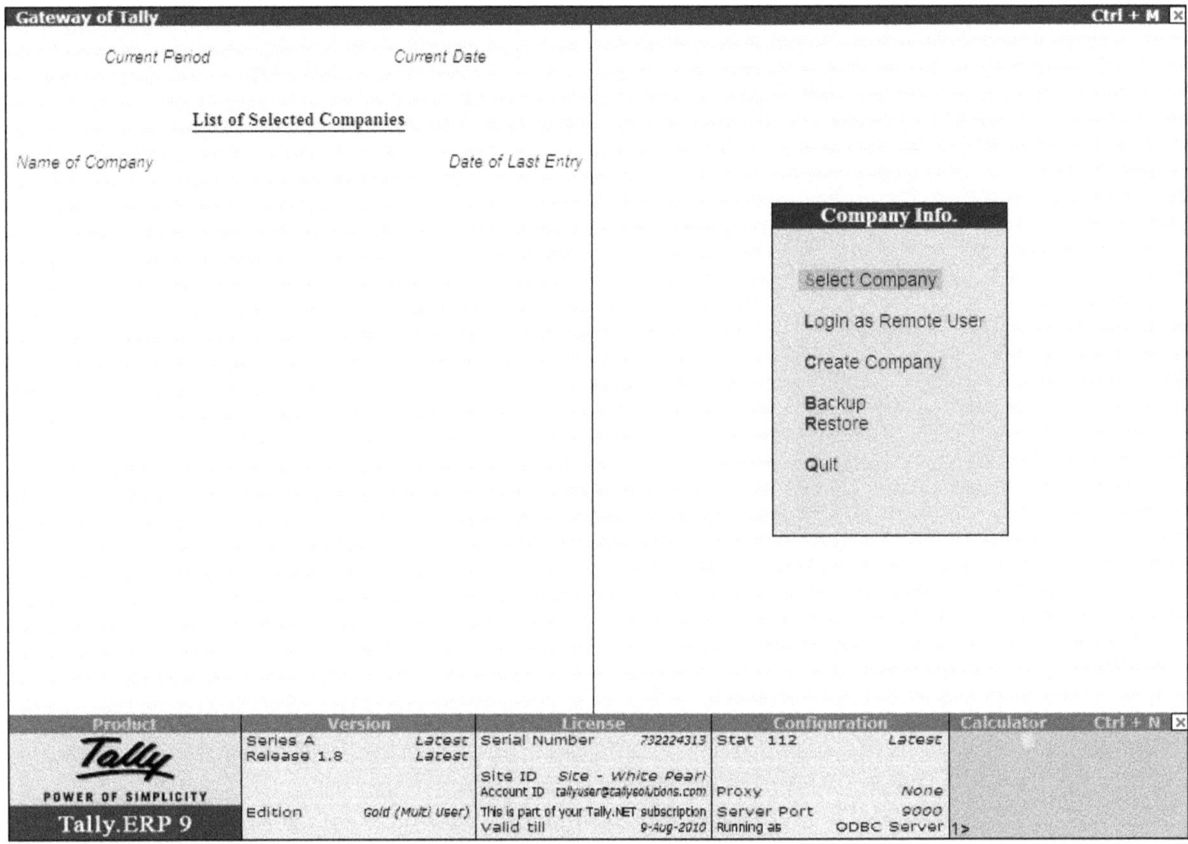

Figure 18.2 Rental License Activated

18.2 Buy Rental License

The user can directly purchase **Tally.ERP 9** rental license by paying the requisite charges for a **Month/Quarter/Year** then activate the rental license and use it.

To purchase a rental license follow the steps shown:

- Start **Tally.ERP 9**

The **Startup** screen appears as shown:

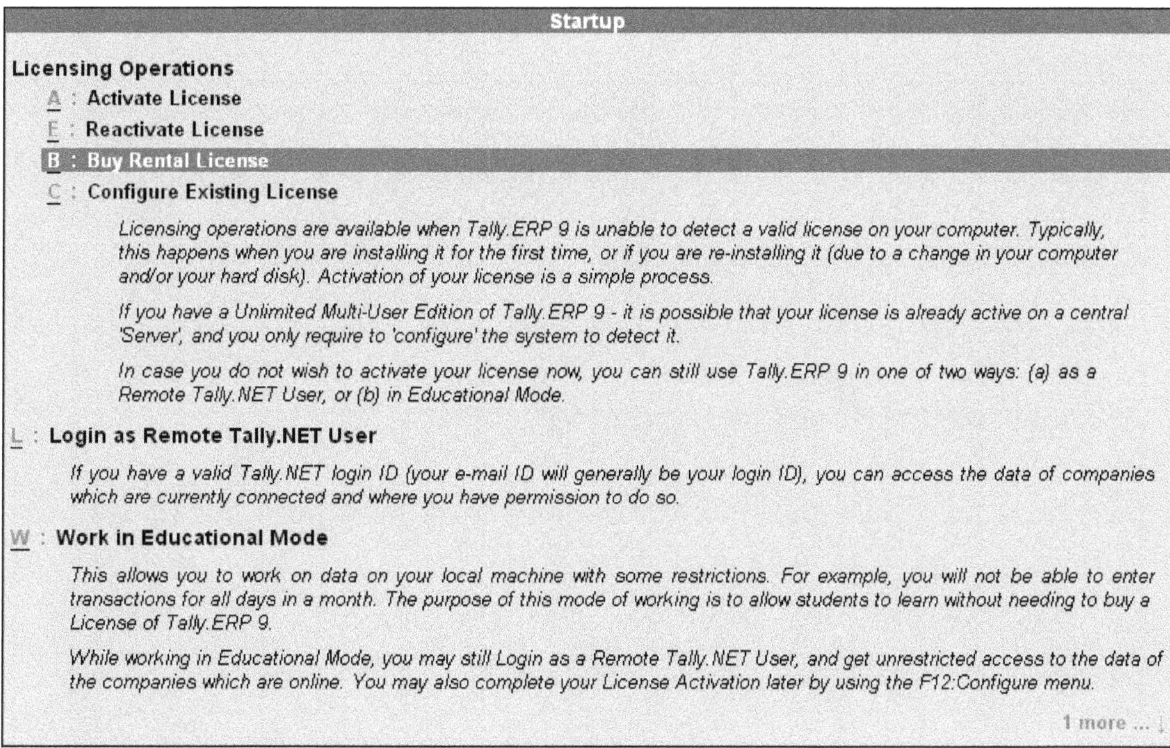

Figure 18.3 Startup

□ Select **Buy Rental License**

The **Buy Rental License** screen appears

□ Enter the Account Administrator's email address in the **E-Mail of Administrator** field.

□ For the purpose of confirmation repeat the same email address in **Repeat(E-Mail ID)**

□ Enter the Company's or Individual's Name in **Billing Name** field. The Billing Name will be printed on the invoice.

□ Enter the required address in the **Address** field, the address will be printed on the Invoice.

□ In the **Country** field select **India** from the **List of Countries**.

□ In the **State** field select the **Karnataka** from the **List of States**

□ In the **City** field select the **Bangalore** from the **List of Cities** or select **Others** and type the name of the city in case it is not listed.

□ Enter the required postal code in **Postal Code** field

□ In **Method of Payment** field select the required payment method from the **List of Payment Methods**.

18.2.1 Payment By Credit Card

- In the **Preferred Partner** field select **New Sales Partner**
- The **Partner Search** screen appears
  - Search for the nearest partner based on the **Location** or **Name** and select the required partner
- In the **Edition** field select the required edition from the **List of Product Types**
- In the **Period to Extend** field enter a number and select the required period (**Months/ Quarters/Years**) from the list of Periods.
- The **Price** field is prefilled to display the rental amount based on the **Edition** and **Period** selected.
- **Accept** to save the details
- The **Credit Card Payment Gateway** appears

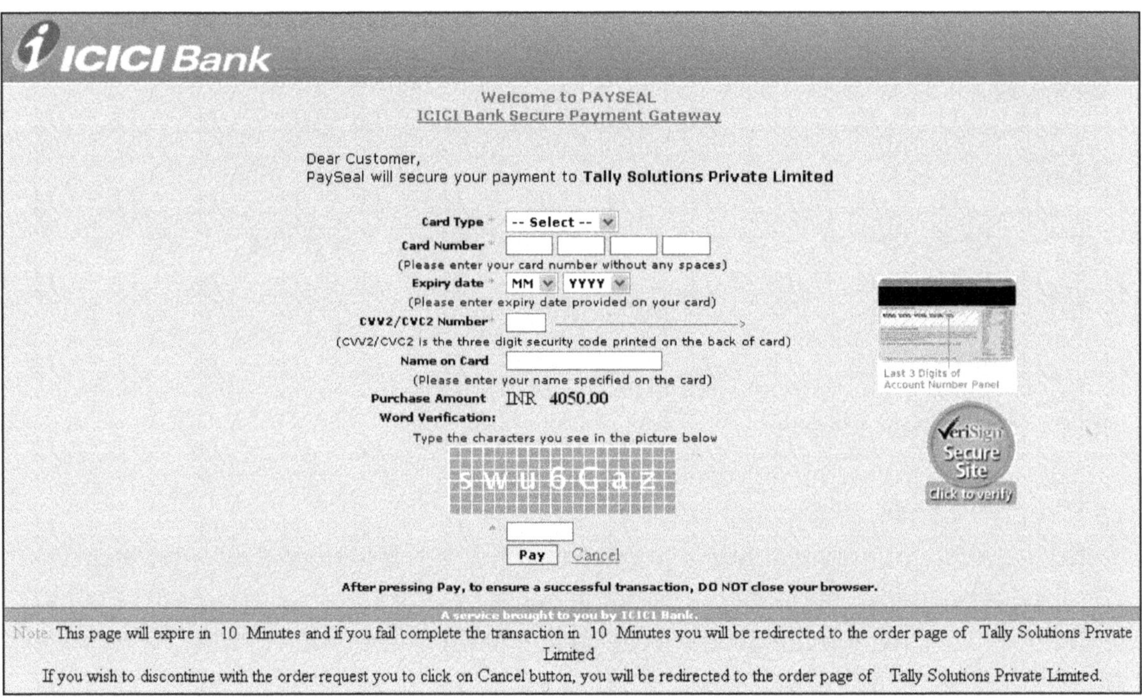

Figure 18.4 Payment Gateway

- Enter the required Credit Card details to purchase **Tally.ERP 9** rental license.
- The payment gateway displays a **Payment Successful Message**. You may print the acknowledgement for future reference.

18.2.2 Payment by TallyCurrency

- In the **Edition** field select the required **Tally.ERP 9 Edition** from the **List of Product Types**
- In the **Period to Buy** field enter the required period number and select the required period from the list of **Periods**.

- The **Price** field is prefilled to display the rental amount based on the **Edition** and period selected.
- Enter the alpha-numeric TallyCurrency key in **Tally Currency Key** field.
- The completed **Buy Rental License** form appears as shown:

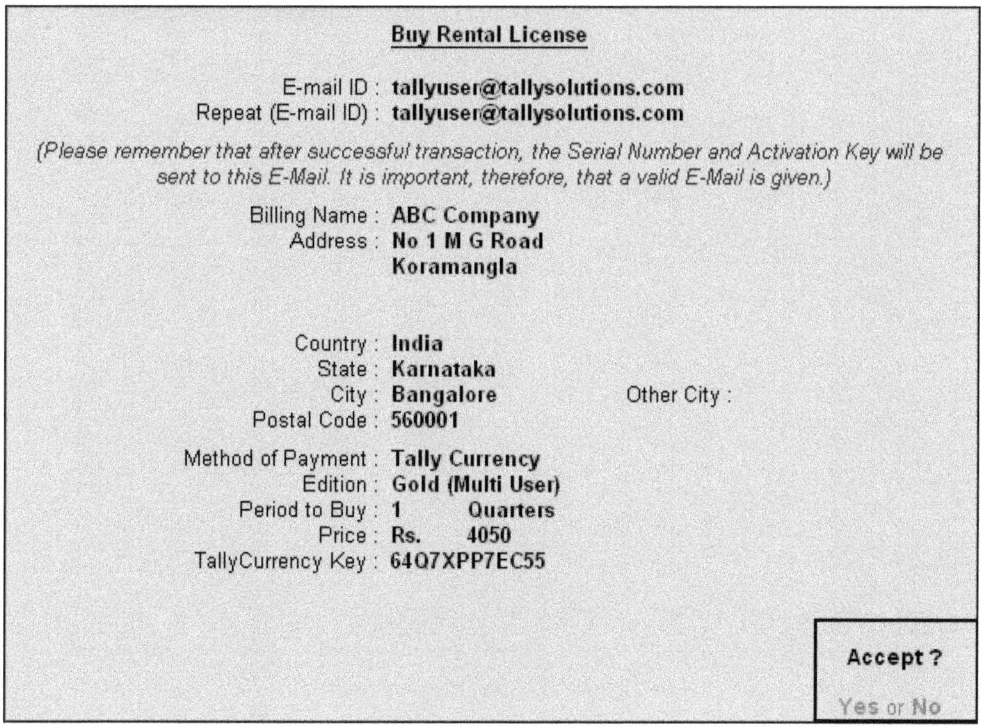

Figure 18.5 Buy Rental License

- **Accept** to purchase **Tally.ERP 9** rental license

*The **Serial Number** and **Activation Key** are mailed to the email id provided while purchasing rental license..*

Tally.ERP 9 displays a message as shown:

Figure 18.6 Congratulations

- Press **Enter** to activate **Tally.ERP 9**

The prefilled **Activate License** form appears as shown

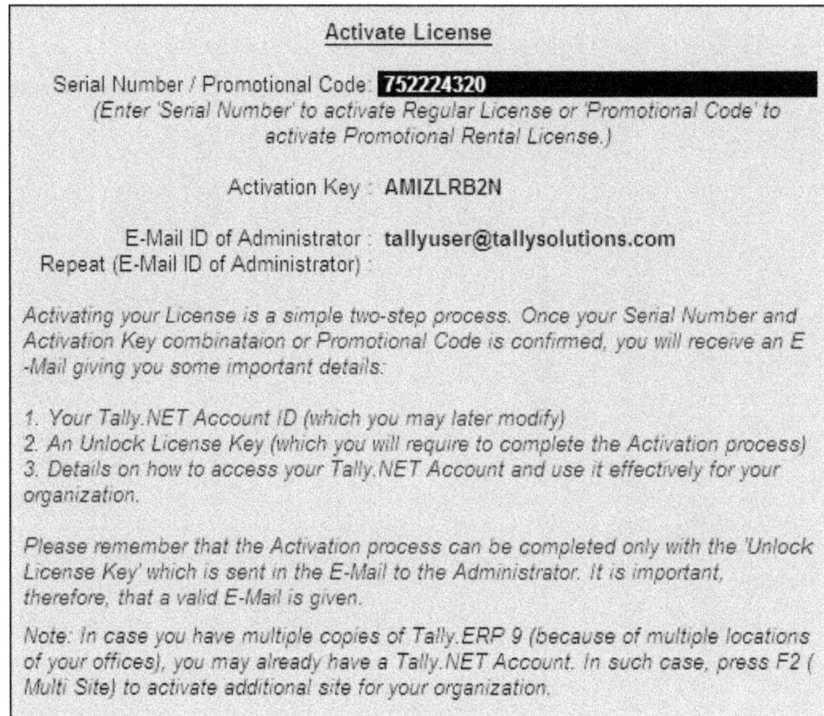

Figure 18.7 Activate License form

- For the purpose of re-confirmation enter the Administrator's E-Mail ID in **Repeat (E-Mail ID of Administrator)** field.
- Press **Enter**

The procedure to activate the rental license is similar to **Activating Single Site**. For a detailed reading refer to **Activating Tally.ERP 9 Single Site** in this book.

18.3 Rental License Resolutions

The **Promotional Rental License** is available with full **Multi User** capabiilities. During promotional rental license activation of Tally.ERP 9, the activation process tries to locate a License Server with the required configurations. In case the license server is not found or the license server configurations do not match the requirement, then the License Server Resolution screen appears. You can select the appropriate option to resolve and continue with Installation of Tally.ERP 9.

The License Server Resolution screen appears as shown:

> You are now activating a Promotional Rental License. Currently Tally.ERP 9 is configured to work in single user license mode. Promotional Rental License comes with multi user license capability and in order to utilize its complete features this license has to be activated through a license server.
>
> Select appropriate option.
>
> **Option 1**
> Install and Start License Server in this system.
> **Option 2**
> Configure existing License Server.
> **Option 3**
> Continue activation in Single User mode.

Figure 18.8 License Server Resolutions

Promotional Rental License comes with multi user license capability and in order to utilize its complete features, the license has to be activated through a license server.

18.3.1 To Install and Start License Server on this computer

Select **Option 1: Install and Start License Server in this system**

- ❑ The **Install and Start License Server** screen appears
- ❑ In the **Tally License Server** executable path field, enter the required **License Server** path
- ❑ Accept to Install and start the License Server

> **Install and start License Server**
>
> Tally License Server executable path : **C:\Tally.ERP9**
>
> Port : **9999**
>
> *A file TallyLicenseServer.exe will be there in the folder in which License Server is installed.*
> *Normally, the Tally.ERP 9 License Server uses port 9999 to operate.*
> *After installation, Tally.ERP 9 will restart for connecting to License server for its license operations and s*
> *Select Activate License option and continue License Activation.*
>
> **Accept ?**
> Yes or No

Figure 18.9 Install and Start License Server

- ❑ *The file TallyLicenseServer.exe has to be available in the path given above.*
- ❑ *By default, the Tally.ERP 9 License Server uses port 9999.*

- **Tally.ERP 9** will re-start to establish a connection with the **License Server** and displays the **Startup** screen.
- You can continue the activation process as described in **Lesson 8**

18.3.2 Configure existing License Server

In case the Tally License server was installed but not configured then :

- Select **Option 2: Configure existing License Server**

The **Configure Existing License** screen appears as shown

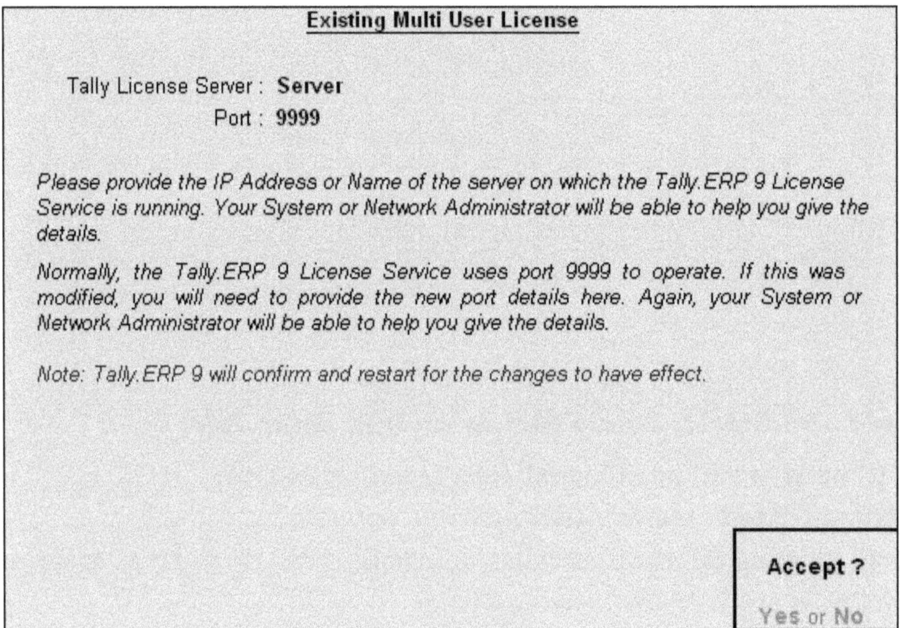

Figure 18.10 Existing Multi User License

- In the **Tally License Sever** field, enter the **Name/IP Address** of the License Server
- By default, the license server uses port **9999**
- **Tally.ERP 9** will re-start to establish a connection with the License server and displays the Startup screen
- You can continue the activation process as described in **Lesson 8**

18.3.3 Continue activation in Single User mode

To activate the **Promotional Rental License** in **Single User** mode:

- Select **Option 3: Continue activation in Single User mode**
- **Tally.ERP 9** will re-start and continue with the activation process
- You can continue the activation process as described in **Activate Tally.ERP 9 Single Site**

18.3.4 Extend Rental License

On expiry of the promotional period, you can either extend the license for a **Month/Quarter/Year** by paying the requisite charges or upgrade to a regular license by purchasing **Tally.ERP 9** from the nearest partner or online from the website using Tally Currency or Credit Card.

To extend the rental license follow the steps shown:

From **Gateway of Tally** or **Company Info** > **F12: Configure** > **Licensing**

The **Licensing** appears as shown:

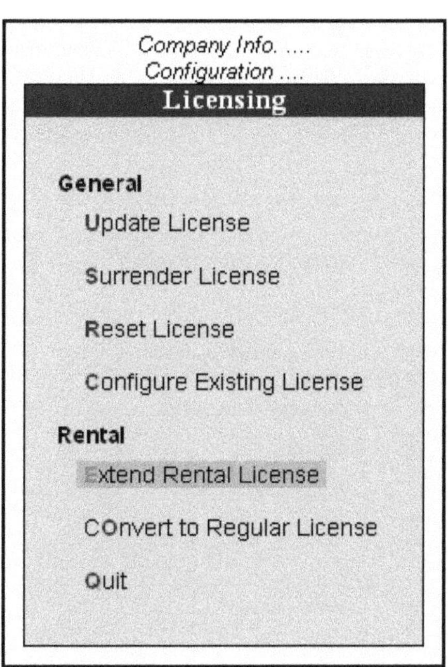

Figure 18.11 Licensing Menu

- Select **Extend Rental License**

The **Extend Rental Period** screen appears
- The **Serial Number**, **Account ID**, **Site ID** (if provided) and **E-Mail ID of the Administrator** are prefilled.
- In the **Billing Name** field enter the name of the Company that has to be printed on the bill.
- In the **Address** field enter the required address of the company.
- In the **Country** field select the required country from the List of Countries
- In the **State** field select the required state from the List of States
- In the **City** field select the required city from the List of Cities
- In the **Postal Code** field enter the required postal code

□ In the **Method of Payment** field select the required payment mode from the List of Payment Methods

18.3.5 Payment by Credit Card

□ In the **Preferred Partner** field select **New Sales Partner**

□ The **Partner Search** screen appears

■ Search for the nearest partner based on the location or the name and select the required partner

□ In the **Edition** field select the required edition from the **List of Product Types**

□ In the **Period to Extend** field enter a number and select the required period (**Months/ Quarters/Years**) from the list of Periods.

□ The **Price** field is prefilled to display the rental amount based on the **Edition** and **Period** selected.

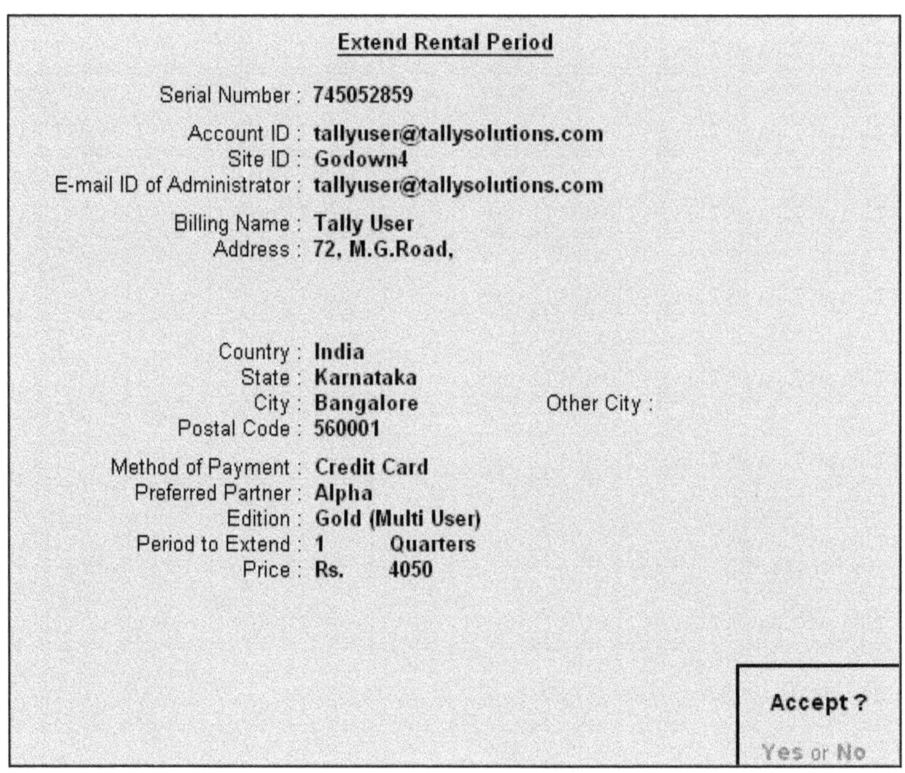

Figure 18.12 Extend Rental License

□ **Accept** to save the details

NIRANJAN JHA SHOWMAN

Founder - Niranjan Jha Showman

cromosys®
Corporation

Education and Technology Research Center
Patankar Park, Nallasopara (W), Mumbai. +91-9561450045
Education, Technology, Publication, Healthcare, Newsmedia, Realtor, Filmmaking
www.facebook.com/cromosys

Cromosys Publication
Teach
Yourself
German
NIRANJAN JHA SHOWMAN

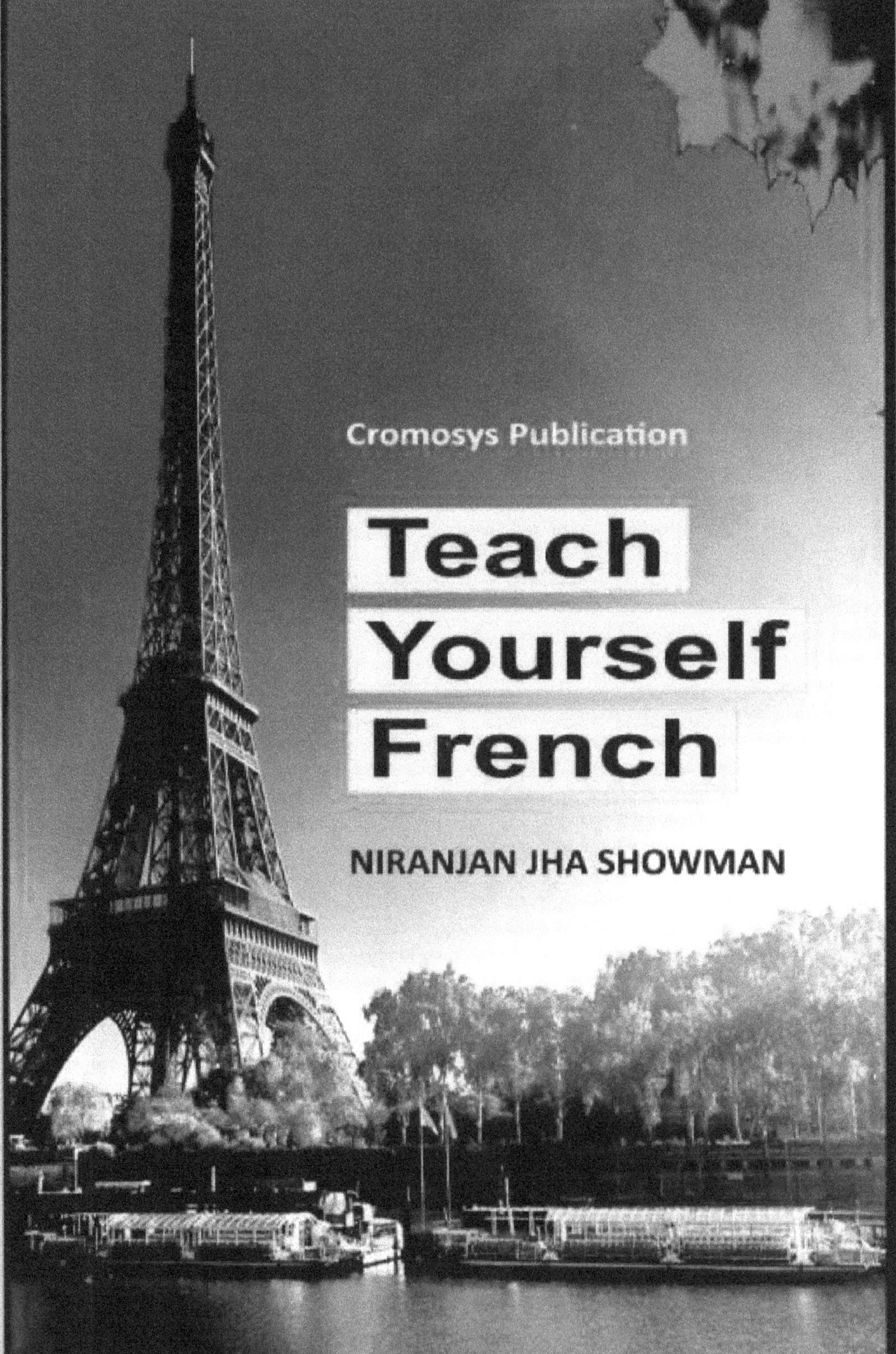
Cromosys Publication

Teach
Yourself
French

NIRANJAN JHA SHOWMAN

Cromosys Publication
Teach
Yourself
Spanish
NIRANJAN JHA SHOWMAN

Cromosys Publication

English
Voice
Accent and
Pronunciation

NIRANJAN JHA SHOWMAN

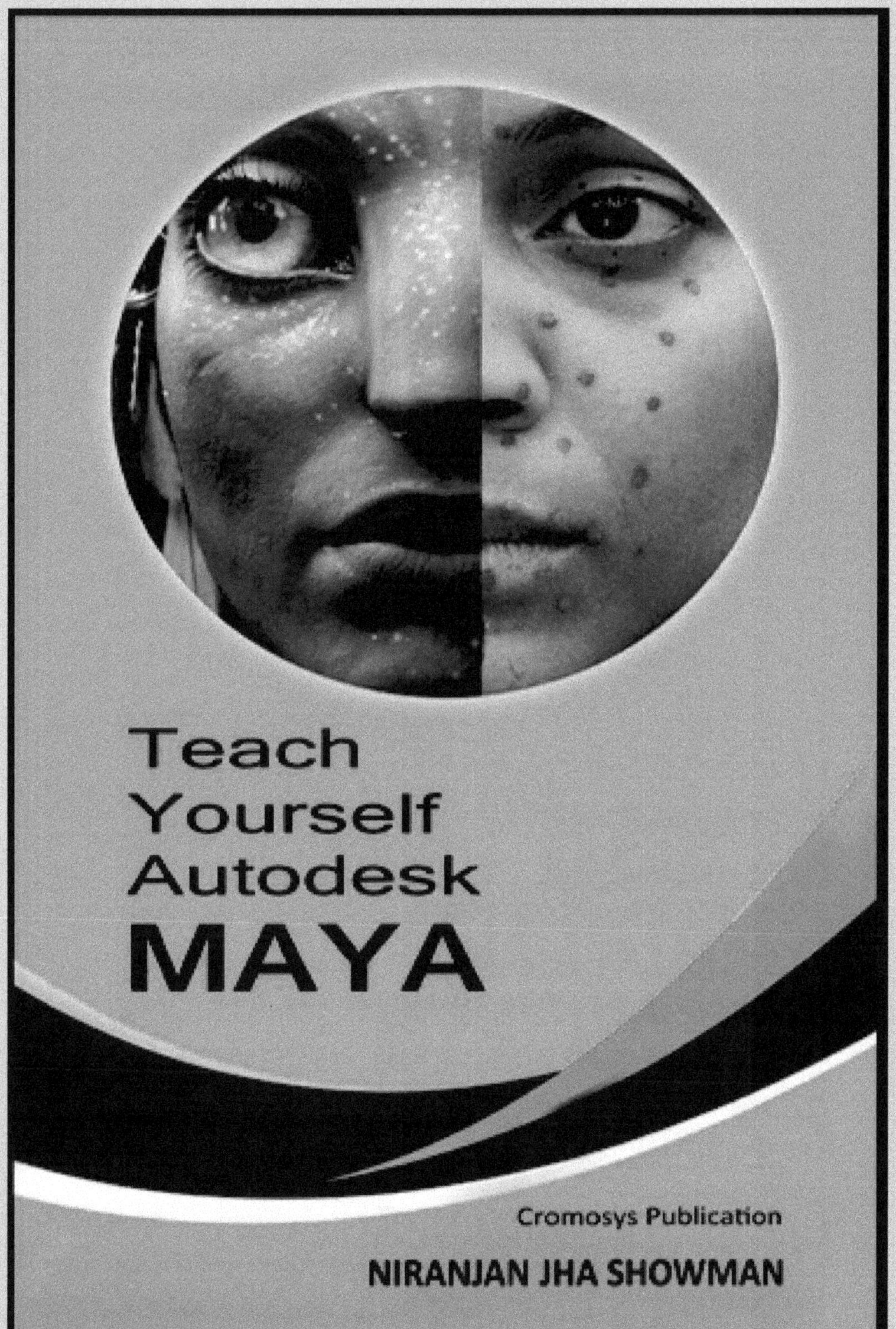

Teach
Yourself
Autodesk
MAYA
Cromosys Publication
NIRANJAN JHA SHOWMAN

Cromosys Publication
Teach
Yourself
Autodesk
3ds Max
NIRANJAN JHA SHOWMAN

Cromosys Publication
CRIMINAL FACTORY
NIRANJAN JHA SHOWMAN

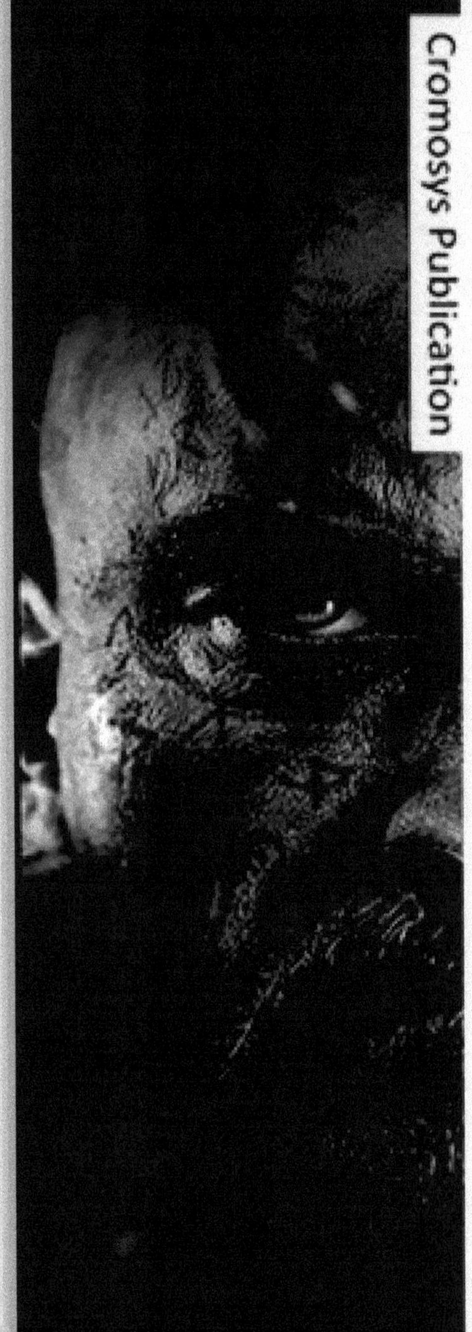

Cromosys Publication
FOCAL DISASTER
NIRANJAN JHA SHOWMAN

Cromosys Publication
Your talents will not help you succeed without your skill of using them.
NIRANJAN JHA SHOWMAN
BE
MILLIONAIRE
LIKE
ME

Copyright Office
Government of India

सत्यमेव जयते

Extracts
from the Register
of Copyrights

Dated : 16/08/2022

1.	Registration Number		**T-91782-2022**
2.	Name, address and nationality of the applicant	:	NIRANJAN JHA SHOWMAN, CROMOSYS PUBLICATION, 001, JAYSATYAM, PATANKAR ROAD, NALLASOPARA (W), MUMBAI, MAHARASHTRA - 401203. INDIAN
3.	Nature of the applicant's interest in the copyright of the work	:	AUTHOR
4.	Class and description of the work	:	LITERARY / BOOK
5.	Title of the work	:	**Teach Yourself Tally**
6.	Language of the work	:	ENGLISH
7.	Name, address and nationality of the author and if the author is deceased, date of his decease	:	NIRANJAN JHA SHOWMAN, CROMOSYS PUBLICATION, 001, JAYSATYAM, PATANKAR ROAD, NALLASOPARA (W), MUMBAI, MAHARASHTRA - 401203. INDIAN
8.	Whether the work is published or unpublished	:	UNPUBLISHED
9.	Year and country of first publication and name, address and nationality of the publisher	:	N.A.
10.	Years and countries of subsequent publications, if any, and names, addresses and nationalities of the publishers	:	N.A. SAME AS ABOVE
11.	Names, addresses and nationalities of the owners of various rights comprising the copyright in the work and the extent of rights held by each, together with particulars of assignments and licences, if any	:	
12.	Names, addresses and nationalities of other persons, if any, authorised to assign or licence of rights comprising the copyright	:	N.A.
13.	If the work is an 'Artistic work', the location of the original work, including name, address and nationality of the person in possession of the work. (In the case of an architectural work, the year of completion of the work should also be shown).	:	N.A.
14.	If the work is an 'Artistic work', whether it is registered under the Designs Act 2000 if yes give details.	:	N.A.
15.	If the work is an 'Artistic work', capable of being registered as a design under the Designs Act 2000.whether it has been applied to an article though an industrial process and ,if yes ,the number of times it is reproduced.	:	N.A.
16.	Remarks, if any	:	

Diary Number :	8823/2020-DF/T
Date of Application :	25/07/2020
Date of Receipt :	25/07/2020

DEPUTY REGISTRAR OF COPYRIGHTS